THE DAILY STUDY BIBLE SERIES

REVISED EDITION

THE GOSPEL OF
JOHN

Volume 1

THE GOSPEL OF
JOHN
Volume 1
(Chapters 1 to 7)

REVISED EDITION

Translated
with an Introduction and Interpretation
by
WILLIAM BARCLAY

THE WESTMINSTER PRESS
PHILADELPHIA

Revised Edition
Copyright © 1975 William Barclay

First published by The Saint Andrew Press
Edinburgh, Scotland

First Edition, July, 1955

Second Edition, November, 1956

Published by The Westminster Press ®
Philadelphia, Pennsylvania

PRINTED IN THE UNITED STATES OF AMERICA

7

Library of Congress Cataloging in Publication Data

Bible. N.T. John. English. Barclay. 1975.
    The Gospel of John.

    (The Daily study Bible series. — Rev. ed.)
    1. Bible. N.T. John — Commentaries. I. Barclay,
William, lecturer in the University of Glasgow, ed.
II. Title. III. Series.
BS2613   1975   226'.5'077   74-30031
ISBN 0-664-21304-9 (v. 1)
ISBN 0-664-24104-2 (v. 1) pbk.

GENERAL INTRODUCTION

The Daily Study Bible series has always had one aim—to convey the results of scholarship to the ordinary reader. A. S. Peake delighted in the saying that he was a " theological middleman ", and I would be happy if the same could be said of me in regard to these volumes. And yet the primary aim of the series has never been academic. It could be summed up in the famous words of Richard of Chichester's prayer—to enable men and women " to know Jesus Christ more clearly, to love him more dearly, and to follow him more nearly "

It is all of twenty years since the first volume of *The Daily Study Bible* was published. The series was the brain-child of the late Rev. Andrew McCosh, M.A., S.T.M., the then Secretary and Manager of the Committee on Publications of the Church of Scotland, and of the late Rev. R. G. Macdonald, O.B.E., M.A., D.D., its Convener.

It is a great joy to me to know that all through the years *The Daily Study Bible* has been used at home and abroad, by minister, by missionary, by student and by layman, and that it has been translated into many different languages. Now, after so many printings, it has become necessary to renew the printer's type and the opportunity has been taken to restyle the books, to correct some errors in the text and to remove some references which have become outdated. At the same time, the Biblical quotations within the text have been changed to use the Revised Standard Version, but my own original translation of the New Testament passages has been retained at the beginning of each daily section.

There is one debt which I would be sadly lacking in courtesy if I did not acknowledge. The work of revision and correction has been done entirely by the Rev. James Martin, M.A., B.D., Minister of High Carntyne Church, Glasgow. Had it not been for him this task would never have been undertaken, and it is impossible for me to thank him enough for the selfless toil he has put into the revision of these books.

It is my prayer that God may continue to use *The Daily Study Bible* to enable men better to understand His word.

Glasgow   WILLIAM BARCLAY

CONTENTS

CONTENTS

INTRODUCTION TO THE
GOSPEL ACCORDING TO SAINT JOHN

THE GOSPEL OF THE EAGLE'S EYE

For many Christian people the Gospel according to *St. John* is the most precious book in the New Testament. It is the book on which above all they feed their minds and nourish their hearts, and in which they rest their souls. Very often on stained glass windows and the like the gospel writers are represented in symbol by the figures of the four beasts whom the writer of the *Revelation* saw around the throne (*Revelation* 4: 7). The emblems are variously distributed among the gospel writers, but a common allocation is that the *man* stands for *Mark*, which is the plainest, the most straightforward and the most human of the gospels; the *lion* stands for *Matthew*, for he specially saw Jesus as the Messiah and the Lion of the tribe of Judah; the ox stands for *Luke*, because it is the animal of service and sacrifice, and Luke saw Jesus as the great servant of men and the universal sacrifice for all mankind; the *eagle* stands for *John*, because it alone of all living creatures can look straight into the sun and not be dazzled, and John has the most penetrating gaze of all the New Testament writers into the eternal mysteries and the eternal truths and the very mind of God. Many people find themselves closer to God and to Jesus Christ in *John* than in any other book in the world.

THE GOSPEL THAT IS DIFFERENT

But we have only to read the Fourth Gospel in the most cursory way to see that it is quite different from the other three. It omits so many things that they include. The Fourth Gospel has no account of the Birth of Jesus, of his baptism, of his temptations; it tells us nothing of the Last Supper, nothing of Gethsemane, and nothing of the Ascension. It has no word of the healing of any people possessed by devils and evil spirits. And, perhaps most surprising of all, it has none of the parable stories Jesus told which are so priceless a part of the other three gospels. In these other three gospels Jesus speaks either in these wonderful stories or in short, epigrammatic, vivid sentences which stick in the memory. But in the Fourth Gospel the speeches of Jesus are often a whole chapter long; and are often involved, argumentative pronouncements quite unlike the pithy, unforgettable sayings of the other three.

Even more surprising, the account in the Fourth Gospel of the facts of the life and ministry of Jesus is often different from that in the other three.

(i) *John* has a different account of the *beginning* of the ministry of Jesus. In the other three gospels it is quite definitely stated that Jesus did not emerge as a preacher until after John the Baptist had been imprisoned. "Now after John was arrested Jesus came into Galilee, preaching the gospel of God" (*Mark* 1: 14; *Luke* 3: 18, 20; *Matthew* 4: 12). But in *John* there is a quite considerable period during which the ministry of Jesus overlapped with the activity of John the Baptist (*John* 3: 22–30; 4: 1, 2).

(ii) *John* has a different account of the *scene* of Jesus's ministry. In the other three gospels the main scene of the ministry is Galilee and Jesus does not reach Jerusalem until the last week of his life. In *John* the main scene of the ministry is Jerusalem and Judaea, with only occasional withdrawals to Galilee (*John* 2: 1–13; 4: 35—5: 1; 6: 1—7: 14). In *John* Jesus is in Jerusalem for a Passover which occurred at the same time as the cleansing of the Temple, as John tells the story (*John* 2: 13); he is in Jerusalem at the time of an unnamed feast (*John* 5: 1); he is there for the Feast of Tabernacles (*John* 7: 2, 10); he is there at the Feast of Dedication in the winter-time (*John* 10: 22). In fact according to the Fourth Gospel Jesus never left Jerusalem after that feast; after chapter 10 he is in Jerusalem all the time, which would mean a stay of months, from the winter-time of the Feast of the Dedication to the spring-time of the Passover at which he was crucified.

In point of fact in this particular matter *John* is surely right. The other gospels show us Jesus mourning over Jerusalem as the last week came on. " O Jerusalem, Jerusalem, killing the prophets and stoning those who are sent to you! How often would I have gathered your children together as a hen gathers her brood under her wings, and you would not!" (*Matthew* 23: 37=*Luke* 13: 34). It is clear that Jesus could not have said that unless he had paid repeated visits to Jerusalem and made repeated appeals to it. It was impossible for him to say that on a first visit. In this *John* is unquestionably right.

It was in fact this difference of scene which provided Eusebius with one of the earliest explanations of the difference between the Fourth Gospel and the other three. He said that in his day (about A.D. 300) many people who were scholars held the following view. Matthew at first preached to the Hebrew people. The day came when he had to leave them and to go to other nations. Before he went he set down his story of the life of Jesus in Hebrew, " and thus compensated those whom he was obliged to leave for the loss of his presence." After Mark and Luke had published their gospels, John was still preaching the story of Jesus orally. " Finally he proceeded to write for the following reason. The three gospels already mentioned having come into the hands of all and into his hands too, they say that he fully accepted them and bore witness to their truthfulness; *but there was lacking in them an account of the deeds done by Christ at the beginning of his ministry*. . . . They therefore say that John, being asked to do it for this reason, gave in his gospel an account of the period which had been omitted by the earlier evangelists, and of the deeds done by the Saviour during that period; that is, of the deeds done before the imprisonment of John the Baptist. . . . John therefore records the deeds of Christ which were performed *before* the Baptist was cast into prison, but the other three evangelists mention the events which happened *after* that time. . . . The *Gospel according to John* contains the *first* acts of Christ, while the others give an account of *the latter part* of his life." (Eusebius, *The Ecclesiastical History* 5: 24.)

So then according to Eusebius there is no contradiction at all between the Fourth Gospel and the other three; the difference is due to the fact that the Fourth Gospel is describing a ministry in Jerusalem, at least in its earlier chapters, which preceded the ministry in Galilee, and which took place while John the Baptist was still at liberty. It may well be that this explanation of Eusebius is at least in part correct.

(iii) *John* has a different account of the *duration* of Jesus's ministry. The other three gospels, on the face of it, imply that it lasted only one year. Within the ministry there is only one Passover Feast. In *John* there are *three* Passovers, one at the Cleansing of the Temple (*John* 2: 13); one near the Feeding of the Five Thousand (*John* 6: 4); and the final Passover at which Jesus went to the Cross. According to *John* the ministry of Jesus would take a minimum of two years, and probably a period nearer three years, to cover its events. Again *John* is unquestionably right. If we read the other three gospels closely and carefully we can see that he is right. When the disciples plucked the ears of corn (*Mark* 2: 23) it must have been spring-time. When the five thousand were fed, they sat down on the *green grass* (*Mark* 6: 39); therefore it was spring-time again, and there must have been a year between the two events. There follows the tour through Tyre and Sidon, and the Transfiguration. At the Transfiguration Peter wished to build three booths and to stay there. It is most natural to think that it was the time of the Feast of Tabernacles or Booths and that that is why Peter made the suggestion (*Mark* 9: 5). That would make the date early in October. There follows the space between that and the last Passover in April. Therefore, behind the narrative of the other three gospels lies the fact that Jesus's ministry actually did last for at least three years, as John represents it.

(iv) It sometimes even happens that *John* differs in matters of fact from the other three. There are two outstanding examples. First, *John* puts the Cleansing of the Temple at the *beginning* of Jesus's ministry (*John* 2: 13–22), the others put it at the *end* (*Mark* 11: 15–17; *Matthew* 21: 12, 13; *Luke* 19: 45, 46).

Second, when we come to study the narratives in detail, we will see that *John* dates the crucifixion of Jesus on the day before the Passover, while the other gospels date it on the day of the Passover.

We can never shut our eyes to the obvious differences between *John* and the other gospels.

JOHN'S SPECIAL KNOWLEDGE

One thing is certain—if John differs from the other three gospels, it is not because of ignorance and lack of information. The plain fact is that, if he omits much that they tell us, he also tells us much that they do not mention. John alone tells of the marriage feast at Cana of Galilee (2: 1–11); of the coming of Nicodemus to Jesus (3: 1–15); of the woman of Samaria (4); of the raising of Lazarus (11); of the way in which Jesus washed his disciples' feet (13: 1–17); of Jesus's wonderful teaching about the Holy Spirit, the Comforter, which is scattered through chapters 14 to 17. It is only in *John* that some of the disciples really come alive. It is in *John* alone that Thomas speaks (11: 16; 14: 5; 20: 24–29); that Andrew becomes a real personality (1: 40, 41; 6: 8, 9; 12: 22); that we get a glimpse of the character of Philip (6: 5–7; 14: 8, 9); that we hear the carping protest of Judas at the anointing at Bethany (12: 4, 5). And the strange thing is that these little extra touches are intensely revealing. *John's* pictures of Thomas and Andrew and Philip are like little cameos or vignettes in which the character of each man is etched in a way we cannot forget.

Further, again and again *John* has little extra details which read like the memories of one who was there. The loaves which the lad brought to Jesus were *barley* loaves (6: 9); when Jesus came to the disciples as they crossed the lake in the storm they had rowed between three and four miles (6: 19); there were six stone waterpots at Cana of Galilee (2: 6); it is only *John* who tells of the four soldiers gambling for the seamless robe as Jesus died (19: 23); he knows the exact weight of the myrrh and aloes which were used to anount the dead body of Jesus (19: 39); he remembers how the perfume of the ointment filled the house at the anointing at Bethany (12: 3). Many of these things are such apparently unimportant details that they are inexplicable unless they are the memories of a man who was there.

However much *John* may differ from the other three gospels, that difference is not to be explained by ignorance but rather by the fact that he had *more* knowledge or better sources or a more vivid memory than the others.

Further evidence of the specialised information of the writer of the Fourth Gospel is his *detailed knowledge of Palestine and of Jerusalem.* He knows how long it took to build the Temple (2: 20); that the Jews and the Samaritans had a permanent quarrel (4: 9); the low Jewish view of women (4: 9); the way in which the Jews regard the Sabbath (5: 10; 7: 21–23; 9: 14). His knowledge of the geography of Palestine is intimate. He knows of two Bethanys, one of which is beyond Jordan (1: 28; 12: 1); he knows that Bethsaida was the home of some of the disciples (1: 44; 12: 21); that Cana is in Galilee (2: 1; 4: 46; 21: 2); that Sychar is near Shechem (4: 5). He has what one might call a street by street knowledge of Jerusalem. He knows the sheep-gate and the pool near it (5: 2); the pool of Siloam (9: 7); Solomon's Porch (10: 23); the brook Kidron (18: 1); the pavement which is called Gabbatha (19: 13); Golgotha, which is like a skull (19: 17). It must be remembered that Jerusalem was destroyed in A.D. 70 and that John did not write until A.D. 100 or thereby; and yet from his memory he knows Jerusalem like the back of his hand.

THE CIRCUMSTANCES IN WHICH JOHN WROTE

We have seen that there are very real differences between the Fourth and the other three gospels; and we have seen that, whatever the reason, it was not lack of knowledge on John's part. We must now go on to ask, What was the aim with which John wrote? If we can discover this we will discover why he selected and treated his facts as he did.

The Fourth Gospel was written in Ephesus about the year A.D. 100. By that time two special features had emerged in the situation of the Christian church. First, *Christianity had gone out into the Gentile world.* By that time the Christian church was no longer predominantly Jewish; it was in fact overwhelmingly gentile. The vast majority of its members now came, not from a Jewish, but an Hellenistic background. That being so, *Christianity had to be restated.* It was not that the truth of Christianity had changed; but the terms and the categories in which if found expression had to be changed.

Take but one instance. A Greek might take up the *Gospel according to St. Matthew.* No sooner had he opened it than he was confronted with a long genealogy. Genealogies were familiar enough to the Jew but quite unintelligible to the Greek. He would read on. He would be confronted with a Jesus who was the Son of David, a king of whom the Greeks had never heard, and the symbol of a racial and nationalist ambition which was nothing to the Greek. He would be faced with the picture of Jesus as Messiah, a term of which the Greek had never heard. Must the Greek who wished to become a Christian be compelled to reorganize his whole thinking into Jewish categories? Must he learn a good deal about Jewish history and Jewish apocalyptic literature (which told about the coming of the Messiah) before he could become a Christian? As E. J. Goodspeed phrased it: " Was there no way in which he might be introduced directly to the values of Christian salvation without being for ever routed, we might even say, detoured, through Judaism? " The Greek was one of the world's great thinkers. Had he to abandon all his own great intellectual heritage in order to think entirely in Jewish terms and categories of thought?

John faced that problem fairly and squarely. And he found one of the greatest solutions which ever entered the mind of man. Later on, in the commentary, we shall deal much more fully with John's great solution. At the moment we touch on it briefly. The Greeks had two great conceptions.

(a) They had the conception of the *Logos.* In Greek *logos* means two things—it means *word* and it means *reason.*The Jew was entirely familiar with the all-powerful word of God. " God said, Let there be light; and there was light " (*Genesis* 1: 3). The

Greek was entirely familiar with the thought of reason. He looked at this world; he saw a magnificent and dependable order. Night and day came with unfailing regularity; the year kept its seasons in unvarying course; the stars and the planets moved in their unaltering path; nature had her unvarying laws. What produced this order? The Greek answered unhesitatingly, The *Logos*, the mind of God, is responsible for the majestic order of the world. He went on, What is it that gives man power to think, to reason and to know? Again he answered unhesitatingly, The *Logos*, the mind of God, dwelling within a man makes him a thinking rational being.

John seized on this. It was in this way that he thought of Jesus. He said to the Greeks, " All your lives you have been fascinated by this great, guiding, controlling mind of God. The mind of God has come to earth in the man Jesus. Look at him and you see what the mind and thought of God are like." John had discovered a new category in which the Greek might think of Jesus, a category in which Jesus was presented as nothing less than God acting in the form of a man.

(*b*) They had the conception of two worlds. The Greek always conceived of two worlds. The one was the world in which we live. It was a wonderful world in its way but a world of shadows and copies and unrealities. The other was the real world, in which the great realities, of which our earthly things are only poor, pale copies, stand for ever. To the Greek the unseen world was the real one; the seen world was only shadowy unreality.

Plato systematized this way of thinking in his doctrine of forms or ideas. He held that in the unseen world there was the perfect pattern of everything, and the things of this world were shadowy copies of these eternal patterns. To put it simply, Plato held that somewhere there was a perfect pattern of a table of which all earthly tables are inadequate copies; somewhere there was the perfect pattern of the good and the beautiful of which all earthly goodness and earthly beauty are imperfect copies. And the great reality, the supreme idea, the pattern of all patterns and the form of all forms was God. The great problem was how to get into this world of reality, how to get out of our shadows into the eternal truths.

John declares that that is what Jesus enables us to do. He *is* reality come to earth. The Greek word for *real* in this sense is *alēthinos*; it is very closely connected with the word *alēthēs*, which means *true*, and *alētheia*, which means *the truth*. The Authorized and Revised Standard Versions translate *alēthinos true*; they would be far better to translate it *real*. Jesus is the *real* light (1: 9); Jesus is the *real* bread (6: 32); Jesus is the *real* vine (15: 1); to Jesus belongs the *real* judgment (8: 16). Jesus alone has reality in our world of shadows and imperfections.

Something follows from that. Every action that Jesus did was, therefore, not only an act in time but a window which allows us to see into reality. That is what John means when he talks of Jesus's miracles as *signs* (*sēmeia*). The wonderful works of Jesus were not simply wonderful; they were windows opening on to the reality which is God. This explains why John tells the miracle stories in a quite different way from the other three gospel writers. There are two differences.

(*a*) In the Fourth Gospel we miss the note of compassion which is in the miracle stories of the others. In the others Jesus is moved with compassion for the leper (*Mark* 1: 41); his sympathy goes out to Jairus (*Mark* 5: 22); he is sorry for the father of the epileptic boy (*Mark* 9: 14); when he raises to life the son of the widow of Nain, Luke says with an infinite tenderness, " He gave him to his mother " (*Luke* 7: 15). But in *John* the miracles are not so much deeds of compassion as deeds which demonstrate the glory of Christ. After the miracle at Cana of Galilee, John comments: " This, the first of his signs, Jesus did at Cana in Galilee, *and manifested his glory* " (*John* 2: 11). The raising of Lazarus happens "*for the glory* of God " (*John* 11: 4). The blind man's blindness existed to allow a demonstration of the glory of the works of God (*John* 9: 3). To John it was not that there was no love and compassion in the miracles; but in every one of them he saw the glory of the reality of God breaking into time and into human affairs.

(*b*) Often the miracles of Jesus in the Fourth Gospel are

accompanied by a long discourse. The feeding of the five thousand is followed by the long discourse on the bread of life (chapter 6); the healing of the blind man springs from the saying that Jesus is the light of the world (chapter 9); the raising of Lazarus leads up to the saying that Jesus is the resurrection and the life (chapter 11). To John the miracles were not simply single events in time; they were insights into what God is always doing and what Jesus always is; they were windows into the reality of God. Jesus did not merely once feed five thousand people; that was an illustration that he is for ever the real bread of life. Jesus did not merely once open the eyes of a blind man; he is for ever the light of the world. Jesus did not merely once raise Lazarus from the dead; he is for ever and for all men the resurrection and the life. To John a miracle was never an isolated act; it was always a window into the reality of what Jesus always was and always is and always did and always does.

It was with this in mind that that great scholar Clement of Alexandria (about A.D. 230) arrived at one of the most famous and true of all verdicts about the origin and aim of the Fourth Gospel. It was his view that the gospels containing the genealogies had been written first—that is, *Luke* and *Matthew*; that then Mark at the request of many who had heard Peter preach composed his gospel, which embodied the preaching material of Peter; and that then " last of all, John, perceiving that what had reference to the bodily things of Jesus's ministry had been sufficiently related, and encouraged by his friends, and inspired by the Holy Spirit, wrote *a spiritual gospel* " (quoted in Eusebius, *The Ecclesiastical History* 6: 14). What Clement meant was that John was not so much interested in the mere facts as in the meaning of the facts, that it was not facts he was after but truth. John did not see the events of Jesus's life simply as events in time; he saw them as windows looking into eternity, and he pressed towards the spiritual meaning of the events and the words of Jesus's life in a way that the other three gospels did not attempt.

That is still one of the truest verdicts on the Fourth Gospel ever reached. John did write, not an historical, but a spiritual gospel.

So then, first of all, John presented Jesus as the mind of God in a person come to earth, and as the one person who possesses reality instead of shadows and able to lead men out of the shadows into the real world of which Plato and the great Greeks had dreamed. The Christianity which had once been clothed in Jewish categories had taken to itself the greatness of the thought of the Greeks.

THE RISE OF THE HERESIES

The second of the great facts confronting the church when the Fourth Gospel was written was *the rise of heresy*. It was now seventy years since Jesus had been crucified. By this time the church was an organisation and an institution. Theologies and creeds were being thought out and stated; and inevitably the thoughts of some people went down mistaken ways and heresies resulted. A heresy is seldom a complete untruth; it usually results when one facet of the truth is unduly emphasised. We can see at least two of the heresies which the writer of the Fourth Gospel sought to combat.

(*a*) There were certain Christians, especially Jewish Christians, who gave too high a place to John the Baptist. There was something about him which had an inevitable appeal to the Jews. He walked in the prophetic succession and talked with the prophetic voice. We know that in later times there was an accepted sect of John the Baptist within the orthodox Jewish faith. In *Acts* 19: 1–7 we come upon a little group of twelve men on the fringe of the Christian church who had never got beyond the baptism of John.

Over and over again the Fourth Gospel quietly, but definitely, relegates John to his proper place. Over and over again John himself denies that he has ever claimed or possessed the highest place, and without qualification yields that place to Jesus. We have already seen that in the other gospels the ministry of Jesus did not begin until John the Baptist had been put into prison, but that in the Fourth Gospel their ministries overlap. The writer of the Fourth Gospel may well have used that arrangement to show John and Jesus in actual meeting and to show that John used these meetings to admit, and to urge others to admit, the supremacy of Jesus. It is carefully pointed out that John is not that light (1: 8). He is shown as quite definitely disclaiming all Messianic aspirations (1: 20ff; 3: 28; 4: 1; 10: 41). It is not even permissible to think of him as the highest witness (5: 36). There is no criticism at all of John the Baptist in the Fourth Gospel; but there is a rebuke to those who would give him a place which ought to belong to Jesus and to Jesus alone.

(*b*) A certain type of heresy which was very widely spread in the days when the Fourth Gospel was written is called by the general name of *Gnosticism*. Without some understanding of it much of John's greatness and much of his aim will be missed. The basic doctrine of Gnosticism was that matter is essentially evil and spirit is essentially good. The Gnostics went on to argue that on that basis God himself cannot touch matter and therefore did not create the world. What he did was to put out a series of emanations. Each of these emanations was further from him, until at last there was one so distant from him that it could touch matter. That emanation was the creator of the world.

By itself that idea is bad enough, but it was made worse by an addition. The Gnostics held that each emanation knew less and less about God, until there was a stage when the emanations were not only ignorant of God but actually hostile to him. So they finally came to the conclusion that the creator god was not only different from the real God, but was also quite ignorant of and actively hostile to him. Cerinthus, one of the leaders of the Gnostics, said that " the world was created, not by God, but by a certain power far separate from him, and far distant from that Power who is over the universe, and ignorant of the God who is over all."

The Gnostics believed that God had nothing to do with the creating of the world. That is why John begins his gospel with the ringing statement: " All things were made through him; and without him was not anything made that was made " (*John* 1: 3). That is why John insists that " God so loved the *world* " (*John* 3: 16). In face of the Gnostics who so mistakenly spiritualized God into a being who could not possibly have anything to do with the world, John presented the Christian doctrine of the God who made the world and whose presence fills the world that he has made.

The beliefs of the Gnostics impinged on their ideas of Jesus.

(*a*) Some of the Gnostics held that Jesus was one of the emanations which had proceeded from God. They held that he was not in any real sense divine; that he was only a kind of demi-god who was more or less distant from the real God; that he was simply one of a chain of lesser beings between God and the world.

(*b*) Some of the Gnostics held that Jesus had no real body. A body is matter and God could not touch matter; therefore Jesus was a kind of phantom without real flesh and blood. They held, for instance, that when he stepped on the ground he left no footprint, for his body had neither weight nor substance. They could never have said: " The Word became *flesh* " (*John* 1: 14). Augustine tells how he had read much in the work of the philosophers of his day; he had found much that was very like what was in the New Testament, but, he said: " ' The Word was made flesh and dwelt among us ' I did not read there." That is why John in his *First Letter* insists that Jesus came *in the flesh*, and declares that any one who denies that fact is moved by the spirit of antichrist (1 *John* 4: 3). This particular heresy is known as *Docetism*. Docetism comes from the Greek word *dokein* which means *to seem* ; and the heresy is so called because it held that Jesus only *seemed* to be a man.

(*c*) Some Gnostics held a variation of that heresy. They held that Jesus was a man into whom the Spirit of God came at his baptism; that Spirit remained with him throughout his life until the end; but since the Spirit of God could never suffer and die, it left him before he was crucified. They gave Jesus's cry on the Cross as : " My power, my power, why hast thou forsaken me? " And in their books they told of people talking on the

Mount of Olives to a form which looked exactly like Jesus while the man Jesus died on the Cross.

So then the Gnostic heresies issued in one of two beliefs. They believed either that Jesus was not really divine but simply one of a series of emanations from God, or that he was not in any sense human but a kind of phantom in the shape of a man. The Gnostic beliefs at one and the same time destroyed the real godhead and the real manhood of Jesus.

THE HUMANITY OF JESUS

The fact that John is out to correct both these Gnostic tendencies explains a curious paradoxical double emphasis in his gospel. On the one hand, there is no gospel which so uncompromisingly stresses the real humanity of Jesus. Jesus was angry with those who bought and sold in the Temple courts (2: 15); he was physically tired as he sat by the well which was near Sychar in Samaria (4: 6); his disciples offered him food in the way in which they would offer it to any hungry man (4: 31); he had sympathy with those who were hungry and with those who were afraid (6: 5, 20); he knew grief and he wept tears as any mourner might do (11: 33, 35, 38); in the agony of the Cross the cry of his parched lips was: " I thirst " (19: 28). The Fourth Gospel shows us a Jesus who was no shadowy, docetic figure; it shows us one who knew the weariness of an exhausted body and the wounds of a distressed mind and heart. It is the truly human Jesus whom the Fourth Gospel sets before us.

THE DEITY OF JESUS

On the other hand, there is no gospel which sets before us such a view of the deity of Jesus.

(*a*) John stresses the *pre-existence* of Jesus. " Before Abraham was," said Jesus, " I am " (8: 58). He talks of the glory which he had with the Father before the world was made (17: 5). Again and again he speaks of his coming down from heaven (6: 33–38). John saw in Jesus one who had always been, even before the world began.

(*b*) The Fourth Gospel stresses more than any of the others the *omniscience* of Jesus. It is John's view that apparently miraculously Jesus knew the past record of the woman of Samaria (4: 16, 17); apparently without anyone telling him he knew how long the man beside the healing pool had been ill (5: 6); before he asked it, he knew the answer to the question he put to Philip (6: 6); he knew that Judas would betray him (6: 61–64); he knew of the death of Lazarus before anyone told him of it (11: 14). John saw in Jesus one who had a special and miraculous knowledge independent of anything which any man might tell him. He needed to ask no questions because he knew all the answers.

(*c*) The Fourth Gospel stresses the fact, as John saw it, that Jesus always acted entirely on his own initiative and uninfluenced by anyone else. It was not his mother's request which moved him to the miracle at Cana of Galilee; it was his own personal decision (2: 4); the urging of his brothers had nothing to do with the visit which he paid to Jerusalem at the Feast of Tabernacles (7: 10); no man took his life from him—no man could; he laid it down purely voluntarily (10: 18; 19: 11). As John saw it, Jesus had a divine independence from all human influence. He was self-determined.

To meet the Gnostics and their strange beliefs John presents us with a Jesus who was undeniably human and who yet was undeniably divine.

THE AUTHOR OF THE FOURTH GOSPEL

We have seen that the aim of the writer of the Fourth Gospel was to present the Christian faith in such a way that it would commend itself to the Greek world to which Christianity had gone out, and also to combat the heresies and mistaken ideas which had arisen within the church..We go on to ask, Who is that writer? Tradition answers unanimously that the author was John the apostle. We shall see that beyond doubt the authority of John lies behind the gospel, although it may well be that its actual form and penmanship did not come from his hand. Let us, then, collect what we know about him.

He was the younger son of Zebedee, who possessed a fishing

boat on the Sea of Galilee and was well enough off to be able to employ hired servants to help him with his work (*Mark* 1: 19, 20). His mother was Salome, and it seems likely that she was the sister of Mary, the mother of Jesus (*Matthew* 27: 56; *Mark* 16: 1). With his brother James he obeyed the call of Jesus (*Mark* 1: 20). It would seem that James and John were in partnership with Peter in the fishing trade (*Luke* 5: 7–10). He was one of the inner circle of the disciples, for the lists of the disciples always begin with the names of Peter, James and John, and there were certain great occasions when Jesus took these three specially with him (*Mark* 3: 17; 5: 37; 9: 2; 14: 33).

In character he was clearly a turbulent and ambitious man. Jesus gave to him and to his brother the name *Boanerges*, which the gospel writers take to mean *Sons of Thunder*. John and his brother James were completely exclusive and intolerant (*Mark* 9: 38; *Luke* 9: 49). So violent was their temper that they were prepared to blast a Samaritan village out of existence because it would not give them hospitality when they were on their journey to Jerusalem (*Luke* 9: 54). Either they or their mother Salome had the ambition that when Jesus came into his kingdom, they might be his principal ministers of state (*Mark* 10: 35; *Matthew* 20: 20). In the other three gospels John appears as a leader of the apostolic band, one of the inner circle, and yet a turbulent ambitious and intolerant character.

In the *Book of Acts* John always appears as the companion of Peter, and he himself never speaks at all. His name is still one of the three names at the head of the apostolic list (*Acts* 1: 13). He is with Peter when the lame man is healed at the Beautiful Gate of the Temple (*Acts* 3: 1ff). With Peter he is brought before the Sanhedrin and faces the Jewish leaders with a courage and a boldness that astonished them (*Acts* 4: 1–13). With Peter he goes from Jerusalem to Samaria to survey the work done by Philip (*Acts* 8: 14).

In Paul's letters he appears only once. In *Galatians* 2: 9 he is named as one of the pillars of the church along with Peter and James, and with them is depicted as giving his approval to the work of Paul.

John was a strange mixture. He was one of the leaders of the Twelve; he was one of the inner circle of Jesus's closest friends; at the same time he was a man of temper and ambition and intolerance, and yet of courage.

We may follow John into the stories told of him in the early church. Eusebius tells us that he was banished to Patmos in the reign of Domitian (Eusebius, *The Ecclesiastical History* 3: 23). In the same passage Eusebius tells a characteristic story about John, a story which he received from Clement of Alexandria. John became a kind of bishop of Asia Minor and was visiting one of his churches near Ephesus. In the congregation he saw a tall and exceptionally fine-looking young man. He turned to the elder in charge of the congregation and said to him: " I commit that young man into your charge and into your care, and I call this congregation to witness that I do so." The elder took the young man into his own house and cared for him and instructed him, and the day came when he was baptized and received into the church. But very soon afterwards he fell in with evil friends and embarked on such a career of crime that he ended up by becoming the leader of a band of murdering and pillaging brigands. Some time afterwards John returned to the congregation. He said to the elder: " Restore to me the trust which I and the Lord committed to you and to the church of which you are in charge." At first the elder did not understand of what John was speaking. " I mean," said John, " that I am asking you for the soul of the young man whom I entrusted to you." " Alas! " said the elder, " he is dead." " Dead? " said John. " He is dead to God," said the elder. " He fell from grace; he was forced to flee from the city for his crimes and now he is a brigand in the mountains." Straightway John went to the mountains. Deliberately he allowed himself to be captured by the robber band. They brought him before the young man who was now the chief of the band and, in his shame, the young man tried to run away from him. John, though an old man, pursued him. " My son," he cried, " are you running away from your father? I am feeble and far advanced in age; have pity on me, my son; fear not; there is yet hope of salvation for you. I will stand for you before the Lord Christ. If need be I will gladly die for you as he died for me. Stop, stay, believe! It is Christ who has sent me to you." The appeal broke the heart of the young man. He stopped, threw away his weapons, and wept. Together he and John came down the mountainside and he was brought back into the church and into the Christian way. There we see the love and the courage of John still in operation.

Eusebius (3: 28) tells another story of John which he got from the works of Irenaeus. We have seen that one of the leaders of the Gnostic heresy was a man called Cerinthus. " The apostle John once entered a bath to bathe; but, when he learned that Cerinthus was within, he sprang from his place and rushed out of the door, for he could not bear to remain under the same roof with him. He advised those who were with him to do the same. ' Let us flee,' he said, ' lest the bath fall, for Cerinthus, the enemy of the truth, is within.' " There we have another glimpse of the temper of John. Boanerges was not quite dead.

Cassian tells another famous story about John. One day he was found playing with a tame partridge. A narrower and more rigid brother rebuked him for thus wasting his time, and John answered: " The bow that is always bent will soon cease to shoot straight."

It is Jerome who tells the story of the last words of John. When he was dying, his disciples asked him if he had any last message to leave them. " Little children," he said, " love one another." Again and again he repeated it; and they asked him if that was all he had to say. " It is enough," he said, " for it is the Lord's command."

Such then is our information about John; and he emerges a figure of fiery temper, of wide ambition, of undoubted courage, and, in the end, of gentle love.

THE BELOVED DISCIPLE

If we have been following our references closely we will have noticed one thing. All our information about John comes from the first three gospels. It is the astonishing fact that the Fourth

Gospel never mentions the apostle John from beginning to end.
But it does mention two other people.

First, it speaks of *the disciple whom Jesus loved*. There are
four mentions of him. He was leaning on Jesus's breast at the
Last Supper (*John* 13: 23–25); it is into his care that Jesus
committed Mary as he died upon his Cross (19: 25–27); it was
Peter and he whom Mary Magdalene met on her return from
the empty tomb on the first Easter morning (20: 2); he was
present at the last resurrection appearance of Jesus by the
lake-side (21: 20).

Second, the Fourth Gospel has a kind of character whom we
might call the *witness*. As the Fourth Gospel tells of the spear
thrust into the side of Jesus and the issue of the water and the
blood, there comes the comment: " He who saw it has borne
witness—his testimony is true, and he knows that he tells the
truth—that you also may believe " (19: 35). At the end of the
gospel comes the statement that it was the beloved disciple who
testified of these things " and we know that his testimony is
true " (21: 24).

Here we are faced with rather a strange thing. In the Fourth
Gospel John is never mentioned, but the beloved disciple is and
in addition there is a witness of some kind to the whole story. It
has never really been doubted in tradition that the beloved
disciple is John. A few have tried to identify him with Lazarus,
for Jesus is said to have loved Lazarus (*John* 11: 3, 5), or with
the Rich Young Ruler, of whom it is said that Jesus, looking on
him, loved him (*Mark* 10: 21). But although the gospel never
says so in so many words, tradition has always identified the
beloved disciple with John, and there is no real need to doubt
the identification.

But a very real point arises—suppose John himself actually
did the writing of the gospel, would he really be likely to speak
of himself as the disciple whom Jesus loved? Would he really be
likely to pick himself out like this, and, as it were, to say: " I
was his favourite; he loved me best of all "? It is surely very
unlikely that John would confer such a title on himself. If it was
conferred by others, it is a lovely title; if it was conferred by

himself, it comes perilously near to an almost incredible self-conceit.

Is there any way then that the gospel can be John's own eye-witness story, and yet at the same time have been actually written down by someone else?

THE PRODUCTION OF THE CHURCH

In our search for the truth we begin by noting one of the outstanding and unique features of the Fourth Gospel. The most remarkable thing about it is the long speeches of Jesus. Often they are whole chapters long, and are entirely unlike the way in which Jesus is portrayed as speaking in the other three gospels. The Fourth Gospel, as we have seen, was written about the year A.D. 100, that is, about seventy years after the crucifixion. Is it possible after these seventy years to look on these speeches as word for word reports of what Jesus said? Or can we explain them in some way that is perhaps even greater than that? We must begin by holding in our minds the fact of the speeches and the question which they inevitably raise.

And we have something to add to that. It so happens that in the writings of the early church we have a whole series of accounts of the way in which the Fourth Gospel came to be written. The earliest is that of Irenaeus who was bishop of Lyons about A.D. 177; and Irenaeus was himself a pupil of Polycarp, who in turn had actually been a pupil of John. There is therefore a direct link between Irenaeus and John. Irenaeus writes:

> " John, the disciple of the Lord, who also leant upon his breast, himself also *published* the gospel in Ephesus, when he was living in Asia."

The suggestive thing there is that Irenaeus does not merely say that John *wrote* the gospel; he says that John *published* (*exedōke*) it in Ephesus. The word that Irenaeus uses makes it sound, not like the private publication of some personal memoir, but like the public issue of some almost official document.

The next account is that of Clement who was head of the great school of Alexandria about A.D. 230. He writes:

" Last of all, John perceiving that the bodily facts had been made plain in the gospel, *being urged by his friends*, composed a spiritual gospel."

The important thing here is the phrase *being urged by his friends*. It begins to become clear that the Fourth Gospel is far more than one man's personal production and that there is a group, a community, a church behind it. On the same lines, a tenth century manuscript called the *Codex Toletanus*, which prefaces the New Testament books with short descriptions, prefaces the Fourth Gospel thus:

" The apostle John, whom the Lord Jesus loved most, last of all wrote this gospel, *at the request of the bishops of Asia*, against Cerinthus and other heretics."

Again we have the idea that behind the Fourth Gospel there is the authority of a group and of a church.

We now turn to a very important document, known as the Muratorian Canon. It is so called after a scholar Muratori who discovered it. It is the first list of New Testament books which the church ever issued and was compiled in Rome about A.D. 170. Not only does it list the New Testament books, it also gives short accounts of the origin and nature and contents of each of them. Its account of the way in which the Fourth Gospel came to be written is extremely important and illuminating.

" At the request of his fellow-disciples and of his bishops, John, one of the disciples, said: ' Fast with me for three days from this time and whatsoever shall be revealed to each of us, whether it be favourable to my writing or not, let us relate it to one another.' On the same night it was revealed to Andrew that John should relate all things, *aided by the revision of all*."

We cannot accept all that statement, because it is not possible that Andrew, the apostle, was in Ephesus in A.D. 100; but the point is that it is stated as clearly as possible that, while the authority and the mind and the memory behind the Fourth Gospel are that of John, it is clearly and definitely the product, not of one man, but of a group and a community.

Now we can see something of what happened. About the year A.D. 100 there was a group of men in Ephesus whose leader was John. They revered him as a saint and they loved him as a father. He must have been almost a hundred years old. Before he died, they thought most wisely that it would be a great thing if the aged apostle set down his memories of the years when he had been with Jesus. But in the end they did far more than that. We can think of them sitting down and reliving the old days. One would say: " Do you remember how Jesus said . . . ? " And John would say: " Yes, and now we know that he meant . . . "

In other words this group was not only writing down what Jesus *said*; that would have been a mere feat of memory. They were writing down what Jesus *meant*; that was the guidance of the Holy Spirit. John had thought about every word that Jesus had said; and he had thought under the guidance of the Holy Spirit who was so real to him. W. M. Macgregor has a sermon entitled: " What Jesus becomes to a man who has known him long." That is a perfect description of the Jesus of the Fourth Gospel. A. H. N. Green Armytage puts the thing perfectly in his book *John who saw*. *Mark*, he says, suits the *missionary* with his clear-cut account of the facts of Jesus's life; *Matthew* suits the *teacher* with his systematic account of the teaching of Jesus; *Luke* suits the *parish minister or priest* with his wide sympathy and his picture of Jesus as the friend of all; but *John* is the gospel of the *contemplative*.

He goes on to speak of the apparent contrast between *Mark* and *John*. " The two gospels are in a sense the same gospel. Only, where Mark saw things plainly, bluntly, literally, John saw them subtly, profoundly, spiritually. We might say that John lit Mark's pages by the lantern of a lifetime's meditation." Wordsworth defined poetry as " Emotion recollected in tranquillity ". That is a perfect description of the Fourth Gospel. That is why *John* is unquestionably the greatest of all the gospels. Its aim is, not to give us what Jesus said like a newspaper report, but to give us what Jesus meant. In it the Risen Christ still speaks. *John* is not so much *The Gospel according to St. John*; it is rather The *Gospel according to the Holy Spirit*. It was not John of Ephesus who wrote the Fourth Gospel; it was the Holy Spirit who wrote it through John.

THE PENMAN OF THE GOSPEL

We have one question still to ask. We can be quite sure that the mind and the memory behind the Fourth Gospel is that of John the apostle; but we have also seen that behind it is a witness who was the writer, in the sense that he was the actual penman. Can we find out who he was? We know from what the early church writers tell us that there were actually two Johns in Ephesus at the same time. There was John the apostle, but there was another John, who was known as John the elder.

Papias, who loved to collect all that he could find about the history of the New Testament and the story of Jesus, gives us some very interesting information. He was Bishop of Hierapolis, which is quite near Ephesus, and his dates are from about A.D. 70 to about A.D. 145. That is to say, he was actually a contemporary of John. He writes how he tried to find out " what Andrew said or what Peter said, or what was said by Philip, by Thomas, or by James, or by John, or by Matthew, or by any other of the disciples of the Lord; and what things Aristion and *the elder John*, the disciples of the Lord, say." In Ephesus there was the *apostle* John, and the *elder* John; and the elder John was so well-loved a figure that he was actually known as *The Elder*. He clearly had a unique place in the church. Both Eusebius and Dionysius the Great tell us that even to their own days in Ephesus there were two famous tombs, the one of John the apostle, and the other of John the elder.

Now let us turn to the two little letters, *Second John* and *Third John*. The *letters* come from the same hand as the gospel, and how do they begin? *The second letter begins*: " The elder unto the elect lady and her children " (2 *John* 1). *The third letter* begins: " The elder unto the beloved Gaius " (3 *John* 1). Here we have our solution. The actual penman of the letters was John the elder; the mind and memory behind them was the aged John the apostle, the master whom John the elder always described as " the disciple whom Jesus loved."

THE PRECIOUS GOSPEL

The more we know about the Fourth Gospel the more precious it becomes. For seventy years John had thought of Jesus. Day by day the Holy Spirit had opened out to him the meaning of what Jesus said. So when John was near the century of life and his days were numbered, he and his friends sat down to remember. John the elder held the pen to write for his master, John the apostle; and the last of the apostles set down, not only what he had heard Jesus say, but also what he now knew Jesus had meant. He remembered how Jesus had said: " I have yet many things to say to you, but you cannot bear them now. When the Spirit of Truth comes, he will guide you into all the truth " (*John* 16: 12, 13). There were many things which seventy years ago he had not understood; there were many things which in these seventy years the Spirit of Truth had revealed to him. These things John set down even as the eternal glory was dawning upon him. When we read this gospel let us remember that we are reading the gospel which of all the gospels is most the work of the Holy Spirit, speaking to us of the things which Jesus meant, speaking through the mind and memory of John the apostle and by the pen of John the elder. Behind this gospel is the whole church at Ephesus, the whole company of the saints, the last of the apostles, the Holy Spirit, the Risen Christ himself

JOHN

THE WORD

John 1: 1–18

When the world had its beginning, the Word was already there; and the Word was with God; and the Word was God. This Word was in the beginning with God. He was the agent through whom all things were made; and there is not a single thing which exists in this world which came into being without him. In him was life and the life was the light of men; and the light shines in the darkness, because the darkness has never been able to conquer it. There emerged a man sent from God whose name was John. He came as a witness, in order to bear witness to the light, that through him all might believe. He himself was not the light; his function was to bear witness to the light. He was the real light, who, in his coming into the world, gives light to every man. He was in the world, and, although the world was made by him, the world did not recognize him. It was into his own home that he came, and yet his own people did not receive him. To all those who did receive him, to those who believe in his name, he gave the right to become the children of God. These were born, not of blood, nor of any human impulse, nor of any man's will, but their birth was of God. So the Word became a person, and took up his abode in our being, full of grace and truth; and we beheld his glory, glory such as an only son receives from his father. John was his witness, for he cried: " This is he of whom I said to you, he who comes after me has been advanced before me, because he was before me. On his fullness we all of us have drawn, and we have received grace upon grace, because it was the law which was given by Moses, but grace and truth came through Jesus Christ. No one has ever seen God. It is the unique one, he who is God, he who is in the bosom of the Father, who has told us all about God."

WE shall go on to study this passage in short sections and in detail; but, before we do so, we must try to understand what John was seeking to say when he described Jesus as *the Word*.

THE WORD BECAME FLESH

THE first chapter of the Fourth Gospel is one of the greatest adventures of religious thought ever achieved by the mind of man.

It was not long before the Christian church was confronted with a very basic problem. It had begun in Judaism. In the beginning all its members had been Jews. By human descent Jesus was a Jew, and, to all intents and purposes, except for brief visits to the districts of Tyre and Sidon, and to the Decapolis, he was never outside Palestine. Christianity began amongst the Jews; and therefore inevitably it spoke in the Jewish language and used Jewish categories of thought.

But although it was cradled in Judaism it very soon went out into the wider world. Within thirty years of Jesus's death it had travelled all over Asia Minor and Greece and had arrived in Rome. By A.D. 60 there must have been a hundred thousand Greeks in the church for every Jew who was a Christian. Jewish ideas were completely strange to the Greeks. To take but one outstanding example, the Greeks had never heard of the Messiah. The very centre of Jewish expectation, the coming of the Messiah, was an idea that was quite alien to the Greeks. The very category in which the Jewish Christians conceived and presented Jesus meant nothing to them. Here then was the problem—how was Christianity to be presented to the Greek world?

Lecky, the historian, once said that the progress and spread of any idea depends, not only on its strength and force but on the predisposition to receive it of the age to which it is presented. The task of the Christian church was to create in the Greek world a predisposition to receive the Christian message. As E. J. Goodspeed put it, the question was, " Must a Greek who was interested in Christianity be routed through Jewish Messianic ideas and through Jewish ways of thinking, or could some new approach be found which would speak out of his background to his mind and heart? " The problem was how to

present Christianity in such a way that a Greek would understand.

Round about the year A.D. 100 there was a man in Ephesus
who was fascinated by that problem. His name was John. He
lived in a Greek city. He dealt with Greeks to whom Jewish
ideas were strange and unintelligible and even uncouth. How
could he find a way to present Christianity to these Greeks in a
way that they would welcome and understand? Suddenly the
solution flashed upon him. In both Greek and Jewish thought
there existed the conception of *the word*. Here was something
which could be worked out to meet the double world of Greek
Jew. Here was something which belonged to the heritage
of both races and that both could understand.

Let us then begin by looking at the two backgrounds of the
conception of *the word*.

THE JEWISH BACKGROUND

In the Jewish background four strands contributed something to the idea of the word.

(i) To the Jew a word was far more than a mere sound; it was
something which had an independent existence and which
actually did things. As Professor John Paterson has put it:
" The spoken word to the Hebrew was fearfully alive. . . . It was
a unit of energy charged with power. It flies like a bullet to its
billet." For that very reason the Hebrew was sparing of words.
Hebrew speech has fewer than 10,000; Greek speech has
200,000.

A modern poet tells how once the doer of an heroic deed was
unable to tell it to his fellow-tribesmen for lack of words.
Whereupon there arose a man " afflicted with the necessary
magic of words," and he told the story in terms so vivid and so
moving that " the words became alive and walked up and down
in the hearts of his hearers." The words of the poet became a
power. History has many an example of that kind of thing.

When John Knox preached in the days of the Reformation in
Scotland it was said that the voice of that one man put more
courage into the hearts of his hearers than ten thousand

trumpets braying in their ears. His words did things to people. In the days of the French Revolution Rouget de Lisle wrote the *Marseillaise* and that song sent men marching to revolution. The words did things. In the days of the Second World War, when Britain was bereft alike of allies and of weapons, the words of the Prime Minister, Sir Winston Churchill, as he broadcast to the nation, did things to people.

It was even more so in the East, and still is. To the eastern people a word is not merely a sound; it is a power which does things. Once when Sir George Adam Smith was travelling in the desert in the East, a group of Moslems gave his party the customary greeting: " Peace be upon you." At the moment they failed to notice that he was a Christian. When they discovered that they had spoken a blessing to an infidel, they hurried back to ask for the blessing back again. The word was like a thing which could be sent out to do things and which could be brought back again. Will Carleton, the poet, expresses something like that:

> " Boys flying kites haul in their white-winged birds;
> You can't do that way when you're flying words:
> ' Careful with fire,' is good advice we know,
> ' Careful with words,' is ten times doubly so.
> Thoughts unexpressed may sometimes fall back dead,
> But God himself can't kill them when they're said."

We can well understand how to the eastern peoples words had an independent, power-filled existence.

(ii) Of that general idea of the power of words, the Old Testament is full. Once Isaac had been deceived into blessing Jacob instead of Esau, nothing he could do could take that word of blessing back again (*Genesis* 27). The word had gone out and had begun to act and nothing could stop it. In particular we see the word of God in action in the Creation story. At every stage of it we read: " And God said ... " (*Genesis* 1: 3, 6, 11). The word of God is the creating power. Again and again we get this idea of the creative, acting, dynamic word of God. " By the word of the Lord the heavens

were made " (*Psalm* 33: 6). " He sent forth his word and healed
them " (*Psalm* 107: 20). " He sent forth his commands to the
earth; his word runs swiftly " (*Psalm* 147: 15). " So shall my
word be that goes forth from my mouth; it shall not return to
me empty, but it shall accomplish that which I purpose, and
prosper in the thing for which I sent it " (*Isaiah* 55: 11). " Is not
my word like fire, and, says the Lord, like a hammer which
breaks the rock in pieces? " (*Jeremiah* 23: 29). " Thou spakest
from the beginning of creation, even the first day, and saidst
thus: ' Let heaven and earth be made.' And thy word was a
perfect work " (2 *Esdras* 6: 38). The writer of the *Book of
Wisdom* addresses God as the one, " who hast made all things
with thy word " (*Wisdom* 9: 1). Everywhere in the Old Testament there is this idea of the powerful, creative word. Even
men's words have a kind of dynamic activity; how much more
must it be so with God?

(iii) There came into Hebrew religious life something which
greatly accentuated the development of this idea of the word of
God. For a hundred years and more before the coming of Jesus
Hebrew was a forgotten language. The Old Testament was
written in Hebrew but the Jews no longer knew the language.
The scholars knew it, but not the ordinary people. They spoke a
development of Hebrew called Aramaic which is to Hebrew
somewhat as modern English is to Anglo-Saxon. Since that was
so the scriptures of the Old Testament had to be translated into
this language that the people could understand, and these
translations were called the *Targums*. In the synagogue the
scriptures were read in the original Hebrew, but then they were
translated into Aramaic and *Targums* were used as translations.

The *Targums* were produced in a time when men were
fascinated by the transcendence of God and could think of
nothing but the distance and the difference of God. Because of
that the men who made the *Targums* were very much afraid of
attributing human thoughts and feelings and actions to God. To
put it in technical language, they made every effort to avoid
anthropomorphism in speaking of him.

Now the Old Testament regularly speaks of God in a human way; and wherever they met a thing like that the *Targums* substituted *the word of God* for the name of God. Let us see how this custom worked. In *Exodus* 19: 17 we read that " Moses brought the people out of the camp *to meet God*." The *Targums* thought that was too human a way to speak of God, so they said that Moses brought the people out of the camp to meet the *word of God*. In *Exodus* 31: 13 we read that God said to the people that the Sabbath " is a sign between me and you throughout your generations." That was far too human a way to speak for the *Targums*, and so they said that the Sabbath is a sign " between *my word* and you." *Deuteronomy* 9: 3 says that God is a consuming fire, but the *Targums* translated it that *the word* of God is a consuming fire. *Isaiah* 48: 13 has a great picture of creation: " My hand laid the foundation of the earth, and my right hand spread out the heavens." That was much too human a picture of God for the *Targums* and they made God say: " By *my word* I have founded the earth; and by my strength I have hung up the heavens." Even so wonderful a passage as *Deuteronomy* 33: 27 which speaks of God's " everlasting arms " was changed, and became: " The eternal God is thy refuge, and by his word the world was created."

In the Jonathan *Targum* the phrase *the word of God* occurs no fewer than about three hundred and twenty times. It is quite true that it is simply a periphrasis for the name of God; but the fact remains that the *word of God* became one of the commonest forms of Jewish expression. It was a phrase which any devout Jew would recognize because he heard it so often in the synagogue when scripture was read. Every Jew was used to speaking of *the Memra, the word* of God.

(iv) At this stage we must look more fully at something we already began to look at in the introduction. The Greek term for *word* is *Logos*; but *Logos* does not only mean *word*; it also means *reason*. For John, and for all the great thinkers who made use of this idea, these two meanings were always closely intertwined. Whenever they used *Logos* the twin ideas of the Word of God and the Reason of God were in their minds.

The Jews had a type of literature called *The Wisdom Literature* which was the concentrated wisdom of sages. It is not usually speculative and philosophical, but practical wisdom for the living and management of life. In the Old Testament the great example of Wisdom Literature is the *Book of Proverbs*. In this book there are certain passages which give a mysterious life-giving and eternal power to *Wisdom* (*Sophia*). In these passages Wisdom has been, as it were, personified, and is thought of as the eternal agent and co-worker of God. There are three main passages.

The first is *Proverbs* 3: 13–26. Out of that passage we may specially note:

" She is a tree of *life* to those who lay hold of her; those who hold her fast are called happy. *The Lord by wisdom* founded the earth; by understanding he established the heavens; by his knowledge the deeps broke forth, and the clouds drop down the dew " (Proverbs 3: 18–20).

We remember that *Logos* means *Word* and also means *Reason*. We have already seen how the Jews thought of the powerful and creative word of God. Here we see the other side beginning to emerge. *Wisdom* is God's agent in enlightenment and in creation; and *Wisdom* and *Reason* are very much the same thing. We have seen how important *Logos* was in the sense of *Word*; now we see it beginning to be important in the sense of *Wisdom* or *Reason*.

The second important passage is *Proverbs* 4: 5–13. In it we may notice:

" Keep hold of instruction, do not let go; guard her, for she is your life."

The *Word* is the *light* of men and *Wisdom* is the *light* of men. The two ideas are amalgamating with each other rapidly now.

The most important passage of all is in *Proverbs* 8: 1—9: 2. In it we may specially note:

" The Lord created me (Wisdom is speaking) at the beginning of his work, the first of his acts of old. Ages ago I was set up, at the first, before the beginning of the earth. When there were no depths I was brought forth, when there were no springs abounding with water. Before the mountains had been shaped, before the hills, I was brought forth; before he had made the earth with its fields, or the first of the dust of the world. When he established the heavens, I was there, when he drew a circle on the face of the deep; when he made firm the skies above; when he established the fountains of the deep; when he assigned to the sea its limit, so that the waters might not transgress his command; when he marked out the foundations of the earth, then I was beside him, like a master workman; and I was daily his delight, rejoicing before him always " (*Proverbs* 8: 22–30).

When we read that passage there is echo after echo of what John says of the *word* in the first chapter of his gospel. *Wisdom* had that eternal existence, that light-giving function, that creative power which John attributed to the *word*, the *Logos*, with which he identified Jesus Christ.

The development of this idea of *wisdom* did not stop here. Between the Old and the New Testament, men went on producing this kind of writing called Wisdom Literature. It had so much concentrated wisdom in it and drew so much from the experience of wise men that it was a priceless guide for life. In particular two very great books were written, which are included in the *Apocrypha* and which it will do any man's soul good to read.

(*a*) The first is called *The Wisdom of Jesus, the son of Sirach*, or, as it is better known, *Ecclesiasticus*. It too makes much of this great conception of the creative and eternal wisdom of God.

> " The sand of the sea, and the drops of the rain,
> And the days of eternity who shall number?
> The height of the heaven and the breadth of the earth
> And the deep and wisdom, who shall search them out?
> *Wisdom hath been created before all things,*
> And the understanding of prudence from everlasting "
> (*Ecclesiasticus* 1: 1–10).

" I came forth from the mouth of the Most High,
    And covered the earth as a mist.
    I dwelt in high places,
    And my throne is in the pillar of the cloud.
    Alone I compassed the circuit of the heaven,
    And walked in the depth of the abyss "

(Ecclesiasticus 24: 3–5).

" He created me from the beginning of the world,
    And to the end I shall not fail "

(Ecclesiasticus 24: 9).

Here again we find wisdom as the eternal, creative power which was at God's side in the days of creation and the beginning of time.

(*b*) *Ecclesiasticus* was written in Palestine about the year 100 B.C.; and at almost the same time an equally great book was written in Alexandria in Egypt, called *The Wisdom of Solomon.* In it there is the greatest of all pictures of *wisdom. Wisdom* is the treasure which men use to become the friends of God (7: 14). *Wisdom* is the artificer of all things (7: 22). She is the breath of the power of God and a pure effluence flowing from the Almighty (7: 25). She can do all things and makes all things new (7: 27).

But the writer does more than talk about *wisdom*; he equates *wisdom* and the *word*. To him the two ideas are the same. He can talk of the *wisdom of God* and the *word of God* in the same sentence and with the same meaning. When he prays to God, his address is:

" O God of my fathers, and Lord of mercy, who hast made all things with *thy word*, and ordained man through *thy wisdom* " (9 : 2).

He can speak of *the word* almost as John was to speak:

" For while all things were in quiet silence, and that night was in the midst of her swift course, *thine Almighty word* leaped down from heaven out of thy royal throne, as a fierce man of war into the midst of a land of destruction, and brought thine unfeigned commandment as a sharp sword, and standing up filled all things

with death; and it touched the heaven but it stood upon the earth "
(18: 14–16).

To the writer of the *Book of Wisdom, wisdom* was God's eternal,
creative, illuminating power; *wisdom* and *the word* were one
and the same. It was *wisdom* and *the word* who were God's
instruments and agents in creation and who ever bring the will
of God to the mind and heart of man.

So when John was searching for a way in which he could
commend Christianity he found in his own faith and in the
record of his own people the idea of *the word*, the ordinary word
which is in itself not merely a sound, but a dynamic thing, the
word of God by which God created the world, the *word* of the
Targums which expressed the very idea of the action of God, the
wisdom of the Wisdom Literature which was the eternal creative and illuminating power of God. So John said: " If you wish
to see that *word* of God, if you wish to see the creative power of
God, if you wish to see that *word* which brought the world
into existence and which gives light and life to every man, *look
at Jesus Christ*. In him the *word* of God came among you."

THE GREEK BACKGROUND

We began by seeing that John's problem was not that of
presenting Christianity to the Jewish world, but of presenting it
to the Greek world. How then did this idea of the *word* fit into
Greek thought? It was already there waiting to be used. In
Greek thought the idea of the *word* began away back about 560
B.C., and, strangely enough, in Ephesus where the Fourth Gospel
was written.

In 560 B.C. there was an Ephesian philosopher called
Heraclitus whose basic idea was that everything is in a state of
flux. Everything was changing from day to day and from
moment to moment. His famous illustration was that it was
impossible to step twice into the same river. You step into a
river; you step out; you step in again; but you do not step into
the same river, for the water has flowed on and it is a different
river. To Heraclitus everything was like that, everything was in
a constantly changing state of flux. But if that be so, why was

life not complete chaos? How can there be any sense in a world where there was constant flux and change?

The answer of Heraclitus was: all this change and flux was not haphazard; it was controlled and ordered, following a continuous pattern all the time; and that which controlled the pattern was the *Logos*, the *word*, the *reason* of God. To Heraclitus, the *Logos* was the principle of order under which the universe continued to exist. Heraclitus went further. He held that not only was there a pattern in the physical world; there was also a pattern in the world of events. He held that nothing moved with aimless feet; in all life and in all the events of life there was a purpose, a plan and a design. And what was it that controlled events? Once again, the answer was *Logos*.

Heraclitus took the matter even nearer home. What was it that in us individually told us the difference between right and wrong? What made us able to think and to reason? What enabled us to choose aright and to recognize the truth when we saw it? Once again Heraclitus gave the same answer. What gave a man reason and knowledge of the truth and the ability to judge between right and wrong was the *Logos* of God dwelling within him. Heraclitus held that in the world of nature and events " all things happen according to the *Logos*," and that in the individual man " the *Logos* is the judge of truth." The *Logos* was nothing less than the mind of God controlling the world and every man in it.

Once the Greeks had discovered this idea they never let it go. It fascinated them, especially the Stoics. The Stoics were always left in wondering amazement at the order of the world. Order always implies a mind. The Stoics asked: " What keeps the stars in their courses? What makes the tides ebb and flow? What makes day and night come in unalterable order? What brings the seasons round at their appointed times? " And they answered; " All things are controlled by the *Logos* of God. The *Logos* is the power which puts sense into the world, the power which makes the world an order instead of a chaos, the power which set the world going and keeps it going in its perfect order. " The *Logos*," said the Stoics, " pervades all things."

There is still another name in the Greek world at which we must look. In Alexandria there was a Jew called Philo who had made it the business of his life to study the wisdom of two worlds, the Jewish and the Greek. No man ever knew the Jewish scriptures as he knew them; and no Jew ever knew the greatness of Greek thought as he knew it. He too knew and used and loved this idea of the *Logos*, the *word*, the *reason* of God. He held that the *Logos* was the oldest thing in the world and the instrument through which God had made the world. He said that the *Logos* was the thought of God stamped upon the universe; he talked about the *Logos* by which God made the world and all things; he said that God, the pilot of the universe, held the *Logos* as a tiller and with it steered all things. He said that man's mind was stamped also with the *Logos*, that the *Logos* was what gave a man reason, the power to think and the power to know. He said that the *Logos* was the intermediary between the world and God and that the *Logos* was the priest who set the soul before God.

Greek thought knew all about the *Logos*; it saw in the *Logos* the creating and guiding and directing power of God, the power which made the universe and kept it going. So John came to the Greeks and said: " For centuries you have been thinking and writing and dreaming about the *Logos*, the power which made the world, the power which keeps the order of the world, the power by which men think and reason and know, the power by which men come into contact with God. Jesus is that *Logos* come down to earth." " The word," said John, " became flesh." We could put it another way—" The Mind of God became a person."

BOTH JEW AND GREEK

Slowly the Jews and Greeks had thought their way to the conception of the *Logos*, the Mind of God which made the world and makes sense of it. So John went out to Jews and Greeks to tell them that in Jesus Christ this creating, illuminating, controlling, sustaining mind of God had come to earth. He came to tell them that men need no longer guess and grope;

all that they had to do was to look at Jesus and see the Mind of God.

THE ETERNAL WORD

John 1: 1, 2

> When the world had its beginning, the word was already there; and the word was with God; and the word was God. This word was in the beginning with God.

THE beginning of John's gospel is of such importance and of such depth of meaning that we must study it almost verse by verse. It is John's great thought that Jesus is none other than God's creative and life-giving and light-giving word, that Jesus is the power of God which created the world and the reason of God which sustains the world come to earth in human and bodily form.

Here at the beginning John says three things about the word; which is to say that he says three things about Jesus.

(i) The word was already there at the very beginning things. John's thought is going back to the first verse of the Bible. " In the beginning God created the heavens and the earth " (*Genesis* 1: 1). What John is saying is this—the word is not one of the created things; the word was there *before creation.* the word is not part of the world which came into being in time; the word is part of eternity and was there with God before time and the world began. John was thinking of what is known as *the pre-existence of Christ*.

In many ways this idea of pre-existence is very difficult, if not altogether impossible, to grasp. But it does mean one very simple, very practical, and very tremendous thing. If the word was with God before time began, if God's word is part of the eternal scheme of things, it means that *God was always like Jesus*. Sometimes we tend to think of God as stern and avenging; and we tend to think that something Jesus did changed God's anger into love and altered his attitude to men.

The New Testament knows nothing of that idea. The whole
New Testament tells us, this passage of John especially, that
God has always been like Jesus. What Jesus did was to open a
window in time that we might see the eternal and unchanging
love of God.

We may well ask, "What then about some of the things
that we read in the Old Testament? What about the passages
which speak about commandments of God to wipe out whole
cities and to destroy men, women and children? What of the
anger and the destructiveness and the jealousy of God that we
sometimes read of in the older parts of Scripture? " The answer
is this—it is not God who has changed; it is men's knowledge
of him that has changed. Men wrote these things because they
did not know any better; that was the stage which their
knowledge of God had reached.

When a child is learning any subject, he has to learn it stage
by stage. He does not begin with full knowledge; he begins with
what he can grasp and goes on to more and more. When he
begins music appreciation, he does not start with a Bach
Prelude and Fugue; he starts with something much more
simple; and goes through stage after stage until his knowledge
grows. It was that way with men and God. They could only
grasp and understand God's nature and his ways in part. It was
only when Jesus came that they saw fully and completely what
God has *always* been like.

It is told that a little girl was once confronted with some of
the more bloodthirsty and savage parts of the Old Testament.
Her comment was: " But that happened before God became a
Christian! " If we may so put it with all reverence, when John
says that the word was always there, he is saying that God was
always a Christian. He is telling us that God was and is and
ever shall be like Jesus; but men could never know and realize
that until Jesus came.

(ii) John goes on to say that *the word was with God.* What
does he mean by that? He means that always there has been the
closest connection between the word and God. Let us put that
in another and a simpler way—there has always been the most

intimate connection between Jesus and God. That means no
one can tell us what God is like, what God's will is for us, what
God's love and heart and mind are like, as Jesus can.

Let us take a simple human analogy. If we want to know
what someone really thinks and feels about something, and if
we are unable to approach the person ourselves, we do not go to
someone who is merely an acquaintance of that person, to
someone who has known him only a short time; we go to
someone whom we know to be an intimate friend of many
years' standing. We know that he will really be able to interpret
the mind and the heart of the other person to us.

It is something like that that John is saying about Jesus. He
is saying that John has always been with God. Let us use very
human language because it is the only language we can use.
John is saying that Jesus is so intimate with God that God has
no secrets from him; and that, therefore, Jesus is the one person
in all the universe who can reveal to us what God is like and
how God feels towards us.

(iii) Finally John says that *the word was God*. This is a
difficult saying for us to understand, and it is difficult because
Greek, in which John wrote, had a different way of saying
things from the way in which English speaks. When Greek uses
a noun it almost always uses the definite article with it. The
Greek for God is *theos* and the definite article is *ho*. When
Greek speaks about God it does not simply say *theos*; it says
ho theos. Now when Greek does not use the definite article with
a noun that noun becomes much more like an adjective. John
did not say that the word was *ho theos*; that would have been to
say that the word was *identical* with God. He said that the word
was *theos*—without the definite article—which means that the
word was, we might say, of the very same character and quality
and essence and being as God. When John said *the word was
God* he was not saying that Jesus was identical with God; he
was saying that Jesus was so perfectly the same as God in
mind, in heart, in being that in him we perfectly see what God is
like.

So right at the beginning of his gospel John lays it down that

in Jesus, and in him alone, there is perfectly revealed to men all
that God always was and always will be, and all that he feels
towards and desires for men.

THE CREATOR OF ALL THINGS

John 1: 3

> He was the agent through whom all things were made; and there is
> not a single thing which exists in this world which came into being
> without him.

IT may seem strange to us that John so stresses the way in
which the world was created; and it may seem strange that he
so definitely connects Jesus with the work of creation. But he
had to do this because of a certain tendency in the thought of
his day.

In the time of John there was a kind of heresy called
Gnosticism. Its characteristic was that it was an intellectual and
philosophical approach to Christianity. To the Gnostics the
simple beliefs of the ordinary Christian were not enough. They
tried to construct a philosophic system out of Christianity.
They were troubled about the existence of sin and evil and
sorrow and suffering in this world, so they worked out a theory
to explain it. The theory was this.

In the beginning two things existed—the one was God and
the other was matter. Matter was always there and was the raw
material out of which the world was made. The Gnostics held
that this original matter was flawed and imperfect. We might
put it that the world got off to a bad start. It was made of
material which had the seeds of corruption in it.

The Gnostics went further. God, they said, is pure spirit, and
pure spirit can never touch matter at all, still less matter which
is imperfect. Therefore it was not possible for God to carry out
the work of creation himself. So he put out from himself a series
of emanations. Each emanation was further and further away
from God and as the emanations got further and further away

from him, they knew less and less about him. About halfway down the series there was an emanation which knew nothing at all about God. Beyond that stage the emanations began to be not only ignorant of but actually hostile to God. Finally in the series there was an emanation which was so distant from God that it was totally ignorant of him and totally hostile to him—and that emanation was the power which created the world, because it was so distant from God that it was possible for it to touch this flawed and evil matter. The creator god was utterly divorced from and utterly at enmity with the real God.

The Gnostics took one step further. They identified the creator god with the God of the Old Testament; and they held that the God of the Old Testament was quite different from, quite ignorant of and quite hostile to the God and Father of Jesus Christ.

In the time of John this kind of belief was widespread. Men believed that the world was evil and that an evil God had created it. It is to combat this teaching that John here lays down two basic Christian truths. In point of fact the connection of Jesus with creation is repeatedly laid down in the New Testament, just because of this background of thought which divorced God from the world in which we live. In *Colossians* 1: 16 Paul writes: " For in him all things were created, in heaven and on earth ... all things were created through him and for him." In 1 *Corinthians* 8: 6 he writes of the Lord Jesus Christ " through whom are all things." The writer to the Hebrews speaks of the one who was the Son, " through whom also God created the world " (*Hebrews* 1: 2). John and the other New Testament writers who spoke like this were stressing two great truths.

(i) Christianity has always believed in what is called *creation out of nothing*. We do not believe that in his creation of the world God had to work with alien and evil matter. We do not believe that the world began with an essential flaw in it. We do not believe that the world began with God and something else. It is our belief that behind everything there is God and God alone.

(ii) Christianity has always believed that this is *God's world*. So far from being so detached from the world that he could have nothing to do with it, God is intimately involved in it. The Gnostics tried to put the blame for the evil of the world on the shoulders of its creator. Christianity believes that what is wrong with the world is due to man's sin. But even though sin has injured the world and kept it from being what it might have been, we can never despise the world, because it is essentially God's. If we believe this it gives us a new sense of the value of the world and a new sense of responsibility to it.

There is a story of a child from the back streets of a great city who was taken for a day in the country. When she saw the bluebells in the woods, she asked: " Do you think God would mind if I picked some of his flowers? " This is God's world; because of that nothing is out of his control; and because of that we must use all things in the awareness that they belong to God. The Christian does not belittle the world by thinking that it was created by an ignorant and a hostile god; he glorifies it by remembering that everywhere God is behind it and in it. He believes that the Christ who re-creates the world was the co-worker of God when the world was first created, and that, in the act of redemption, God is seeking to win back that which was always his own.

LIFE AND LIGHT

John 1: 4

In him was life and the life was the light of men.

IN a great piece of music the composer often begins by stating the themes which he is going to elaborate in the course of the work. That is what John does here. *Life* and *light* are two of the great basic words on which the Fourth Gospel is built up. They are two of the main themes which it is the aim of the gospel to develop and to expound. Let us look at them in detail.

The Fourth Gospel begins and ends with *life*. At the very

beginning we read that in Jesus was *life*; and at the very end we read that John's aim in writing the gospel was that men might " believe that Jesus is the Christ, the Son of God, and that believing you may have *life* in his name " (*John* 20: 31). The word is continually on the lips of Jesus. It is his wistful regret that men will not come to him that they might have *life* (5:40). It is his claim that he came that men might have *life* and that they might have it abundantly (10: 10). He claims that he gives men *life* and that they will never perish because no one will snatch them out of his hand (10: 28). He claims that he is the way, the truth and the *life* (14: 6). In the gospel the word *life* (*zōē*) occurs more than thirty-five times and the verb *to live* or *to have life* (*zēn*) more than fifteen times. What then does John mean by *life*?

(i) Quite simply he means that *life* is the opposite of destruction, condemnation and death. God sent his Son that the man who believes should not perish but have eternal *life* (3: 16). The man who hears and believes has eternal *life* and will not come into judgment (5: 24). There is a contrast between the resurrection to *life* and the resurrection to *judgment* (5: 29). Those to whom Jesus gives *life* will never perish (10: 28). There is in Jesus that which gives a man security in this life and in the life to come. Until we accept Jesus and take him as our saviour and enthrone him as our king we cannot be said to live at all. The man who lives a Christless life *exists*, but he does not know what *life* is. Jesus is the one person who can make life worth living, and in whose company death is only the prelude to fuller life.

(ii) But John is quite sure that, although Jesus is the bringer of this *life*, the giver of life is God. Again and again John uses the phrase *the living God*, as indeed the whole Bible does. It is the will of the Father who sent Jesus that everyone who sees him and believes on him should have life (6: 40). Jesus is the giver of life because the Father has set his own seal of approval upon him (6: 27). He gives life to as many as God has given him (17: 2). At the back of it all there is God. It is as if God was saying: " I created men that they should have real life; through their sin they have ceased to live and only exist; I have sent them my Son to enable them to know what real life is."

(iii) We must ask what this life is. Again and again the Fourth Gospel uses the phrase *eternal life*. We shall discuss the full meaning of that phrase later. At present we note this. The word John uses for *eternal* is *aiōnios*. Clearly whatever else *eternal* life is, it is not simply life which lasts for ever. A life which lasted for ever could be a terrible curse; often the thing for which men long is release from life. In eternal life there must be more than *duration* of life; there must be a certain *quality* of life.

Life is not desirable unless it is a certain kind of life. Here we have the clue. *Aiōnios* is the adjective which is repeatedly used to describe God. In the true sense of the word *only* God is *aiōnios*, *eternal*; therefore *eternal life is that life which God lives*. What Jesus offers us from God is God's own life. Eternal life is life which knows something of the serenity and power of the life of God himself. When Jesus came offering men *eternal life*, he was inviting them to enter into the very life of God.

(iv) How, then, do we enter into that life? We enter into it *by believing in Jesus Christ*. The word *to believe* (*pisteuein*) occurs in the Fourth Gospel no fewer than seventy times. " He who believes in the Son has eternal life " (3: 36). " He who believes," says Jesus, " has eternal life " (6: 47). It is God's will that men should see the Son, and believe in him, and have eternal life (5: 24). What does John mean by *to believe*? He means two things.

(*a*) He means that we must be convinced that Jesus is really and truly the Son of God. He means that we must make up our minds about him. After all, if Jesus is only a man, there is no reason why we should give him the utter and implicit obedience that he demands. We have to think out for ourselves who he was. We have to look at him, learn about him, study him, think about him until we are driven to the conclusion that this is none other than the Son of God. (*b*) But there is more than intellectual belief in this. To believe in Jesus means to take Jesus at his word, to accept his commandments as absolutely binding, to believe without question that what he says is true.

For John, belief means the conviction of the mind that Jesus is the Son of God, the trust of the heart that everything he says is true and the basing of every action on the unshakable assurance that we must take him at his word. When we do that we stop existing and begin living. We know what *Life* with a capital L really means.

LIFE AND LIGHT

John 1: 4 (*continued*)

In him was life and the life was the light of men.

THE second of the great Johannine key-words which we meet here is the word *light*. This word occurs in the Fourth Gospel no fewer than twenty-one times. Jesus is the *light* of men. .The function of John the Baptist was to point men to that *light* which was in Christ. Twice Jesus calls himself the *light* of the world (8: 12; 9: 5). This *light* can be in men (11: 10), so that they can become children of the *light* (12: 36), " I have come," said Jesus, " as light into the world " (12: 46). Let us see if we can understand something of this idea of the *light* which Jesus brings into the world. Three things stand out.

(i) The *light* Jesus brings is the *light* which puts chaos to flight. In the creation story God moved upon the dark, formless chaos which was before the world began and said: " Let there be light " (*Genesis* 1: 3). The new-created light of God routed the empty chaos into which it came. So Jesus is *the light which shines in the darkness* (1: 5). He is the one person who can save life from becoming a chaos. Left to ourselves we are at the mercy of our passions and our fears.

When Jesus dawns upon life, light comes. One of the oldest fears in the world is the fear of the dark. There is a story of a child who was to sleep in a strange house. His hostess, thinking to be kind, offered to leave the light on when he went to bed. Politely he declined the offer. " I thought," said his hostess, " that you might be afraid of the dark." " Oh, no," said the lad,

" you see, it's God's dark." With Jesus the night is light about us as the day.

(ii) The *light* which Jesus brings is a revealing *light*. It is the condemnation of men that they loved the darkness rather than the *light*; and they did so because their deeds were evil; and they hated the *light* lest their deeds should be exposed (3: 19, 20). The *light* which Jesus brings is something which shows things as they are. It strips away the disguises and the concealments; it shows things in all their nakedness; it shows them in their true character and their true values.

Long ago the Cynics said that men hate the truth for the truth is like the light to sore eyes. In Caedmon's poem there is a strange picture. It is a picture of the last day and in the centre of the scene there is the Cross; and from the Cross there flows a strange blood-red light, and the mysterious quality of that light is such that it shows things as they are. The externals, the disguises, the outer wrappings and trappings are stripped away; and everything stands revealed in the naked and awful loneliness of what it essentially is.

We never see ourselves until we see ourselves through the eyes of Jesus. We never see what our lives are like until we see them in the light of Jesus. Jesus often drives us to God by revealing us to ourselves.

(iii) The *light* which Jesus brings is a guiding *light*. If a man does not possess that *light* he walks in darkness and does not know where he is going (12: 36). When a man receives that *light* and believes in it, he walks no more in darkness (12: 46). One of the features of the gospel stories which no one can miss is the number of people who came running to Jesus asking: " What am I to do? " When Jesus comes into life the time of guessing and of groping is ended, the time of doubt and uncertainty and vacillation is gone. The path that was dark becomes light; the decision that was wrapped in a night of uncertainty is illumined. Without Jesus we are like men groping on an unknown road in a black-out. With him the way is clear.

THE HOSTILE DARK

John 1: 5

> And the light shines in the darkness, and the darkness did not put
> it out.

HERE we meet another of John's key-words—*darkness* (*skotos*,
skotia). This word occurs seven times in the gospel. To John
there was a *darkness* in the world that was as real as the *light*.

(i) The *darkness* is hostile to the *light*. The light shines in the
darkness, but, however hard the *darkness* tries, it cannot
extinguish it. Sinning man loves the *darkness* and hates the
light, because the light shows up too many things.

It may well be that in John's mind there is a borrowed
thought here. John, as we know, was prepared to go out and to
take in new ideas, if by so doing he could present and commend
the Christian message to men. The great Persian religion of
Zoroastrianism had at this time a very great influence on men's
thoughts. It believed that there were two great opposing powers
in the universe, the god of the light and the god of the dark,
Ahriman and Ormuzd. This whole universe was a battle-ground
in the eternal, cosmic conflict between the light and the dark;
and all that mattered in life was the side a man chose.

So John is saying: " Into this world there comes Jesus, the
light of the world; there is a darkness which would seek to
eliminate him, to banish him from life, to extinguish him. But
there is a power in Jesus that is undefeatable. The darkness can
hate him, but it can never get rid of him." As has been truly
said: " Not all the darkness in the world can extinguish the
littlest flame." The unconquerable light will in the end defeat the
hostile dark. John is saying: " Choose your side in the eternal
conflict and choose aright."

(ii) The *darkness* stands for the natural sphere of all those
who hate the good. It is men whose deeds are evil who fear the
light (3: 19, 20). The man who has something to hide loves the
dark; but it is impossible to hide anything from God. His

searchlight sweeps the shadows and illuminates the skulking evils of the world.

(iii) There are certain passages where the *darkness* seems to stand for *ignorance*, especially for that wilful ignorance which refuses the light of Jesus Christ. Jesus says: " I am the light of the world; he who follows me will not walk in *darkness* " (8: 12). He says to his disciples that the light will be with them only for so short a time; let them walk in it; if they do not, the *darkness* comes and a man who walks in *darkness* does not know where he is going (12: 35). He says that he came with his light that men should not abide in *darkness* (12: 46). Without Jesus Christ a man cannot find or see the way. He is like a blindfolded man or even a blind man. Without Jesus Christ life goes lost. It was Goethe who cried out for: " Light, more light! " It was one of the old Scots leaders who said to his friends towards the end: " Light the candle that I may see to die." Jesus is the light which shows a man the road, and which lights the road at every step of the way.

There are times when John uses this word *darkness* symbolically. He uses it at times to mean more than merely the dark of an earthly night. He tells of Jesus walking on the water. He tells how the disciples had embarked on their boat and were crossing the lake without Jesus; and then he says, " *And it was now dark*, and Jesus had not yet come to them " (6: 17). Without the presence of Jesus there was nothing but the threatening dark. He tells of the Resurrection morning and of the hours before those who had loved Jesus realized that he had risen from the dead. He begins the story: " Now on the first day of the week Mary Magdalene came, *while it was still dark* " (20: 1). She was living at the moment in a world from which she thought Jesus had been eliminated, and a world like that was dark. He tells the story of the Last Supper. He tells how Judas received the sop and then went out to do his terrible work and arrange for the betrayal of Jesus; and he says with a kind of terrible symbolism: " So, after receiving the morsel, he immediately went out; *and it was night* " (13: 30). Judas was going out into the night of a life which had betrayed Christ.

To John the Christless life was life in the dark. The *darkness* stands for life without Christ, and especially for that which has turned its back on Christ.

Before we leave this passage there is one other thing to note. The word which we have translated *put out* is in Greek *katalambanein*. This word can have three meanings.

(*a*) It can mean that the darkness never *understood* the light. There is a sense in which the man of the world simply cannot understand the demands of Christ and the way Christ offers him. To him it seems sheer foolishness. A man cannot understand Christ until he first submits to him.

(*b*) It can mean the darkness never *overcame* the light. *Katalambanein* can mean *to pursue until one overtakes and so lays hold on and overcomes*. This could mean that the darkness of the world had done everything possible to eliminate Jesus Christ, even to crucifying him, but it could never destroy him. This could be a reference to the crucified and conquering Christ.

(*c*) It can be used of *extinguishing a fire or flame*. That is the sense in which we have taken it here. Although men did all they could to obscure and extinguish the light of God in Christ, they could not quench it. In every generation the light of Christ still shines in spite of the efforts of men to extinguish the flame.

THE WITNESS TO JESUS CHRIST

John 1: 6–8

> There emerged a man sent from God whose name was John. He came as a witness, in order to bear witness to the light, that through him all might believe. He himself was not the light; his function was to bear witness to the light.

IT is a strange fact that in the Fourth Gospel every reference to John the Baptist is a reference of depreciation. There is an explanation of that. John was a prophetic voice; for four

hundred years the voice of prophecy had been silent, and in
John it spoke again. It seems that certain people were so
fascinated by John that they gave him a higher place than he
ought to have had. There are, in fact, indications that there was
actually a sect who put John the Baptist in the highest place.
We find an echo of them in *Acts* 19: 3, 4. In Ephesus Paul came
upon certain people who knew nothing but the baptism of John.
It was not that the Fourth Gospel wished to criticize John or
that it under-rated his importance. It was simply that John
knew that there were certain people who gave John the Baptist
a place that encroached upon the place of Jesus himself.

So all through the Fourth Gospel John is careful to point out
that the place of John the Baptist in the scheme of things was
high, but that nonetheless it was still subordinate to the place of
Jesus Christ. Here he is careful to say that John was not that
light, but only a witness to the light (1: 8). He shows us John
denying that he was the Christ, or even that he was the great
prophet whom Moses had promised (1: 20). When the Jews
came to John and told him that Jesus had begun his career as a
teacher they must have expected John to resent this intrusion.
But the Fourth Gospel shows us John denying that the first
place was his and declaring that he must decrease while Jesus
increased (3: 25–30). It is pointed out that Jesus was more
successful in his appeal to men than John was (4: 1). It is
pointed out that even the people said that John was not able to
do the things that Jesus did (10: 41).

Somewhere in the church there was a group of men who
wished to give John the Baptist too high a place. John the
Baptist himself gave no encouragement to that but rather did
everything to discourage it. But the Fourth Gospel knew that
that tendency was there and took steps to guard against it. It
can still happen that men may worship a preacher rather than
Christ. It can still happen that men's eyes may be fixed upon the
herald rather than upon the King of whom he is the messenger.
John the Baptist was not in the least to blame for what had
happened; but John the evangelist was determined to see that
none should shoulder Christ from out the topmost niche.

It is more important to note that in this passage we come
upon another of the great key-words of the Fourth Gospel. That
is the word *witness*. The Fourth Gospel presents us with witness
after witness to the supreme place of Jesus Christ, eight no less.

(i) There is the witness of the *Father*. Jesus said: " The
Father who sent me has himself borne witness to me " (5: 37).
" The Father who sent me bears witness to me " (8: 18). What
did Jesus mean by this? He meant two things.

He meant something which affected *himself*. In his heart the
inner voice of God spoke, and that voice left him in no doubt as
to who he was and what he was sent to do. Jesus did not regard
himself as having himself chosen his task. His inner conviction
was that God had sent him into the world to live and to die for
men.

He meant something which affected *men*. When a man is
confronted with Christ there comes an inner conviction that
this is none other than the Son of God. Father Tyrrell has said
that the world can never get away from that " strange man
upon the Cross." That inner power which always brings our
eyes back to Christ even when we wish to forget him, that inner
voice which tells us that this Jesus is none other than the Son of
God and the Saviour of the world is the witness of God within
our souls.

(ii) There is the witness of *Jesus himself*. " I bear witness," he
said, " to myself " (8: 18). " Even if I do bear witness to
myself," he said, " my testimony is true " (8: 14). What does
this mean? It means that it was what Jesus was that was his
best witness. He claimed to be the light and the life and the truth
and the way. He claimed to be the Son of God and one with the
Father. He claimed to be the Saviour and the Master of all men.
Unless his life and character had been what they were, such
claims would have been merely shocking and blasphemous.
What Jesus was in himself was the best witness that his claims
were true.

(iii) There is the witness of *his works*. He said: " The works
which the Father has granted me to accomplish . . . bear me
witness " (5: 36). " The works that I do in my Father's name,

they bear witness to me " (10: 25). He tells Philip of his
complete identity with the Father, and then goes on to say:
" Believe me for the sake of the works themselves " (14: 11).
One of the condemnations of men is that they have seen his
works, and have not believed (15: 24). We must note one
thing—when John spoke of the works of Jesus, he was not
speaking *only* of the miracles of Jesus; he was thinking of
Jesus's whole life. He was thinking not only of the great
outstanding moments, but of the life that Jesus lived every
minute of the day. No man could have done the mighty works
that Jesus did unless he was closer to God than any other man
ever was; but, equally, no man could have lived that life of love
and pity, compassion and forgiveness, service and help in the life
of the everyday unless he had been in God and God in him. It is
not by working miracles that we can prove that we belong to
Christ, but by living a Christ-like life every moment of every
day. It is in the ordinary things of life that we show that we
belong to him.

(iv) There is the witness which *the Scriptures* bear to him.
Jesus said: " Search the scriptures, because you think that in
them you have eternal life; and it is they that bear witness to
me " (5: 39). " If you believed Moses, you would believe me; for
he wrote of me " (5: 46). It is Philip's conviction that he has
found him of whom Moses and the law and the prophets wrote
(1: 45). All through the history of Israel men had dreamed of
the day when God's Messiah would come. They had drawn
their pictures and set down their ideas of him. And now in Jesus
all these dreams and pictures and hopes were finally and fully
realized. He for whom the world was waiting had come.

(v) There is the witness of *the last of the prophets*, John the
Baptist. " He came for testimony to bear witness to the light "
(1: 7, 8). John bore witness that he saw the Spirit descending
upon Jesus. The one in whom the prophetic witness culminated
was the one who bore witness to Jesus to whom all the
prophetic witness pointed.

(vi) There is the witness of *those with whom Jesus came into
contact*. The woman of Samaria bore witness to the insight and

to the power of Jesus (4: 39). The man born blind bore witness to his healing power (9: 25, 38). The people who witnessed his miracles told of their wonder at the things he did (12: 17). There is a legend which tells how the Sanhedrin sought for witnesses when Jesus was on trial. There came a crowd of people saying: " I was a leper and he healed me "; " I was blind and he opened my eyes "; " I was deaf and he made me able to hear." That was precisely the kind of witness the Sanhedrin did *not* want. In every age and in every generation there have always been a great crowd ready to bear witness to what Christ had done for them.

(vii) There is the witness of *the disciples and especially of the writer of the gospel himself*. It was Jesus's commission to his disciples: " You also are witnesses, because you have been with me from the beginning " (15: 27). The writer of the gospel is a personal witness and guarantor of the things he relates. Of the crucifixion he writes: " He who saw it has borne witness—his testimony is true " (19: 35). " This " he says, " is the disciple who is bearing witness to these things, and who has written these things " (21: 24). The story he tells is no carried story, no second-hand tale, but what he had seen and experienced himself. The best kind of witness of all is the one which can say: " This is true, because I know it from my own experience."

(viii) There is the witness of *the Holy Spirit*. " When the Counsellor comes ... even the Spirit of truth ... he will bear witness to me " (15: 26). In the *First Epistle* John writes: " And the Spirit is the witness, because the Spirit is the truth " (1 *John* 5: 7). To the Jew the Spirit had two functions. The Spirit brought God's truth to men, and the Spirit enabled men to recognize that truth when they saw it. It is the work of the Spirit within our hearts which enables us to recognize Jesus for what he is and to trust him for what he can do.

John wrote his gospel to present the unanswerable witness that Jesus Christ is the mind of God fully revealed to men.

THE LIGHT OF EVERY MAN

John 1: 9

> He was the real light, who, in his coming into the world, gives
> light to every man.

IN this verse John uses a very significant word to describe
Jesus. He says that Jesus was the *real* light. In Greek there are
two words which are very like each other. The Authorized
Version and the Revised Standard use the word *true* to translate
both of them; but they have different shades of meaning. The
first is *alēthēs. Alēthēs* means *true* as opposed to *false*; it is the
word that would be used of a statement which is true. The other
word is *alēthinos. Alēthinos* means *real* or *genuine* as opposed
to unreal.

So what John is saying is that Jesus is the real light come to
illumine men. Before Jesus came there were other lights which
men followed. Some were flickers of the truth; some were faint
glimpses of reality; some were will o' the wisps which men
followed and which led them out into the dark and left them
there. It is still the case. There are still the partial lights; and
there are still the false lights; and men still follow them. Jesus is
the only genuine light, the real light to guide men on their way.

John says that Jesus, by his coming into the world, brought
the real light to men. His coming was like a blaze of light. It was
like the coming of the dawn. A traveller tells how once in Italy
he was standing on a hill overlooking the Bay of Naples. It was
so dark that nothing could be seen; then all a sudden there came
a lightning flash and everything, in every detail, was lit up.
When Jesus came into this world he came like a light in the
dark.

(i) His coming dissipated the shadows of *doubt.* Until he
came men could only guess about God. " It is difficult to find
out about God," said one of the Greeks, " and when you have
found out about him it is impossible to tell anyone else about
him." To the pagan, God either dwelt in the shadows that no

man can penetrate or in the light that no man can approach. But when Jesus came men saw full-displayed what God is like. The shadows and the mists were gone; the days of guessing were at an end; there was no more need for a wistful agnosticism. The light had come.

(ii) His coming dissipated the shadows of *despair*. Jesus came to a world that was in despair. " Men," as Seneca said, " are conscious of their helplessness in necessary things." They were longing for a hand let down to help them up. " They hate their sins but cannot leave them." Men despaired of ever making themselves or the world any better. But with the coming of Jesus a new power came into life. He came not only with knowledge but with power. He came not only to show them the right way but to enable them to walk in it. He gave them not only instruction but a presence in which all the impossible things had become possible. The darkness of pessimism and despair was gone for ever.

(iii) His coming dissipated the darkness of *death*. The ancient world feared death. At the best, death was annihilation and the soul of man shuddered at the thought. At the worst, it was torture by whatever gods there be and the soul of man was afraid. But Jesus by his coming, by his life, his death, his Resurrection showed that death was only the way to a larger life. The darkness was dispelled. Stevenson has a scene in one of his stories in which he draws the picture of a young man who has almost miraculously escaped in a duel in which he was certain he would be killed. As he walks away his heart is singing: " The bitterness of death is past." Because of Jesus the bitterness of death is past for every man.

Further, Jesus is the light who lights *every* man who comes into the world. The ancient world was exclusive. The Jew hated the Gentile and held that Gentiles were created for no other purpose than to be fuel for the fires of hell. True, there was a lonely prophet who saw that Israel's destiny was to be a light to the Gentiles (*Isaiah* 42: 6; 49: 6) but that was a destiny which Israel had always definitely refused. The Greek world never dreamed that knowledge was for every man. The Roman world looked down on the barbarians, the lesser breeds without the law. But Jesus came to be a light to *every* man. Only the God and Father of our Lord Jesus Christ has a heart big enough to hold all the world.

UNRECOGNIZED

John 1: 10, 11

> He was in the world, and, although the world came into being through him, the world did not recognize him. It was into his own home that he came, and his own people did not welcome him.

WHEN John wrote this passage two thoughts were in his mind.

(i) He was thinking of the time before Jesus Christ came into the world in the body. From the beginning of time God's *Logos* has been active in the world. In the beginning God's creating, dynamic *word* brought the world into being; and ever since it is the *word*, the *Logos*, the *reason* of God which has made the world an ordered whole and man a thinking being. If men had only had the sense to see him, the *Logos* was always recognizable in the universe.

The Westminster Confession of Faith begins by saying that " the lights of nature, and the works of creation and providence do so far manifest the goodness, wisdom and power of God as to leave men inexcusable." Long ago Paul had said that the visible things of the world were so designed by God as to lead men's thoughts to the invisible things, and that if men had looked with open eyes and an understanding heart at the world their thoughts would have been inevitably led to the creator of the world (*Romans* 1: 19, 20). The world has always been such that, looked at in the right way, it would lead men's minds to God.

Theology has always made a distinction between *natural* theology and *revealed* theology. Revealed theology deals with the truths that came to us directly from God in the words of the prophets, the pages of his book, and supremely in Jesus Christ.

Natural theology deals with the truths that man could discover by the exercise of his own mind and intellect on the world in which he lives. How, then, can we see God's *word*, God's *Logos*, God's *reason*, God's *mind* in the world in which we live?

(*a*) We must look *outwards*. It was always a basic Greek thought that where there is order there must be a mind. When we look at the world we see an amazing order. The planets keep to their appointed courses. The tides observe their appointed times. Seed times and harvest, summer and winter, day and night come in their appointed order. Clearly there is order in nature, and, therefore, equally clearly there must be a mind behind it all. Further, that mind must be greater than any human mind because it achieves results that the human mind can never achieve. No man can make day into night, or night into day; no man can make a seed that will have in it the power of growth; no man can make a living thing. If in the world there is order, there must be mind; and if in that order there are things which are beyond the mind of man to do, then the mind behind the order of nature must be a mind above and beyond the mind of man—and straightway we have reached God. To look outwards upon the world is to come face to face with the God who made it.

(*b*) We must look *upwards*. Nothing demonstrates the amazing order of the universe so much as the movement of the world. Astronomers tell us that there are as many stars as there are grains of sand upon the seashore. If we may put it in human terms, think of the traffic problem of the heavens; and yet the heavenly bodies keep their appointed courses and travel their appointed way. An astronomer is able to forecast to the minute and to the inch when and where a certain planet will appear. An astronomer can tell us when and where an eclipse of the sun will happen hundreds of years from now, and he can tell us to the second how long it will last. It has been said that " no astronomer can be an atheist." When we look upwards we see God.

(*c*) We must look *inwards*. Where did we get the power to think, to reason and to know? Where did we get our knowledge of right and of wrong? Why does even the most evil-ridden man know in his heart of hearts when he is doing a wrong thing? Kant said long ago that two things convinced him of the existence of God—the starry heavens above him and the moral law within him. We neither gave ourselves life, nor did we give ourselves the reason which guides and directs life. It must have come from some power outside ourselves. Where do remorse and regret and the sense of guilt come from? Why can we never do what we like and be at peace? When we look inwards we find what Marcus Aurelius called " the god within," and what Seneca called " the holy spirit which sits within our souls." No man can explain himself apart from God.

(d) We must look *backwards*. Froude, the great historian, said that the whole of history is a demonstration of the moral law in action. Empires rise and empires collapse. As Kipling wrote:

> " Lo, all our pomp of yesterday
> Is one with Nineveh and Tyre! "

And it is a demonstrable fact of history that moral degeneration and national collapse go hand in hand. " No nation," said George Bernard Shaw, " has ever outlived the loss of its gods." All history is the practical demonstration that there is a God.

So, then, even if Jesus Christ had never come into this world in bodily form, it would still have been possible for men to see God's *word*, God's *Logos*, God's *reason* in action. But, although the action of the *word* was there for all to see, men never recognized him.

UNRECOGNIZED

John 1: 10, 11 (*continued*)

He was in the world, and, although the world came into being through him, the world did not recognize him. It was into his own home that he came, and his own people did not welcome him.

(ii) In the end God's creating and directing *word* did come into this world in the form of the man Jesus. John says that the *word* came to his own home and his own people gave him no welcome. What does he mean by that? He means that when God's *word* entered this world, he did not come to Rome or to Greece or to Egypt or to the Eastern Empires. *He came to Palestine*; Palestine was specially God's land and the Jews were specially God's people.

The very titles by which the Old Testament calls the land and the people show that. Palestine is repeatedly called *the holy land* (*Zechariah* 2: 12; *2 Maccabees* 1: 7; *Wisdom* 12: 3). It is called *the Lord's land*; God speaks of it as *his land* (*Hosea* 9: 3; *Jeremiah* 2: 7; 16: 18; *Leviticus* 25: 23). The Jewish nation is called *God's peculiar treasure* (*Exodus* 19: 5; *Psalm* 135: 4). The Jews are called *God's special people* (*Deuteronomy* 7: 6). They are called God's *peculiar people* (*Deuteronomy* 14: 2; 26: 18). They are called *the Lord's portion* (*Deuteronomy* 32: 9).

Jesus came to a land which was peculiarly God's land and a people who were peculiarly God's people. He ought, therefore, to have been coming to a nation that would welcome him with open arms; the door should have been wide open for him; he should have been welcomed like a wayfarer coming home; or, even more, like a king coming to his own—but *he was rejected*. He was received with hate and not with adoration.

Here is the tragedy of a people being prepared for a task and then refusing that task. It may be that parents plan and save and sacrifice to give a son or a daughter a chance in life, to prepare that son or daughter for some special task and opportunity—and then when the chance comes, the one for whom so much sacrifice was made refuses to grasp the opportunity, or fails miserably when confronted with the challenge. Therein is tragedy. And that is what happened to God.

It would be wrong to think that God prepared only the Jewish people. God is preparing every man and woman and child in this world for some task that he has in store for them. A novelist tells of a girl who refused to touch the soiling things of life. When she was asked why, she said: " Some day something fine is going to come into my life, and I want to be ready for it." The tragedy is that so many people refuse the task God has for them.

We may put it in another way—a way that strikes home—there are so few people who become what they have it in them to be. It may be through lethargy and laziness, it may be through timidity and cowardice, it may be through lack of discipline and self-indulgence, it may be through involvement in second-bests and byways; but the world is full of people who have never realized the possibilities which are in them. We need not think of the task God has in store for us in terms of some great act or achievement of which all men will know. It may be to fit a child for life; it may be at some crucial moment to speak that word and exert that influence which will stop someone ruining his life; it may be to do some quite small job superlatively well; it may be to touch the lives of many by our hands, our voices or our minds. The fact remains that God is preparing us by all the experiences of life for *something*; and many refuse the task when it comes and never even realize that they are refusing it.

There is all the pathos in the world in the simple saying: " He came to his own home—and his own people gave him no welcome." It happened to Jesus long ago—and it is happening yet.

CHILDREN OF GOD

John 1: 12, 13

> To all those who did receive him, to those who believe in his name, he gave the right to become the children of God. These were born not of blood, nor of any human impulse, nor of any man's will, but their birth was of God.

Not everyone rejected Jesus when he came; there were some who did receive him and welcome him; and to them Jesus gave the right to become children of God.

There is a sense in which a man is not naturally a child of God. There is a sense in which he has to *become* a child of God.

We may think of this in human terms, because human terms are the only ones open to us.

There are two kinds of sons. There is the son who never does anything else but use his home. All through his youth he takes everything that the home has to offer and gives nothing in return. His father may work and sacrifice to give him his chance in life, and he takes it as a right, never realizing what he is taking and making no effort to deserve it or repay it. When he leaves home, he makes no attempt to keep in touch. The home has served his purpose and he is finished with it. He realizes no bond to be maintained and no debt to be paid. He is his father's son; to his father he owes his existence; and to his father he owes what he is; but between him and his father there is no bond of love and intimacy. The father has given all in love; but the son has given nothing in return.

On the other hand there is the son who all his life realizes what his father is doing and has done for him. He takes every opportunity to show his gratitude by trying to be the son his father would wish him to be; as the years go on he grows closer and closer to his father; the relationship of father and son becomes the relationship of fellowship and friendship. Even when he leaves home the bond is still there and he is still conscious of a debt that can never be repaid.

In the one case the son grows further and further away from the father; in the other he grows nearer and nearer the father. Both are sons, but the sonship is very different. The second has *become* a son in a way that the first never was.

We may illustrate this kind of relationship from another, but a kindred, sphere. The name of a certain younger man was mentioned to a famous teacher, whose student the younger man claimed to be. The older man answered: " He may have attended my lectures, but he was not one of my students." There is a world of difference between sitting in a teacher's class room and being one of his students. There can be contact without communion; there can be relationship without fellowship. All men are the sons of God in the sense that they owe to him the creation and the preservation of their lives; but only some men *become* the sons of God in the depth and intimacy of the true father and son relationship.

It is the claim of John that men can enter into that true and real sonship only through Jesus Christ. When he says that it does not come from blood, he is using Jewish thought, for the Jews believed that a physical son was born from the union of the seed of the father with the blood of the mother. This sonship does not come from any human impulse or desire or from any act of the human will; it comes entirely from God. We cannot make ourselves sons of God; we have to enter into a relationship which God offers us. No man can ever enter into friendship with God by his own will and power; there is a great gulf fixed between the human and the divine. Man can only enter into friendship with God when God himself opens the way.

Again let us think in human terms. A commoner cannot approach a king with the offer of friendship; if there is ever to be such a friendship it must depend entirely on the approach of the king. It is so with us and God. We cannot by will or achievement enter into fellowship with God, for we are men and he is God. We can enter into it only when God in his totally undeserved grace condescends to open the way to himself.

But there is a human side to this. What God offers, man has to appropriate. A human father may offer his son his love, his advice, his friendship, and the son may refuse it and prefer to take his own way. It is so with God; God offers us *the right* to become sons but we need not accept it.

We do accept it through believing in the name of Jesus Christ. What does that mean? Hebrew thought and language had a way of using *the name* which is strange to us. By that expression Jewish thought did not so much mean the name by which a person was called as his nature in so far as it was revealed and known. For instance, in *Psalm 9: 10* the psalmist says: " Those who know *thy name* put their trust in thee." Clearly that does not mean that those who know that God is called Jehovah will trust him; it means that those who know God's character, God's nature, who know what God is like, will be ready and willing to trust him for everything. In *Psalm 20: 7* the psalmist says: " Some boast of chariots and some of horses: but we boast of *the name* of the Lord our God." Clearly that does not mean that we will boast that God is called Jehovah. It means that some people will put their trust in human aids, but we will put our trust in God because we know what he is like.

To trust in the name of Jesus therefore means to put our trust in what he is. He was the embodiment of kindness and love and gentleness and service. It is John's great central doctrine that in Jesus we see the very mind of God, the attitude of God to men. If we believe that, then we also believe that God is like Jesus, as kind, as loving as Jesus was. To believe in the name of Jesus is to believe that God is like him; and it is only when we believe that, that we can submit ourselves to God and become his children. Unless we had seen in Jesus what God is like we would never even have dared to think of ourselves as being able to become the children of God. It is what Jesus is that opens to us the possibility of becoming the children of God.

THE WORD BECAME FLESH

John 1: 14

> So the Word of God became a person, and took up his abode in our being, full of grace and truth; and we looked with our own eyes upon his glory, glory like the glory which an only son receives from a father.

HERE we come to the sentence for the sake of which John wrote his gospel. He has thought and talked about the word of God, that powerful, creative, dynamic word which was the agent of creation, that guiding, directing, controlling word which puts order into the universe and mind into man. These were ideas which were known and familiar to both Jew and Greek. Now he says the most startling and incredible thing that he could have said. He says quite simply: " This word which created the world, this reason which controls the order of the world, has become a person and with our own eyes we saw him." The word that John uses for *seeing* this word is *theasthai*; it is used in the New Testament more than twenty times and is always used of *actual physical sight*. This is no spiritual vision seen with the eye of the soul or of the mind. John declares that the word actually came to earth in the form of a man and was seen by human eyes. He says: " If you want to see what this creating word, this controlling reason, is like, look at Jesus of Nazareth."

This is where John parted with all thought which had gone before him. This was the entirely new thing which John brought to the Greek world for which he was writing. Augustine afterwards said that in his pre-Christian days he had read and studied the great pagan philosophers and had read many things, but he had never read that the word became flesh.

To a Greek this was the impossible thing. The one thing that no Greek would ever have dreamed of was that God could take a body. To the Greek the body was an evil, a prison-house in which the soul was shackled, a tomb in which the spirit was confined. Plutarch, the wise old Greek, did not even believe that God could control the happenings of this world directly; he had to do it by deputies and intermediaries, for, as Plutarch saw it, it was nothing less than blasphemy to involve God in the affairs of the world. Philo could never have said it. He said: " The life of God has not descended to us; nor has it come as far as the necessities of the body." The great Roman Stoic Emperor, Marcus Aurelius, despised the body in comparison with the spirit. " Therefore despise the flesh—blood and bones and a net-work, a twisted skein of nerves and veins and arteries." "The composition of the whole body is under corruption."

Here was the shatteringly new thing—that God could and would become a human person, that God could enter into this life that we live, that eternity could appear in time, that somehow the Creator could appear in creation in such a way that men's eyes could actually see him.

So staggeringly new was this conception of God in a human form that it is not surprising that there were some even in the church who could not believe it. What John says is that the word became *sarx*. Now *sarx* is the very word Paul uses over and over again to describe what he called *the flesh*, human nature in all its weakness and in all its liability to sin. The very thought of taking this word and applying it to God, was something that their minds staggered at. So there arose in the church a body of people called *Docetists*.

Dokein is the Greek word for *to seem to be*. These people held that Jesus in fact was only a phantom; that his human body was not a real body; that he could not really feel hunger and weariness, sorrow and pain; that he was in fact a disembodied spirit in the apparent form of a man. John dealt with these people much more directly in his First Letter. " By this you know the Spirit of God: every spirit which confesses that Jesus Christ has come *in the flesh* is of God, and every spirit which does not confess Jesus is not of God. This is the spirit of Antichrist " (1 *John* 4: 2, 3). It is true that this heresy was born of a kind of mistaken reverence which recoiled from saying that Jesus was really, fully and truly human. To John it contradicted the whole Christian gospel.

It may well be that we are often so eager to conserve the fact that Jesus was fully God that we tend to forget the fact that he was fully man. *The word became flesh*—here, perhaps as nowhere else in the New Testament, we have the full manhood of Jesus gloriously proclaimed. In Jesus we see the creating word of God, the controlling reason of God, taking manhood upon himself. In Jesus we see God living life as he would have lived it if he had been a man. Supposing we said nothing else about Jesus we could still say that he shows us how God would live this life that we have to live.

THE WORD BECAME FLESH

John 1: 14 (*continued*)

> So the word of God became a person, and took up his abode in our being, full of grace and truth; and we looked with our own eyes upon his glory, glory like the glory which an only son receives from a father.

IT might well be held that ths is the greatest single verse in the New Testament; we must therefore spend much time upon it so that we may enter the more fully into its riches.

We have already seen how John has certain great words which haunt his mind and dominate his thought and we are the themes out of which his whole message is elaborated. Here we have three more of these words.

(i) The first is *grace*. This word has always two basic ideas in it.

(*a*) It always has the idea of something completely undeserved. It always has the idea of something that we could never have earned or achieved for ourselves. The fact that God came to earth to live and to die for men is not something which humanity deserved; it is an act of pure love on the part of God. The word grace emphasizes at one and the same time the helpless poverty of man and the limitless kindness of God.

(*b*) It always has the idea of beauty in it. In modern Greek the word means *charm*. In Jesus we see the sheer winsomeness of God. Men had thought of God in terms of might and majesty and power and judgment. They had thought of the power of God which could crush all opposition and defeat all rebellion; but in Jesus men are confronted with the sheer loveliness of God.

(ii) The second is *truth*. This word is one of the dominant notes of the Fourth Gospel. We meet it again and again. Here we can only briefly gather together what John has to say about Jesus and the truth.

(*a*) Jesus is the embodiment of the truth. He said: " I am the truth " (14: 6). To see truth we must look at Jesus. Here is something infinitely precious for every simple mind and soul. Very few people can grasp abstract ideas; most people think in pictures. We could think and argue for ever and we would very likely be no nearer arriving at a definition of beauty. But if we can point at a beautiful person and say that *is* beauty, the thing becomes clear. Ever since men began to think about God they have been trying to define just who and what he is—and their puny minds get no nearer a definition. But we can cease our thinking and look at Jesus Christ and say: "That is what God is like." Jesus did not come to *talk* to men about God; he came to *show* men what God is like, so that the simplest mind might know him as intimately as the mind of the greatest philosopher.

(*b*) Jesus is the communicator of the truth. He told his disciples that if they continued with him they would know the truth (8: 31). He told Pilate that his object in coming into this world was to witness to the truth (18: 37). Men will flock to a teacher or preacher who can really give them guidance for the tangled business of thinking and living. Jesus is the one who, amidst the shadows, makes things clear; who, at the many crossroads of life, shows us the right way; who, in the baffling moments of decision, enables us to choose aright; who, amidst the many voices which clamour for our allegiance, tells us what to believe.

(*c*) Even when Jesus left this earth in the body, he left us his Spirit to guide us into the truth. His Spirit is the Spirit of truth (14: 17; 15: 26; 16: 13). He did not leave us only a book of instruction and a body of teaching. We do not need to search through some unintelligible textbook to find out what to do. Still, to this day, we can ask Jesus what to do, for his Spirit is with us every step of the way.

(*d*) The truth is what makes us free (8: 32). There is always a certain liberating quality in the truth. A child often gets queer, mistaken notions about things when he thinks about them himself; and often he becomes afraid. When he is told the truth he is emancipated from his fears. A man may fear that he is ill; he goes to the doctor; even if the verdict is bad he is at least liberated from the vague fears which haunted his mind. The truth which Jesus brings liberates us from estrangement from God; it liberates us from frustration; it liberates us from our fears and weaknesses and defeats. Jesus Christ is the greatest liberator on earth.

(*e*) The truth can be resented. They sought to kill Jesus because he told them the truth (8: 40). The truth may well condemn a man; it may well show him how far wrong he was. " Truth," said the Cynics, " can be like the light to sore eyes."

The Cynics declared that the teacher who never annoyed anyone never did anyone any good. Men may shut their ears and their minds to the truth; they may kill the man who tells them the truth—but the truth remains. No man ever destroyed the truth by refusing to listen to the voice that told it to him; and the truth will always catch up with him in the end.

(*f*) The truth can be disbelieved (8: 45). There are two main reasons why men disbelieve the truth. They may disbelieve it because it seems to good to be true; or they may disbelieve it because they are so fastened to their half-truths that they will not let them go. In many instances a half-truth is the worst enemy of a whole truth.

(*g*) The truth is not something abstract; it is something which must be done (3: 21). It is something which must be known with the mind, accepted with the heart, and acted out in the life.

THE WORD BECAME FLESH

John 1: 14 (*continued*)

> So the word of God became a person, and took up his abode in our being, full of grace and truth; and we looked with our own eyes upon his glory, glory like the glory which an only son receives from a father.

A life-time of study and thought could not exhaust the truth of this verse. We have already looked at two of the great theme words in it; now we look at the third—*glory*. Again and again John uses this word in connection with Jesus Christ. We shall first look at what John says about the glory of Christ, and then we shall go on to see if we can understand a little of what he means.

(i) The life of Jesus Christ was a manifestation of glory. When he performed the miracle of the water and the wine at Cana of Galilee, John says that he manifested forth his glory (2: 11). To look at Jesus and to experience his power and love was to enter into a new glory.

(ii) The glory which he manifests is the glory of God. It is not from men that he receives it (5: 41). He seeks not his own glory but the glory of him who sent him (7: 18). It is his Father who glorifies him (8: 50, 54). It is the glory of God that Martha will see in the raising of Lazarus (11: 4). The raising of Lazarus is for the glory of God, that the Son may be glorified thereby (11: 4). The glory that was on Jesus, that clung about him, that shone through him, that acted in him is the glory of God.

(iii) Yet that glory was uniquely his own. At the end he prays that God will glorify him with the glory that he had before the world began (17: 5). He shines with no borrowed radiance; his glory is his and his by right.

(iv) The glory which is his he has transmitted to his disciples. The glory which God gave him he has given to them (17: 22). It is as if Jesus shared in the glory of God and the disciple shares in the glory of Christ. The coming of Jesus is the coming of God's glory among men.

What does John mean by all this? To answer that we must turn to the Old Testament. To the Jew the idea of the *Shechinah* was very dear. The *Shechinah* means *that which dwells*; and it is the word used for the visible presence of God among men. Repeatedly in the Old Testament we come across the idea that there were certain times when God's glory was visible among men. In the desert, before the giving of the manna, the children of Israel " looked toward the wilderness, and, behold, the glory of the Lord appeared in the cloud " (*Exodus* 16: 10). Before the giving of the Ten Commandments, " the glory of the Lord settled upon Mount Sinai " (*Exodus* 24: 16). When the Tabernacle had been erected and equipped, " the glory of the Lord filled the tabernacle " (*Exodus* 40: 34). When Solomon's Temple was dedicated the priests could not enter in to minister " for the glory of the Lord filled the house of the Lord " (1 *Kings* 8: 11). When Isaiah had his vision in the Temple, he heard the angelic choir singing that " the whole earth is full of his glory " (*Isaiah* 6: 3). Ezekiel in his ecstasy saw " the likeness of the glory of the Lord " (*Ezekiel* 1: 28). In the Old Testament the glory of the Lord came at times when God was very close.

The glory of the Lord means quite simply the presence of God. John uses a homely illustration. A father gives to his eldest son his own authority, his own honour. The heir apparent to the throne, the king's heir, is invested with all the royal glory of his father. It was so with Jesus. When he came to this earth men saw in him the splendour of God, and at the heart of that splendour was love. When Jesus came to this earth men saw the wonder of God, and the wonder was love. They saw that God's glory and God's love were one and the same thing. The glory of God is not that of a despotic eastern tyrant, but the splendour of love before which we fall not in abject terror but lost in wonder, love and praise.

THE INEXHAUSTIBLE FULLNESS

John 1: 15–17

> John was his witness and his statement still sounds out: " This is he of whom I said to you, he who comes after me has been advanced before me, because he was before me." On his fullness we all of us have drawn, and from him we have received grace upon grace, for it was the law which was given by Moses, but grace and truth came through Jesus Christ.

WE have already seen that the Fourth Gospel was written in a situation where it was necessary to make sure that John the Baptist did not occupy an exaggerated position in men's thoughts. So John begins this passage with a saying of John the Baptist which gives to Jesus the first place.

John the Baptist says of Jesus: " He who comes after me was before me." He may mean more than one thing by that. (*a*) Jesus was actually six months younger in age than John, and John may be saying quite simply: " He who is my junior has been advanced beyond me." (*b*) John may be saying: " I was in the field before Jesus; I occupied the centre of the stage before he did; my hand was laid to work before his was; but all that I was doing was to prepare the way for his coming; I was only

the advance guard of the main force and the herald of the king."
(*c*) It may be that John is thinking in terms much more deep
than that. He may be thinking not in terms of time but of
eternity. He may be thinking of Jesus as the one who existed
before the world began, and beside whom any human figure has
no standing at all. It may be that all three ideas are in John's
mind. It was not he who had exaggerated his own position; that
was the mistake that some of his followers had made. To John
the topmost place belonged to Jesus.

This passage then goes on to say three great things about
Jesus.

(i) On his fullness we all have drawn. The word that John
uses for *fullness* is a great word; it is *plērōma*, and it means the
sum total of all that is in God. It is a word which Paul uses
often. In *Colossians* 1: 19 he says that all *plērōma* dwelt in
Christ. In *Colossians* 2: 9 he says in Christ there dwelt the
plērōma of deity in a bodily form. He meant that in Jesus there
dwelt the totality of the wisdom, the power, the love of God.
Just because of that Jesus is inexhaustible. A man can go to
Jesus with any need and find that need supplied. A man can go
to Jesus with any ideal and find that ideal realized. In Jesus the
man in love with beauty will find the supreme beauty. In Jesus
the man to whom life is the search for knowledge will find the
supreme revelation. In Jesus the man who needs courage will
find the pattern and the secret of being brave. In Jesus the man
who feels that he cannot cope with life will find the Master of
life and the power to live. In Jesus the man who is conscious of
his sin will find the forgiveness for his sin and the strength to be
good. In Jesus the *plērōma*, the fullness of God, all that is in
God, what Westcott called " the spring of divine life," becomes
available to men.

(ii) From him we have received grace upon grace. Literally
the Greek means *grace instead of grace*. What does that strange
phrase mean?

(*a*) It may mean that in Christ we have found one wonder
leading to another. One of the old missionaries came to one of
the ancient Pictish kings. The king asked him what he might

expect if he became a Christian. The missionary answered:
" You will find wonder upon wonder and every one of them
true." Sometimes when we travel a very lovely road, vista after
vista opens to us. At every view we think that nothing could be
lovelier, and then we turn another corner and an even greater
loveliness opens before us. When a man enters on the study of
some great subject, like music or poetry or art, he never gets to
the end of it. Always there are fresh experiences of beauty
waiting for him. It is so with Christ. The more we know of him,
the more wonderful he becomes. The longer we live with him,
the more loveliness we discover. The more we think about him
and with him, the wider the horizon of truth becomes. This
phrase may be John's way of expressing the limitlessness of
Christ. It may be his way of saying that the man who
companies with Christ will find new wonders dawning upon his
soul and enlightening his mind and enchaining his heart every
day.

(*b*) It may be that we ought to take this expression quite
literally. In Christ we find *grace instead of grace*. The different
ages and the different situations in life demand a different kind
of grace. We need one grace in the days of prosperity and another
in the days of adversity. We need one grace in the sunlit days of youth
and another when the shadows of age begin to lengthen. The church
needs one grace in the days of persecution and another when
the days of acceptance have come. We need one grace when we
feel that we are on the top of things and another when we are
depressed and discouraged and near to despair. We need one
grace to bear our own burdens and another to bear one
another's burdens. We need one grace when we are sure of
things and another when there seems nothing certain left in the
world. The grace of God is never a static but always a dynamic
thing. It never fails to meet the situation. One need invades life
and one grace comes with it. That need passes and another need
assaults us and with it another grace comes. All through life we
are constantly receiving grace instead of grace, for the grace of
Christ is triumphantly adequate to deal with any situation.

(iii) The law was given by Moses, but grace and truth came

through Jesus Christ. In the old way, life was governed by law.
A man had to do a thing whether he liked it or not, and whether
he knew the reason for it or not; but with the coming of Jesus
we no longer seek to obey the law of God like slaves; we seek to
answer the love of God like sons. It is through Jesus Christ that
God the law-giver has become God the Father, that God the
judge has become God the lover of the souls of men.

THE REVELATION OF GOD

John 1: 18

> No one has ever seen God. It is the unique one, he who is God, he
> who is in the bosom of the Father, who has told us all about God.

WHEN John said that no man has ever seen God, everyone in
the ancient world would fully agree with him. Men were
fascinated and depressed and frustrated by what they regarded
as the infinite distance and the utter unknowability of God. In
the Old Testament God is represented as saying to Moses:
" You cannot see my face; for man shall not see me and live "
(*Exodus* 33: 20). When God reminds the people of the giving of
the law, he says: " You heard the sound of words, but saw
no form; there was only a voice " (*Deuteronomy* 4: 12). No
one in the Old Testament thought it possible to see God. The
great Greek thinkers felt exactly the same. Xenophanes said:
" Guesswork is over all." Plato said: " Never man and God can
meet." Celsus laughed at the way that the Christians called God
Father, because " God is away beyond everything." At the best,
Apuleius said, men could catch a glimpse of God as a lightning
flash lights up a dark night—one split second of illumination,
and then the dark. As Glover said: " Whatever God was, he
was far from being within the reach of ordinary men." There
might be very rare moments of ecstasy when men caught a
glimpse of what they called " Absolute Being," but ordinary
men were the prisoners of ignorance and fancy. There would be

none to disagree with John when he said that no man has ever seen God.

But John does not stop there; he goes on to make the startling and tremendous statement that Jesus has fully revealed to men what God is like. What has come to men is what J. H. Bernard calls " the exhibition to the world of God in Christ." Here again the keynote of John's gospel sounds: " If you want to see what God is like, look at Jesus."

Why should it be that Jesus can do what no one else has ever done? Wherein lies his power to reveal God to men? John says three things about him.

(i) Jesus is *unique*. The Greek word is *monogenēs*, which the Authorized Version translates *only-begotten*. It is true that that is what *monogenēs* literally means; but long before this it had lost its purely physical sense, and had come to have two special meanings. It had come to mean *unique* and *specially beloved*. Obviously an only son has a unique place and a unique love in his father's heart. So this word came to express *uniqueness* more than anything else. It is the conviction of the New Testament that there is no one like Jesus. He alone can bring God to men and bring men to God.

(ii) Jesus is *God*. Here we have the very same form of expression as we had in the first verse of the chapter. This does not mean that Jesus is identical with God; it does mean that in mind and character and being he is one with God. In this case it might be better if we thought of it as meaning that Jesus is divine. To see him is to see what God is.

(iii) Jesus is *in the bosom of the Father*. To be in the bosom of someone is the Hebrew phrase which expresses the deepest intimacy possible in human life. It is used of mother and child; it is used of husband and wife; a man speaks of the wife of his bosom (*Numbers* 11: 12; *Deuteronomy* 13: 6); it is used of two friends who are in complete communion with one another. When John uses this phrase about Jesus, he means that between Jesus and God there is complete and uninterrupted intimacy. It is because Jesus is so intimate with God, that he is one with God and can reveal him to men.

In Jesus Christ the distant, unknowable, invisible, unreachable God has come to men; and God can never be a stranger to us again.

THE WITNESS OF JOHN

John 1: 19–28

This is the witness of John, when the Jews sent priests and Levites to him from Jerusalem to ask him: " Who are you? " He quite definitely affirmed and stated: " *I* am not the Messiah." So they asked him: " What then are we to think? Are you Elijah? " He said: " I am not." " Are you the promised prophet? " He answered: " No." So they said to him: " Who are you? Tell us, so that we can give an answer to those who sent us. What claim do you make for yourself? " He said: " I am the voice of one crying in the wilderness, ' Make the Lord's road straight,' as Isaiah the prophet said." Now they had been sent by the Pharisees. So they asked him and said to him: " If you are neither the Messiah, nor Elijah, nor the promised prophet, why then do you baptize? " John answered: " *I* baptize with water. But there is one standing among you, whom you do not know, I mean the one who is coming after me, the straps of whose sandals I am not worthy to unloose." These things happened at Bethany, on the far side of Jordan, where John was baptizing.

WITH this passage John begins the narrative part of his gospel. In the prologue he has shown what he intends to do; he is writing his gospel to demonstrate that Jesus is the Mind, the Reason, the Word of God come into this world in the form of a human person. Having set down his central thought, he now begins the story of the life of Jesus.

No one is so careful of details of time as John is. Starting from this passage and going on to 2: 11 he tells step by step the story of the first momentous week in the public life of Jesus. The events of the first day are in 1: 19–28; the story of the second day is 1: 29–34; the third day is unfolded in 1: 35–39. The three verses 1: 40–42 tell the story of the fourth day. The events of the fifth day are told in 1: 43–51. The sixth day is left a blank. And the events of the last day of the week are told in 2: 1–11.

In this same section from 1: 19 to 2: 11 the Fourth Gospel gives us three different kinds of witness to the greatness and the uniqueness of Jesus. (i) There is the witness of John the Baptist (1: 19–34). (ii) There is the witness of those who accepted Jesus as their Master, and who became his disciples (1: 41–51). (iii) There is the witness of Jesus's own wonderful powers (2: 1–11). John is setting Jesus before us in three different contexts, and in each showing us his supreme wonder.

We have already seen that the Fourth Gospel had to take account of a situation in which John the Baptist was given a position far higher than he himself had claimed. As late as A.D. 250 the *Clementine Recognitions* tell us that " there were some of John's disciples who preached about him as if their master was the Messiah." In this passage we see that that was a view that John the Baptist himself would have definitely repudiated.

Let us now turn to the passage itself. Right at the beginning we come upon a characteristic of the Fourth Gospel. It is emissaries of the *Jews* who come to cross-question John. The word *Jews* (*Ioudaioi*) occurs in this gospel no fewer than seventy times; and always the Jews are the opposition. They are the people who have set themselves against Jesus. The mention of the *Jews* brings the opposition thus early upon the stage. The Fourth Gospel is two things. First, as we have seen, it is the exhibition of God in Jesus Christ. But, second, it is equally the story of the rejection of Jesus Christ by the Jews, the story of God's offer and man's refusal, the story of God's love and man's sin, the story of Jesus Christ's invitation and man's rejection. The Fourth Gospel is the gospel in which love and warning are uniquely and vividly combined.

The deputation which came to interview John was composed of two kinds of people. First, there were the priests and the Levites. Their interest was very natural, for John was the son of Zacharias, and Zacharias was a priest (*Luke* 1: 5). In Judaism the only qualification for the priesthood was descent. If a man was not a descendant of Aaron nothing could make him a priest; if he was a descendant of Aaron nothing could stop him being one. Therefore, in the eyes of the authorities John the Baptist was in fact a priest and it was very natural that the priests should come to find out why he was behaving in such an unusual way. Second, there were emissaries of the Pharisees. It may well be that behind them was the Sanhedrin. One of the functions of the Sanhedrin was to deal with any man who was suspected of being a false prophet. John was a preacher to whom the people were flocking in hordes. The Sanhedrin may well have felt it their duty to check up on this man in case he was a false prophet.

The whole thing shows how suspicious orthodoxy was of anything unusual. John did not conform to the normal idea of a priest; and he did not conform to the normal idea of a preacher; therefore the ecclesiastical authorities of the day looked upon him askance. The church always runs the danger of condemning a new way just because it is new. In one sense there is hardly any institution in the world which resents change so much as the church does. It has often rejected a great teacher and often refused some great adventure simply because it suspected all things new.

THE WITNESS OF JOHN

John 1: 19–28 (*continued*)

THE emissaries of the orthodox could think of three things that John might claim to be.

(i) They asked him if he was the Messiah. The Jews were waiting, and are waiting to this day, for the Messiah. There was no one idea of the Messiah. Some people expected one who would bring peace over all the earth. Some expected one who would bring in the reign of righteousness. Most expected one who would be a great national champion to lead the armies of the Jews as conquerors over all the world. Some expected a

supernatural figure straight from God. Still more expected a
prince to rise from David's line. Frequently Messianic pre-
tenders arose and caused rebellions. The time of Jesus was an
excited age. It was natural to ask John if he claimed to be the
Messiah. John completely rejected that claim; but he rejected it
with a certain hint. In the Greek the word *I* is stressed by its
position. It is as if John said: " *I* am not the Messiah, but, if you
only knew, the Messiah is here."

(ii) They asked him if he was Elijah. It was the Jewish belief
that, before the Messiah came, Elijah would return to herald his
coming and to prepare the world to receive him. Particularly,
Elijah was to come to arrange all disputes. He would settle what
things and what people were clean and unclean; he would settle
who were Jews and who were not Jews; he would bring together
again families which were estranged. So much did the Jews
believe this that the traditional law said that money and
property whose owners were disputed, or anything found whose
owner was unknown, must wait " until Elijah comes." The
belief that Elijah would come before the Messiah goes back to
Malachi 4: 5. It was even believed that Elijah would anoint the
Messiah to his kingly office, as all kings were anointed, and that
he would raise the dead to share in the new kingdom; but John
denied that any such honour was his.

(iii) They asked him if he was the expected and promised
prophet. It was sometimes believed that Isaiah and, especially,
Jeremiah would return at the coming of the Messiah. But this is
really a reference to the assurance which Moses gave to the
people in *Deuteronomy* 18: 15: " The Lord your God will raise
up for you a prophet like me from among you, from your
brethren—him you shall heed." That was a promise that no Jew
ever forgot. They waited and longed for the emergence of the
prophet who would be the greatest of all prophets, *the Prophet
par excellence*. But once again John denied that this honour
was his.

So they asked him who he was; his answer was that he was
nothing but a voice bidding men prepare the way for the king.
The quotation is from *Isaiah* 40: 3. All the gospels cite it (*Mark*

1: 3; *Matthew* 3: 3; *Luke* 3: 4). The idea behind it is this. Eastern roads were not surfaced and metalled. They were mere tracks. When a king was about to visit a province, when a conqueror was about to travel through his domains, the roads were smoothed and straightened out and put in order. What John was saying was: " I am nobody; I am only a voice telling you to get ready for the coming of the king, for he is on the way."

John was what every true preacher and teacher ought to be—only a voice, a pointer to the king. The last thing that he wanted men to do was to look at him; he wanted them to forget him and see only the king.

But the Pharisees were puzzled about one thing—what right had John to baptize? If he had been the Messiah, or even Elijah or the prophet, he might have baptized. Isaiah had written: " So shall he sprinkle many nations " (*Isaiah* 52: 15). Ezekiel had said: " I will sprinkle clean water upon you, and you shall be clean " (*Ezekiel* 36: 25). Zechariah had said: " On that day there shall be a fountain opened for the house of David and the inhabitants of Jerusalem to cleanse them from sin and uncleanness " (*Zechariah* 13: 1). But why should John baptize?

What made the matter still more strange was this. Baptism at the hands of men was not for Israelites at all. It was *proselytes*, incomers from other faiths, who were baptized. An Israelite was never baptized; he was God's already and did not need to be washed. But *Gentiles* had to be washed in baptism. John was making Israelites do what only Gentiles had to do. He was suggesting that *the chosen people had to be cleansed*. That was indeed precisely what John believed. But he did not answer directly.

He said: " I am baptizing only with water; but there is One among you—you don't recognize him—and I am not worthy to untie the straps of his shoes." John could not have cited a more menial office. To untie the straps of sandals was slaves' work. There was a Rabbinic saying which said that a disciple might do for his master anything that a servant did, *except* only to untie his sandals. That was too menial a service for even a disciple to render. So John said: " One is coming whose slave I am not fit to be." We are to understand that by this time the baptism of Jesus had taken place at which John had recognized Jesus. So here John is saying again: " The king is coming. And, for his coming, you need to be cleansed as much as any Gentile. Prepare yourself for the entry into history of the king."

John's function was to be only the preparer of the way. Any greatness he had came from the greatness of the one whose coming he foretold. He is the great example of the man prepared to obliterate himself in order that Jesus Christ may be seen. He was only, as he saw it, a finger-post pointing to Christ. God give *us* grace to forget ourselves and to remember only Christ.

THE LAMB OF GOD

John 1: 29–31

> On the next day, John saw Jesus as he was coming towards him, and said: " See! The Lamb of God who is taking away the sin of the world! This is he of whom I said to you: ' There is a man who is coming after me, who has been advanced before me, because he was before me.' Even I did not know him. All the same, the reason that I came baptizing with water is that he might be shown forth to Israel."

HERE we come to the second day of this momentous week in the life of Jesus. By this time his baptism and his temptations were past and he was about to set his hand to the work which he came into the world to do. Once again the Fourth Gospel shows us John paying spontaneous tribute to Jesus. He calls him by that tremendous title which has become woven into the very language of devotion—*The Lamb of God*. What was in John's mind when he used that title? There are at least four pictures which may well contribute something to it.

(i) It may well have been that John was thinking of the Passover Lamb. The Passover Feast was not very far away (*John* 2: 13). The old story of the Passover was that it was the blood of the slain lamb which protected the houses of the Israelites on the night when they left Egypt (*Exodus* 12: 11–13). On that night when the Angel of Death walked abroad and slew the first-born of the Egyptians, the Israelites were to smear their doorposts with the blood of the slain lamb, and the angel, seeing it, would pass over that house. The blood of the lamb delivered them from destruction. It has been suggested that even as John the Baptist saw Jesus, there passed by flocks of lambs, being driven up to Jerusalem from the country districts to serve as sacrifices for the Passover Feast. The blood of the Passover Lamb delivered the Israelites in Egypt from death; and it may be that John was saying: " There is the one true sacrifice who can deliver you from death." Paul too thought of Jesus as the Passover Lamb (1 *Corinthians* 5: 7). There is a deliverance that only Jesus Christ can win for us.

(ii) John was the son of a priest. He would know all the ritual of the Temple and its sacrifices. Every morning and every evening a lamb was sacrificed in the Temple for the sins of the people (*Exodus* 29: 38–42). So long as the Temple stood this daily sacrifice was made. Even when the people were starving in war and in siege they never omitted to offer the lamb until in A.D. 70 the Temple was destroyed. It may be that John is saying: " In the Temple a lamb is offered every night and every morning for the sins of the people; but in this Jesus is the only sacrifice which can deliver men from sin."

(iii) There are two great pictures of the lamb in the prophets. Jeremiah writes: " But I was like a gentle lamb led to the slaughter " (*Jeremiah* 11: 19). And Isaiah has the great picture of the one who was brought " like a lamb to the slaughter " (*Isaiah* 53: 7). Both these great prophets had the vision of one who by his sufferings and his sacrifice, meekly and lovingly borne, would redeem his people. Maybe John is saying: " Your prophets dreamed of the one who was to love and suffer and die for the people; that one is come." It is certainly true that in later times the picture of *Isaiah* 53 became to the church one of the most precious forecasts of Jesus in all the Old Testament. It may be that John the Baptist was the first to see it so.

(iv) There is a fourth picture which would be very familiar to the Jews, although very strange to us. Between the Old and New Testaments there were the days of the great struggles of the Maccabees. In those days the lamb, and especially the horned lamb, was the symbol of a great conqueror. Judas Maccabaeus is so described, as are Samuel and David and Solomon. The lamb—strange as it may sound to us—stood for the conquering champion of God. It may well be that this is no picture of gentle and helpless weakness, but rather a picture of conquering majesty and power. Jesus was the champion of God who fought with sin and mastered it in single contest.

There is sheer wonder in this phrase, the Lamb of God. It haunted the writer of the Revelation. Twenty-nine times he used it. It becomes one of the most precious titles of Christ. In one word it sums up the love, the sacrifice, the suffering and the triumph of Christ.

John says that he did not know Jesus. Now John was a relation of Jesus (*Luke* 1: 36), and he must have been acquainted with him. What John is saying is not that he did not know *who* Jesus was, but that he did not know *what* Jesus was. It had suddenly been revealed to him that Jesus was none other than the Son of God.

Once again John makes clear what his only function was. It was to point men to Christ. He was nothing and Christ was everything. He claimed no greatness and no place for himself; he was only the man who, as it were, drew back the curtain and left Jesus occupying the lonely centre of the stage.

THE COMING OF THE SPIRIT

John 1: 32, 34

So John bore his witness. " With my own eyes," he said, " I saw the Spirit coming down from heaven, as it mght have been a dove, and the Spirit remained upon him. And I did not know him. But it was he who sent me to baptize with water who said to me: ' The one on whom you see the Spirit coming down and remaining is the one who baptizes with the Holy Spirit.' And I saw it happen; and my witness stands that this is the Son of God."

SOMETHING had happened at the baptism of Jesus which had convinced John beyond all doubt that Jesus was the Son of God. As the fathers of the church saw centuries ago, it was something which only the eye of the mind and soul could see. But John saw it and was convinced.

In Palestine the dove was a sacred bird. It was not hunted and it was not eaten. Philo noticed the number of doves at Ascalon, because it was not permitted to catch and kill them, and they were tame. In *Genesis* 1: 2 we read of the creative Spirit of God moving upon the face of the waters. The Rabbis used to say that the Spirit of God moved and fluttered like a dove over the ancient chaos breathing order and beauty into it. The picture of the dove was one which the Jews knew and loved.

It was at his baptism that the Spirit came down upon Jesus with power. We must remember that at this time the *Christian* doctrine of the Spirit had not yet come into being. We have to wait for the last chapters of John's gospel and for Pentecost for that to emerge. When John the Baptist spoke of the Spirit coming upon Jesus, he must have been thinking in *Jewish* terms. What then was the Jewish idea of the Spirit?

The Jewish word for Spirit is *ruach*, the word which means *wind*. To the Jew there were always three basic ideas of the Spirit. The Spirit was *power*, power like a mighty rushing wind; the Spirit was *life*, the very dynamic of the existence of man; the Spirit was *God*; the power and the life of the Spirit were beyond mere human achievement and attainment; the coming of the Spirit into a man's life was the coming of God. Above all it was the Spirit who controlled and inspired the prophets. " I am filled with power, with the Spirit of the Lord, and with justice and might to declare to Jacob his transgression and to Israel his sin " (Micah 3: 8). God speaks to Isaiah of " My Spirit which is upon you and my words which I have put in your mouth " (*Isaiah* 59: 21). " The Spirit of the Lord God is upon me

because the Lord has anointed me to bring good tidings "
(*Isaiah* 61: 1). " A new heart I will give you and a new spirit I
will put within you.... I will put my Spirit within you "
(*Ezekiel* 36: 26, 27). We may say that the Spirit of God did
three things for the man on whom he came. First, he brought to
men the truth of God. Second, he gave men the power to
recognize that truth when they saw it. Third, he gave them the
ability and the courage to preach that truth to men. To the Jew
the Spirit was God coming into a man's life.

At his baptism the Spirit came upon Jesus in a different way
from that in which he ever came on any other person. Most men
have what might be called spasmodic experiences of the Spirit.
They have their moments of dazzling illumination, of extraordinary power, of superhuman courage. But these moments
come and go. Twice (verses 32, 33) John goes out of his way to
point out that the Spirit *remained* on Jesus. Here was no
momentary inspiration. In Jesus the Spirit took up his permanent abode. That is still another way of saying that the mind
and the power of God were uniquely in Jesus.

Here we can learn a great deal of what the word *baptism*
means. The Greek verb *baptizein* means *to dip* or *to submerge*.
It can be used of clothes being *dipped* in dye; it can be used of a
ship *submerged* beneath the waves; it can be used of a person
who is so drunk that he is *soaked* in drink. When John says that
Jesus will baptize men with the Holy Spirit, he means that Jesus
can bring God's Spirit to us in such a way that we are saturated
and our life and being are flooded with that Spirit.

Now what did this baptism mean for John? His own baptism
meant two things. (i) It meant *cleansing*. It meant that a man
was being washed from the impurities that clung to him. (ii) It
meant *dedication*. It meant that he went out to a new and a
different and a better life. But Jesus's baptism was *a baptism of
the Spirit*. If we remember the Jewish conception of the Spirit
we can say that when the Spirit takes possession of a man
certain things happen.

(i) His life is *illumined*. There comes to him the knowledge of
God and God's will. He knows what God's purpose is, what life

means, where duty lies. Some of God's wisdom and light has come into him.

(ii) His life is *strengthened*. Knowledge without power is a haunting and frustrating thing. But the Spirit gives us not only knowledge to know the right, but also strength and power to do it. The Spirit gives us a triumphant adequacy to cope with life.

(iii) His life is *purified*. Christ's baptism with the Spirit was to be a baptism of *fire* (*Matthew* 3: 11; *Luke* 3: 16). The dross of evil things, the alloy of the lower things, the base admixture is burned away until a man is clean and pure.

Often our prayers for the Spirit are a kind of theological and liturgical formality; but when we know that for which we are praying, these prayers become a desperate cry from the heart.

THE FIRST DISCIPLES

John 1: 35–39

> On the next day John was again standing with two of his disciples. John looked at Jesus as he walked. " See! " he said, " The Lamb of God! " And the two disciples heard him speaking and followed Jesus. Jesus turned and saw them following him. " What are you looking for? " he said to them. " Rabbi " (the word means Teacher), they said to him, " where are you staying? " He said to them: " Come and see! " They came and saw where he was staying, and they stayed with him throughout that day. And it was about four o'clock in the afternoon.

NEVER was a passage of scripture fuller of little revealing touches than this.

Once again we see John the Baptist pointing beyond himself. He must have known very well that to speak to his disciples about Jesus like that was to invite them to leave him and transfer their loyalty to this new and greater teacher; and yet he did it. There was no jealousy in John. He had come to attach men not to himself but to Christ. There is no harder task than to take the second place when once the first place was enjoyed.

But as soon as Jesus emerged on the scene John never had any other thought than to send men to him.

So the two disciples of John followed Jesus. It may well be that they were too shy to approach him directly and followed respectfully some distance behind. Then Jesus did something entirely characteristic. He turned and spoke to them. That is to say, he met them half way. He made things easier for them. He opened the door that they might come in.

Here we have the symbol of the divine initiative. It is always God who takes the first step. When the human mind begins to seek and the human heart begins to long, God comes to meet us far more than half way. God does not leave a man to search and search until he comes to him; God goes out to meet the man. As Augustine said, we could not even have begun to seek for God unless he had already found us. When we go to God we do not go to one who hides himself and keeps us at a distance; we go to one who stands waiting for us, and who even takes the initiative by coming to meet us on the road.

Jesus began by asking these two men the most fundamental question in life. " What are you looking for? " he asked them. It was very relevant to ask that question in Palestine in the time of Jesus. Were they legalists, looking only for subtle and recondite conversations about the little details of the Law, like the scribes and Pharisees? Were they ambitious time-servers looking for position and power like the Sadducees? Were they nationalists looking for a political demagogue and a military commander who would smash the occupying power of Rome like the Zealots? Were they humble men of prayer looking for God and for his will, like the Quiet in the Land? Or were they simply puzzled, bewildered sinful men looking for light on the road of life and forgiveness from God?

It would be well if every now and again we were to ask ourselves: " What am I looking for? What's my aim and goal? What am I really trying to get out of life? "

Some are searching for *security*. They would like a position which is safe, money enough to meet the needs of life and to put some past for the time when work is done, a material security which will take away the essential worry about material things. This is not a wrong aim, but it is a low aim, and an inadequate thing to which to direct all life; for, in the last analysis, there is no safe security in the chances and the changes of this life.

Some are searching for what they would call a *career*, for power, prominence, prestige, for a place to fit the talents and the abilities they believe themselves to have, for an opportunity to do the work they believe themselves capable of doing. If this be directed by motives of personal ambition it can be a bad aim; if it be directed by motives of the service of our fellow men it can be a high aim. But it is not enough, for its horizon is limited by time and by the world.

Some are searching for some kind of *peace*, for something to enable them to live at peace with themselves, and at peace with God, and at peace with men. This is the search for God; this aim only Jesus Christ can meet and supply.

The answer of John's disciples was that they wished to know where Jesus stayed. They called him *Rabbi*; that is a Hebrew word which literally means *My great one*. It was the title of respect given by students and seekers after knowledge to their teachers and to wise men. John, the evangelist, was writing for Greeks. He knew they would not recognize that Hebrew word, so he translated it for them by the Greek word *didaskalos*, *teacher*. It was not mere curiosity which made these two ask this question. What they meant was that they did not wish to speak to Jesus only on the road, in the passing, as chance acquaintances might stop and exchange a few words. They wished to linger long with him and talk out their problems and their troubles. The man who would be Jesus's disciple can never be satisfied with a passing word. He wants to meet Jesus, not as an acquaintance in the passing, but as a friend in his own house.

Jesus's answer was: " Come and see! " The Jewish Rabbis had a way of using that phrase in their teaching. They would say: " Do you want to know the answer to this question? Do you want to know the solution to this problem? Come and see, and we will think about it together." When Jesus said: " Come and see! " he was inviting them, not only to come and talk, but to come and find the things that he alone could open out to them.

John who wrote the gospel finishes the paragraph—" It was about four o'clock in the afternoon." It may very well be that he finishes that way because he was one of the two himself. He could tell you the very hour of the day and no doubt the very stone of the road he was standing on when he met Jesus. At four o'clock on a spring afternoon in Galilee life became a new thing for him.

SHARING THE GLORY

John 1: 40–42

> Andrew, Simon Peter's brother, was one of the two who had heard John speaking about Jesus, and who had followed him. First thing in the morning, he went and found his own brother Simon. " We have found the Messiah," he said to him. (The word *Messiah* means the same as the word *Christ*.) He brought him to Jesus. Jesus looked intently at him. " You are Simon, Jona's son," he said. " You will be called Cephas." *Cephas* is the same name as *Peter* and means a *rock*.

THE Revised Standard Version has it that Andrew " *first* found his brother Simon." In the Greek manuscripts there are two readings. Some manuscripts have the word *prōton*, which means *first*, and that is the reading that the Revised Standard Version has translated. Other manuscripts have *prōi*, which means *early in the morning*. In our translation we have taken the second reading because it suits better the story of the first momentous week in Jesus's life to regard this event as taking place on the next day.

Again John explains a Hebrew word in order to help his Greek readers to understand better. *Messiah* and *Christ* are the same word. *Messiah* is Hebrew and *Christ* is Greek; both mean *anointed*. In the ancient world, as today in our own country,

kings were anointed with oil at their coronation. *Messiah* and
Christos both mean *God's Anointed King.*

We do not possess a great deal of information about
Andrew, but even the little that we know perfectly paints his
character. He is one of the most attractive men in the apostolic
band. He has two outstanding characteristics.

(i) Andrew was characteristically the man who was prepared
to take the second place. Again and again he is identified as
Simon Peter's brother. It is clear that he lived under the shadow
of Peter. People might not know who Andrew was, but everyone knew Peter; and when men spoke of Andrew they described
him as Peter's brother. Andrew was not one of the inner circle
of the disciples. When Jesus healed Jairus's daughter, when he
went up to the Mount of Transfiguration, when he underwent
his temptation in Gethsemane, it was Peter, James and John
whom he took with him. It would have been so easy for Andrew
to resent this. Was he not one of the first two disciples who ever
followed Jesus? Did Peter not owe his meeting with Jesus to
him? Might he not reasonably have expected a foremost place
in the apostolic band? But all that never even occurred to
Andrew. He was quite content to stand back and let his brother
have the limelight; he was quite content to play a humble part in
the company of the Twelve. To Andrew matters of precedence
and place and honour mattered nothing at all. All that mattered
was to be with Jesus and to serve him as well as he could.
Andrew is the patron saint of all who humbly and loyally and
ungrudgingly take the second place.

(ii) Andrew is characteristically the man who was always
introducing others to Jesus. There are only three times in the
gospel story when Andrew is brought into the centre of the
stage. There is this incident here, in which he brings Peter to
Jesus. There is the incident in *John* 6: 8, 9 when he brings to
Jesus the boy with the five loaves and two small fishes. And
there is the incident in *John* 12: 22 when he brings the enquiring Greeks into the presence of Jesus. It was Andrew's great
joy to bring others to Jesus. He stands out as the man whose
one desire was to share the glory. He is the man with the mis-

sionary heart. Having himself found the friendship of Jesus, he
spent all his life in introducing others to that friendship. Andrew
is our great example in that he could not keep Jesus to himself.

When Andrew brought Peter to Jesus, Jesus looked at Peter.
The word used of that look is *emblepein*. It describes a
concentrated, intent gaze, the gaze which does not see only the
superficial things that lie on the surface, but which reads a
man's heart. When Jesus saw Simon, as he was then called, he
said to him: " Your name is Simon; but you are going to be
called Cephas, which means a rock."

In the ancient world nearly everyone had two names. Greek
was the universal language and nearly everyone had a name in
his own native tongue, by which he was known to his friends
Thomas was the *Aramaic* and *Didymus* the *Greek* for a *twin*;
Tabitha was the *Aramaic* and *Dorcas* the *Greek* for a *gazelle*.
Sometimes the Greek name was chosen because it sounded like
the Aramaic name. A Jew who was called *Eliakim* or *Abel* in
his own tongue might become *Alcimus* or *Apelles* to his Greek
circle of acquaintances. So then *Peter* and *Cephas* are not
different names; they are the same name in different languages.

In the Old Testament a change of name often denoted a new
relationship with God. For instance, *Jacob* became *Israel*
(*Genesis* 32: 28), and *Abram* became *Abraham* (*Genesis* 17: 5)
when they entered into a new relationship with God. When a
man enters into a new relationship with God, it is as if life
began all over again and he became a new man, so that he needs
a new name.

But the great thing about this story is that it tells us *how
Jesus looks at men*. He does not only see what a man *is*; he also
sees what a man *can become*. He sees not only the *actualities* in
a man; he also sees the *possibilities*. Jesus looked at Peter and
saw in him not only a Galilaean fisherman but one who had it
in him to become the rock on which his church would be built.
Jesus sees us not only as we are, but as we can be; and he says:
" Give your life to me, and I will make you what you have it in
you to be." Once someone came on Michelangelo chipping
away with his chisel at a huge shapeless piece of rock. He asked

the sculptor what he was doing. " I am releasing the angel imprisoned in this marble," he answered. Jesus is the one who sees and can release the hidden hero in every man.

THE SURRENDER OF NATHANAEL

John 1: 43–51

On the next day Jesus determined to go away to Galilee; and there he found Philip. Jesus said to him: " Follow me! " Now Philip came from Bethsaida, which was the town from which Andrew and Peter came. Philip went and found Nathanael and said to him: " We have found the One about whom Moses wrote in the law, and about whom the prophets spoke—I mean Jesus, the son of Joseph, the man from Nazareth." Nathanael said to him: " Can anything good come out of Nazareth? " Philip said to him: " Come and see! " When Jesus saw Nathanael coming towards him, he said: " See! A man who is really an Israelite! A man in whom there is no guile! " Nathanael said to him: " How do you know me? " " Before Philip called you," said Jesus, " I saw you when you were under the fig-tree." ": Rabbi," answered Nathanael, " you are the Son of God; you are the King of Israel." Jesus answered: " Do you believe because I said to you, ' I saw you under the fig-tree '? You will see greàter things than these." He said to him: " This is the truth I tell you—you will see the heavens opened, and the angels of God ascending and descending on the Son of Man."

AT this point in the story Jesus left the south and went north to Galilee. There, perhaps in Cana, he found and called Philip. Philip, like Andrew, could not keep the good news to himself. As Godet said: " One lighted torch serves to light another." So Philip went and found his friend Nathanael. He told him that he believed that he had discovered the long promised Messiah in Jesus, the man from Nazareth. Nathanael was contemptuous. There was nothing in the Old Testament which foretold that God's Chosen One should come from Nazareth. Nazareth was a quite undistinguished place. Nathanael himself came from Cana, another Galilaean town, and, in country places, jealousy between town and town, and rivalry between village and village, is notorious. Nathanael's reaction was to declare that Nazareth was not the kind of place that anything good was likely to come out of. Philip was wise. He did not argue. He said simply: " Come and see! "

Not very many people have ever been argued into Christianity. Often our arguments do more harm than good. The only way to convince a man of the supremacy of Christ is to confront him with Christ. On the whole it is true to say that it is not argumentative and philosophical preaching and teaching which have won men for Christ; it is the presentation of the story of the Cross.

There is a story which tells how, towards the end of the nineteenth century, Huxley, the great agnostic, was a member of a house-party at a country house. Sunday came round, and most of the members prepared to go to church; but, very naturally, Huxley did not propose to go. Huxley approached a man known to have a simple and radiant Christian faith. He said to him: " Suppose you don't go to church today. Suppose you stay at home and you tell me quite simply what your Christian faith means to you and why you are a Christian." " But," said the man, " you could demolish my arguments in an instant. I'm not clever enough to argue with you." Huxley said gently: " I don't want to argue with you; I just want you to tell me simply what this Christ means to you." The man stayed at home and told Huxley most simply of his faith. When he had finished there were tears in the great agnostic's eyes. " I would give my right hand," he said, " if only I could believe that."

It was not clever argument that touched Huxley's heart. He could have dealt efficiently and devastatingly with any argument that that simple Christian was likely to have produced, but the simple presentation of Christ caught him by the heart. The best argument is to say to people: " Come and see! " Of course, we have to know Christ ourselves before we can invite others to come to him. The true evangelist must himself have met Christ first.

So Nathanael came; and Jesus could see into his heart. " Here," said Jesus, " is a genuine Israelite, a man in whose heart there is no guile." That was a tribute that any devout Israelite would recognize. " Blessed is the man," said the Psalmist, " to whom the Lord imputes no iniquity, and in whose spirit there is no deceit " (*Psalm* 32: 2). " He had done no violence," said the prophet of the Servant of the Lord " and there was no deceit in his mouth " (*Isaiah* 53: 9).

Nathanael was surprised that anyone could give a verdict like that on so short an acquaintance, and he demanded how Jesus could possibly know him. Jesus told him that he had already seen him under the fig-tree. What is the significance of that? To the Jews the fig-tree always stood for peace. Their idea of peace was when a man could be undisturbed under his own vine and his own fig-tree (cp. 1 *Kings* 4: 25; *Micah* 4: 4). Further, the fig-tree was leafy and shady and it was the custom to sit and meditate under the roof of its branches. No doubt that was what Nathanael had been doing; and no doubt as he sat under the fig-tree he had prayed for the day when God's Chosen One should come. No doubt he had been meditating on the promises of God. And now he felt that Jesus had seen into the very depths of his heart.

It was not so much that Jesus had seen him under the fig-tree that surprised Nathanael; it was the fact that Jesus had read the thoughts of his inmost heart. Nathanael said to himself: " Here is the man who understands my dreams! Here is the man who knows my prayers1 Here is the man who has seen into my most intimate and secret longings, longings which I have never even dared put into words! Here is the man who can translate the inarticulate sigh of my soul! This must be God's promised anointed one and no other." Nathanael capitulated for ever to the man who read and understood and satisfied his heart.

It may be that Jesus smiled. He quoted the old story of Jacob
at Bethel who had seen the golden ladder leading up to heaven
(*Genesis* 28: 12, 13). It was as if Jesus said: " Nathanael, I can
do far more than read your heart. I can be for you and for all
men the way, the ladder that leads to heaven." It is through
Jesus and Jesus alone that the souls of men can mount the
ladder which leads to heaven.

This passage presents us with a problem. Who was
Nathanael? In the Fourth Gospel he is one of the first group of
disciples; in the other three gospels he never appears at all.
More than one explanation has been given.

(i) It has been suggested that Nathanael is not a real figure at
all, but an ideal figure standing for all the true Israelites who
burst the bonds of national pride and prejudice and gave themselves to Jesus Christ.

(ii) On the same basis, it has been suggested that he stands
either for Paul or for the beloved disciple. Paul was the great
example of the Israelite who had accepted Christ; the beloved
disciple was the ideal disciple. Again the supposition is that
Nathanael stands for an ideal; that he is a type and not a
person. If this were the only mention of Nathanael that might
be true; but Nathanael appears again in *John* 21: 2 and there is
no thought of him as an ideal there.

(iii) He has been identified with Matthew, because both
Matthew and *Nathanael* mean *the gift of God*. We saw that in
those days most people had two names; but then one name was
Greek and the other Jewish. In this case both *Matthew* and
Nathanael are Jewish names.

(iv) There is a simpler explanation. *Nathanael* was brought
to Jesus by *Philip*. *Nathanael's* name is never mentioned in the
other three gospels; and in the Fourth Gospel *Bartholomew's*
name is never mentioned. Now, in the list of the disciples in
Matthew 10: 3 and *Mark* 3: 18, *Philip* and *Bartholomew* come
together, as if it was natural and inevitable to connect them.
Moreover, *Bartholomew* is really a *second* name. It means *Son
of Tholmai* or *Ptolemy*. *Bartholomew* must have had another
name, a first name; and it is at least possible that *Bartholomew*

and *Nathanael* are the same person under different names. That certainly fits the facts.

Whatever else, it is true that Nathanael stands for the Israelite whose heart was cleansed of pride and prejudice and who saw in Jesus the one who satisfied the longing of his waiting, seeking heart.

THE NEW EXHILARATION

John 2: 1–11

Two days after this there was a wedding in Cana of Galilee; and Jesus's mother was there. And Jesus was invited to the wedding and so were his disciples. When the wine had run short, Jesus's mother said to him: " They have no wine." Jesus said to her: " Lady, let me handle this in my own way. My hour has not yet come." His mother said to the servants: " Do whatever he tells you to do." There were six stone waterpots standing there—they were needed for the Jewish purifying customs—and each of them held about twenty or thirty gallons. Jesus said to them: " Fill the waterpots with water." They filled them up to the very brim. He said to them: " Draw from them now, and take what you draw to the steward in charge." They did so. When the steward had tasted the water which had become wine—he did not know where it came from, but the servants who had drawn the water knew—the steward called the bridegroom and said to him: " Everyone first sets before the guests the good wine, and then, when they have drunk their fill, he sets before them the inferior wine. You have kept the good wine until now."

Jesus did the first of his signs in Cana of Galilee, and displayed his glory; and his disciples believed on him.

THE very richness of the Fourth Gospel presents those who would study it and him who would expound it with a problem. Always there are two things. There is a simple surface story that anyone can understand and re-tell; but there is also a wealth of deeper meaning for him who has the eagerness to search and the eye to see and the mind to understand. There is so much in a passage like this that we must take three days to study it. We shall look at it first of all quite simply to set it within its background and to see it come alive. We shall then look at certain of the things it tells us about Jesus and his work. And finally we shall look at the permanent truth which John is seeking to tell us in it.

Cana of Galilee is so called to distinguish it from Cana in Coelo-Syria. It was a village quite near to Nazareth. Jerome, who stayed in Palestine, says that he saw it from Nazareth. In Cana there was a wedding feast to which Mary went and at which she held a special place. She had something to do with the arrangements, for she was worried when the wine ran done; and she had authority enough to order the servants to do whatever Jesus told them to do. Some of the later gospels which never got into the New Testament add certain details to this story. One of the Coptic gospels tells us that Mary was a sister of the bridegroom's mother. There is an early set of Prefaces to the books of the New Testament called the Monarchian Prefaces which tell us that the bridegroom was no other than John himself, and that his mother was Salome, the sister of Mary. We do not know whether these extra details are true or not, but the story is st vividly told that it is clearly an eye-witness account.

There is no mention of Joseph. The explanation most probably is that by this time Joseph was dead. It would seem that Joseph died quite soon, and that the reason why Jesus spent eighteen long years in Nazareth was that he had to take upon himself the support of his mother and his family. It was only when his younger brothers and sisters were able to look after themselves that he left home.

The scene is a village wedding feast. In Palestine a wedding was a really notable occasion. It was the Jewish law that the wedding of a virgin should take place on a Wednesday. This is interesting because it gives us a date from which to work back; and if this wedding took place on a Wednesday it must have been the Sabbath day when Jesus first met Andrew and John and they stayed the whole day with him. The wedding festivities lasted far more than one day. The wedding ceremony itself took place late in the evening, after a feast. After the ceremony the young couple were conducted to their new home. By that time it was dark and they were conducted through the village streets by the light of flaming torches and with a canopy over their heads. They were taken by as long a route as possible so that as many people as possible would have the opportunity to wish them well. But a newly married couple did not go away for their honeymoon; they stayed at home; and for a week they kept open house. They wore crowns and dressed in their bridal robes. They were treated like a king and queen, were actually addressed as king and queen, and their word was law. In a life where there was much poverty and constant hard work, this week of festivity and joy was one of the supreme occasions.

It was in a happy time like this that Jesus gladly shared. But something went wrong. It is likely that the coming of Jesus caused something of a problem. He had been invited to the feast, but he had arrived not alone but with five disciples. Five extra people may well have caused complications. Five unexpected guests might provide any festival with a problem, and the wine went done.

For a Jewish feast wine was essential. " Without wine," said the Rabbis, " there is no joy." It was not that people were drunken, but in the East wine was an essential. Drunkenness was in fact a great disgrace, and they actually drank their wine in a mixture composed of two parts of wine to three parts of water. At any time the failure of provisions would have been a problem, for hospitality in the East is a sacred duty; but for the provisions to fail at a wedding would be a terrible humiliation for the bride and the bridegroom.

So Mary came to Jesus to tell him that it was so. The Authorized Version translation of Jesus's reply makes it sound very discourteous. It makes him say: " Woman, what have I to do with thee? " That is indeed a translation of the *words*, but it does not in any way give the *tone*.

The phrase, " What have I to do with thee? " was a common conversational phrase. When it was uttered angrily and sharply it did indicate complete disagreement and reproach, but when it was spoken gently it indicated not so much reproach but misunderstanding. It means: " Don't worry; you don't quite understand what is going on; leave things to me, and I will settle them in my own way." Jesus was simply telling Mary to leave things to him, that he would have his own way of dealing with the situation.

The word *Woman* (*gunai*) is also misleading. It sounds to us very rough and abrupt. But it is the same word as Jesus used on the Cross to address Mary as he left her to the care of John (*John* 19: 26). In Homer it is the title by which Odysseus addresses Penelope, his well-loved wife. It is the title by which Augustus, the Roman Emperor, addressed Cleopatra, the famous Egyptian queen. So far from being a rough and discourteous way of address, it was a title of respect. We have no way of speaking in English which exactly renders it; but it is better to translate it *Lady* which gives at least the courtesy in it.

However Jesus spoke, Mary was confident of him. She told the servants to do as Jesus told them to do. At the door there were six great water jars. The word that the Authorized Version translates *firkin* represents the Hebrew measure called the *bath* which was a measure equivalent to between eight and nine gallons. The jars were very large; they would hold about twenty gallons of water apiece.

John was writing his gospel for Greeks and so he explains that these jars were there to provide water for the purifying ceremonies of the Jews. Water was required for two purposes. First, it was required for cleansing the feet on entry to the house. The roads were not surfaced. Sandals were merely a sole attached to the foot by straps. On a dry day the feet were covered by dust and on a wet day they were soiled with mud; and the water was used for cleansing them. Second, it was required for the handwashing. Strict Jews washed the hands before a meal and between each course. First the hand was held upright and the water was poured over it in such a way that it ran right to the wrist; then the hand was held pointing down and the water was poured in such a way that it ran from the wrist to the finger-tips. This was done with each hand in turn;

and then each palm was cleansed by rubbing it with the fist of the other hand. The Jewish ceremonial law insisted that this should be done not only at the beginning of a meal but also between courses. If it was not done the hands were technically *unclean*. It was for this footwashing and handwashing that these great stone jars of water stood there.

John commanded that the jars should be filled to the brim. John mentions that point to make it clear that nothing else but water was put into them. He then told them to draw out the water and to take it to the *architriklinos*, the steward in charge. At their banquets the Romans had a toast-master called the *arbiter bibendi*, the arranger of the drinking. Sometimes one of the guests acted as a kind of master of ceremonies at a Jewish wedding. But our equivalent of the *architriklinos* is really the head-waiter. He was responsible for the seating of the guests and the correct running of the feast. When he tasted the water which had become wine he was astonished. He called the bridegroom—it was the bridegroom's parents who were responsible for the feast—and spoke jestingly. " Most people," he said, " serve the good wine first; and then, when the guests have drunk a good deal, and their palates are dulled and they are not in much of a condition to appreciate what they are drinking, they serve the inferior wine, but you have kept the best until now."

So it was at a village girl's wedding in a Galilaean village that Jesus first showed his glory; and it was there that his disciples caught another dazzling glimpse of what he was.

THE NEW EXHILARATION

John 2: 1–11 (*continued*)

WE note three general things about this wonderful deed which Jesus did.

(i) We note *when* it happened. It happened at a wedding feast. Jesus was perfectly at home at such an occasion. He was

no severe, austere killjoy. He loved to share in the happy rejoicing of a wedding feast.

There are certain religious people who shed a gloom wherever they go. They are suspicious of all joy and happiness.
To them religion is a thing of black clothes, the lowered voice, the
expulsion of social fellowship. It was said of Alice Freeman
Palmer by one of her scholars: " She made me feel as if I was
bathed in sunshine." Jesus was like that. C. H. Spurgeon in his
book *Lectures to my Students* has some wise, if caustic, advice.
" Sepulchral tones may fit a man to be an undertaker, but
Lazarus is not called out of his grave by hollow moans." " I
know brethren who from head to foot, in garb, tone, manner,
necktie and boots are so utterly *parsonic* that no particle of
manhood is visible.... Some men appear to have a white
cravat twisted round their souls, their manhood is throttled with
that starched rag." " An individual who has no geniality about
him had better be an undertaker, and bury the dead, for he will
never succeed in influencing the living." " I commend cheerful-
ness to all who would win souls; not levity and frothiness,
but a genial, happy spirit. There are more flies caught with
honey than with vinegar, and there will be more souls led to
heaven by a man who wears heaven in his face than by one who
bears Tartarus in his looks."

Jesus never counted it a crime to be happy. Why should his
followers do so?

(ii) We note *where* it happened. It happened in a humble
home in a village in Galilee. This miracle was not wrought
against the background of some great occasion and in the
presence of vast crowds. It was wrought in a home. A. H. N.
Green Armytage in his book, *A Portrait of St. Luke*, speaks of
how Luke delighted to show Jesus against a background of
simple, homely things and people. In a vivid phrase he says that
St. Luke's gospel " domesticated God "; it brought God right
into the home circle and into the ordinary things of life. Jesus's
action at Cana of Galilee shows what he thought of a home. As
the Revised Standard Version has it, he " manifested forth his
glory," and that manifestation took place within a home.

There is a strange paradox in the attitude of many people to the place they call home. They would admit at once that there is no more precious place in all the world; and yet, at the same time, they would also have to admit that in it they claim the right to be far more discourteous, far more boorish, far more selfish, far more impolite than they would dare to be in any society of strangers. Many of us treat the ones we love most in a way that we would never dare to treat a chance acquaintance. So often it is strangers who see us at our best and those who live with us who see us at our worst. We ought ever to remember that it was in a humble home that Jesus manifested forth his glory. To him home was a place for which nothing but his best was good enough.

(iii) We note *why* it happened. We have already seen that in the East hospitality was always a sacred duty. It would have brought embarrassed shame to that home that day if the wine had run done. It was to save a humble Galilaean family from hurt that Jesus put forth his power. It was in sympathy, in kindness, in understanding for simple folk that Jesus acted.

Nearly everyone can do the big thing on the big occasion; but it takes Jesus to do the big thing on a simple, homely occasion like this. There is a kind of natural human maliciousness which rather enjoys the misfortunes of others and which delights to make a good story of them over the teacups. But Jesus, the Lord of all life, and the King of glory, used his power to save a simple Galilaean lad and lass from humiliation. It is just by such deeds of understanding, simple kindliness that we too can show that we are followers of Jesus Christ.

Further, this story shows us very beautifully two things about Mary's faith in Jesus.

(i) Instinctively Mary turned to Jesus whenever something went wrong. She knew her son. It was not till he was thirty years old that Jesus left home; and all these years Mary lived with him. There is an old legend which tells of the days when Jesus was a little baby in the home in Nazareth. It tells how in those days when people felt tired and worried and hot and bothered and upset, they would say: " Let us go and look at

Mary's child," and they would go and look at Jesus, and somehow all their troubles rolled away. It is still true that those who know Jesus intimately instinctively turn to him when things go wrong—and they never find him wanting.

(ii) Even when Mary did not understand what Jesus was going to do, even when it seemed that he had refused her request, Mary still believed in him so much that she turned to the serving folk and told them to do whatever Jesus told them to do. Mary had the faith which could trust even when it did not understand. She did not know what Jesus was going to do, but she was quite sure that he would do the right thing. In every life come periods of darkness when we do not see the way. In every life come things which are such that we do not see why they came or any meaning in them. Happy is the man who in such a case still trusts even when he cannot understand.

Still further, this story tells us something about Jesus. In answer to Mary he said: " My hour has not yet come." All through the gospel story Jesus talks about *his hour*. In *John* 7: 6, 8 it is the hour of his emergence as the Messiah. In *John* 12: 23 and 17: 1, and in *Matthew* 26: 18, 45 and in *Mark* 14: 41 it is the hour of his crucifixion and his death. All through his life Jesus knew that he had come into this world for a definite purpose and a definite task. He saw his life not in terms of his wishes, but in terms of God's purpose for himself. He saw his life not against the shifting background of time, but against the steady background of eternity. All through his life he went steadily towards that hour for which he knew that he had come into the world. It is not only Jesus who came into this world to fulfil the purpose of God. As someone has said: " Every man is a dream and an idea of God." We, too, must think not of our own wishes and our own desires, but of the purpose for which God sent us into his world.

THE NEW EXHILARATION

John 2: 1–11 (*continued*)

Now we must think of the deep and permanent truth which John is seeking to teach when he tells this story.

We must remember that John was writing out of a double background. He was a Jew and he was writing for Jews; but his great object was to write the story of Jesus in such a way that it would come home also to the Greeks.

Let us look at it first of all from the *Jewish* point of view. We must always remember that beneath John's simple stories there is a deeper meaning which is open only to those who have eyes to see. In all his gospel John never wrote an unnecessary or an insignificant detail. Everything means something and everything points beyond.

There were six stone waterpots; and at the command of Jesus the water in them turned to wine. According to the Jews *seven* is the number which is complete and perfect; and *six* is the number which is unfinished and imperfect. The six stone waterpots stand for all the imperfections of the Jewish law. Jesus came to do away with the imperfections of the law and to put in their place the new wine of the gospel of his grace. Jesus turned the imperfection of the law into the perfection of grace.

There is another thing to note in this connection. There were six waterpots; each held between twenty and thirty gallons of water; Jesus turned the water into wine. That would give anything up to one hundred and eighty gallons of wine. Simply to state that fact is to show that John did not mean the story to be taken with crude literalness. What John did mean to say is that when the grace of Jesus comes to men there is enough and to spare for all. No wedding party on earth could drink one hundred and eighty gallons of wine. No need on earth can exhaust the grace of Christ; there is a glorious superabundance in it.

John is telling us that in Jesus the imperfections have become perfection, and the grace has become illimitable, sufficient and more than sufficient for every need.

Let us look at it now from the Greek point of view. It so happens that the Greeks actually possessed stories like this. Dionysos was the Greek god of wine. Pausanias was a Greek who wrote a description of his country and of its ancient ceremonies. In his description of Elis, he describes an old ceremony and belief: " Between the market-place and the Menius is an old theatre and a sanctuary of Dionysos; the image is by Praxiteles. No god is more revered by the Eleans than Dionysos is, and they say that he attends their festival of the Thyia. The place where they hold the festival called the Thyia is about a mile from the city. Three empty kettles are taken into the building and deposited there by the priests in the presence of the citizens and of any strangers who may happen to be staying in the country. On the doors of the buildings the priests, and all who choose to do so, put their seals. Next day they are free to examine the seals, and on entering the building they find the kettles full of wine. I was not there myself at the time of the festival, but the most respectable men of Elis, and strangers too, swore that the facts were as I have said."

So the Greeks, too, had their stories like this; and it is as if John said to them: " You have your stories and your legends about your gods. They are only stories and you know that they are not really true. But Jesus has come to do what you have always dreamed that your gods could do. He has come to make the things you longed for come true."

To the Jews John said: " Jesus has come to turn the imperfection of the law into the perfection of grace." To the Greeks he said: " Jesus has come really and truly to do the things you only dreamed the gods could do."

Now we can see what John is teaching us. Every story tells us not of something Jesus did once and never again, but of something which he is for ever doing. John tells us not of things that Jesus once did in Palestine, but of things that he still does today. And what John wants us to see here is not that Jesus once on a day turned some waterpots of water into wine; he wants us to see that whenever Jesus comes into a man's life, there comes a new quality which is like turning water into wine. Without Jesus, life is dull and stale and flat; when Jesus comes into it, life becomes vivid and sparkling and exciting. Without Jesus, life is drab and uninteresting; with him it is thrilling and exhilarating.

When Sir Wilfred Grenfell was appealing for volunteers for his work in Labrador, he said that he could not promise them much money, but he could promise them the time of their lives. That is what Jesus promises us. Remember that John was writing seventy years after Jesus was crucified. For seventy years he had thought and meditated and remembered, until he saw meanings and significances that he had not seen at the time. When John told this story he was remembering what life with Jesus was like; and he said, " Wherever Jesus went and whenever he came into life it was like water turning into wine." This story is John saying to *us*: " If you want the new exhilaration, become a follower of Jesus Christ, and there will come a change in your life which will be like water turning into wine."

THE ANGER OF JESUS

John 2: 12–16

After this Jesus went down to Capernaum with his mother and his brothers and his disciples; and they stayed there for a short time.

The Passover Feast of the Jews was near, and Jesus went up to Jerusalem. In the Temple he found those who were selling oxen and sheep and doves, and the money-changers sitting at their tables. He made a scourge of cords and drove them all out of the Temple, and the sheep and the oxen as well. He scattered the coins of the exchangers and overturned their tables. He said to those who were selling doves: " Take these away and stop making my Father's house a house of trade."

AFTER the wedding feast at Cana of Galilee, Jesus and his friends returned for a short visit to Capernaum, on the north shore of the Sea of Galilee and about twenty miles distant.

Shortly after this Jesus set out to observe the Passover Feast in Jerusalem. The Passover fell on the 15th Nisan, which is about the middle of April; and, according to the law, it was obligatory for every adult male Jew who lived within fifteen miles of Jerusalem to attend the feast.

Here we have a very interesting thing. At first sight John has a quite different chronology of the life of Jesus from that of the other three gospels. In them Jesus is depicted as going to Jerusalem only once. The Passover Feast at which he was crucified is the only one they mention, and his only visit to Jerusalem except the visit to the Temple when he was a boy. But in John we find Jesus making frequent visits to Jerusalem. John tells us of no fewer than three Passovers—this present one, the one in *John* 6: 4 and the one in *John* 11: 55. In addition, according to John's story, Jesus was in Jerusalem for an unnamed feast in 5: 1; for the Feast of Tabernacles in 7: 2, 10; and for the Feast of the Dedication in 10: 22. In point of fact in the other three gospels the main ministry of Jesus is in Galilee; in John Jesus is in Galilee only for brief periods (2: 1–12; 4: 43—5: 1; 6: 1—7: 14), and his main ministry is in Jerusalem.

The truth is that there is no real contradiction here. John and the others are telling the story from different points of view. They do not contradict but complement each other. Matthew, Mark and Luke concentrate on the ministry in Galilee; John concentrates on the ministry in Jerusalem. Although the other three tell us of only one visit to Jerusalem and one Passover there, they imply that there must have been many others. At his last visit they show us Jesus mourning over Jerusalem: " O Jerusalem, Jerusalem, killing the prophets and stoning those who are sent to you! How often would I have gathered your children together as a hen gathers her brood under her wings, and you would not! " (*Matthew* 23: 37). Jesus could never have spoken like that if he had not made repeated appeals to

Jerusalem and if the visit at which he was crucified was his first. We ought not to talk about the contradictions between the Fourth Gospel and the other three, but to use them all to get as complete a picture of the life of Jesus as possible.

But there is a real difficulty we must face. This passage tells of the incident known as the Cleansing of the Temple. John sets it right at the *beginning* of the ministry of Jesus, while the other three gospel writers set it right at the *end* (*Matthew* 21: 12, 13; *Mark* 11: 15–17; *Luke* 19: 45, 46). This definitely needs explanation and various explanations have been put forward.

(i) It is suggested that Jesus cleansed the Temple twice, once at the beginning and once at the end of his ministry. That is not very likely, because if he had done this staggering thing once, it is very unlikely that he would ever have had the chance to do it again. His reappearance in the Temple would have been a sign for such precautions to be taken that a repetition of it would not have been possible.

(ii) It is suggested that John is right and that the other three are wrong. But the incident fits in much better at the end of Jesus's ministry. It is the natural succession to the blazing courage of the Triumphal Entry and the inevitable prelude to the Crucifixion. If we have to choose between John's dating and the dating of the other three, we must choose the dating of the three.

(iii) It is suggested that when John died he left his gospel not completely finished; that he left the various incidents written out on separate sheets of papyrus and not bound together. It is then suggested that the sheet containing the account of this incident got out of place and was inserted near the beginning of the manuscript instead of near the end. That is quite possible, but it involves assuming that the person who arranged the manuscript did not know the correct order, which is difficult to believe when he must have known at least some of the other gospels.

(iv) We must always remember that John, as someone has said, is more interested in the truth than in the facts. He is not interested in writing a chronological biography of Jesus but supremely interested in showing Jesus as the Son of God and the Messiah. It is probable that John was thinking back to the great prophecies of the coming of the Messiah. " And the Lord whom you seek will suddenly come to his temple; the messenger of the covenant in whom you delight; behold he is coming, says the Lord of Hosts. But who can endure the day of his coming and who can stand when he appears? For he is like a refiner's fire, and like fullers' soap ... he will purify the sons of Levi ... till they present right offerings to the Lord. Then the offering of Judah and Jerusalem will be pleasing to the Lord, as in the days of old, and as in former years " (*Malachi* 3: 1–4). John had these tremendous prophecies ringing in his mind. He was not interested to tell men *when* Jesus cleansed the Temple; he was supremely interested in telling men that Jesus *did* cleanse the Temple, because that cleansing was the act of the promised Messiah of God. All the likelihood is that John put this tremendous incident here to set in the very forefront of his story the great fact that Jesus was the Messiah of God come to cleanse the worship of men and to open the door to God. It is not the date that John is interested in; the date does not matter; his great concern is to show that Jesus's actions prove him to be the promised one of God. Right at the beginning he shows us Jesus acting as God's Messiah must act.

THE ANGER OF JESUS

John 2: 12–16 (*continued*)

Now let us see why Jesus acted as he did. His anger is a terrifying thing; the picture of Jesus with the whip is an awe-inspiring sight. We must see what moved Jesus to this white-hot anger in the Temple Courts.

The passover was the greatest of all the Jewish feasts. As we have already seen, the law laid it down that every adult male Jew who lived within fifteen miles of Jerusalem was bound to attend it. But it was not only the Jews in Palestine who came to the Passover. By this time Jews were scattered all over the

world, but they never forgot their ancestral faith and their
ancestral land; and it was the dream and aim of every Jew, no
matter in what land he stayed, to celebrate at least one Passover
in Jerusalem. Astonising as it may sound, it is likely that as
many as two and a quarter million Jews sometimes assembled
in the Holy City to keep the Passover.

There was a tax that every Jew over nineteen years of age
must pay. That was the Temple tax. It was necessary that all
should pay that tax so that the Temple sacrifices and the
Temple ritual might be carried out day by day. The tax was one
half-shekel. We must always remember, when we are thinking
of sums of money, that at this time a working man's wage was
about less than 4p per day. The value of a half-shekel was about
6p. It was, therefore, equivalent to almost two days' wages. For
all ordinary purposes in Palestine all kinds of currency were
valid. Silver coins from Rome and Greece and Egypt and Tyre
and Sidon and Palestine itself all were in circulation and all
were valid. But the Temple tax had to be paid either in
Galilaean shekels or in shekels of the sanctuary. These were
Jewish coins, and so could be used as a gift to the Temple; the
other currencies were foreign and so were unclean; they might
be used to pay ordinary debts, but not a debt to God.

Pilgrims arrived from all over the world with all kinds of
coins. So in the Temple courts there sat the *money-changers*. If
their trade had been straightforward they would have been
fulfilling an honest and a necessary purpose. But what they did
was to charge one ma'ah, a coin worth about 1p, for every
half-shekel they changed, and to charge another ma'ah on every
half-shekel of change they had to give if a larger coin was
tendered. So, if a man came with a coin the value of which was
two shekels, he had to pay 1p to get it changed, and other 3p
to get his change of three half-shekels. In other words the
money-changers made 4p out of him—and that, remember,
was one day's wage.

The wealth which accrued from the Temple tax and from this
method of money-changing was fantastic. The annual revenue
of the Temple from the Temple tax has been estimated at

£75,000, and the annual profit of the money-changers at £9,000. When Crassus captured Jerusalem and raided the Temple treasury in 54 B.C. he took from it £2,500,000 without coming near to exhausting it.

The fact that the money-changers received some discount when they changed the coins of the pilgrims was not in itself wrong. The *Talmud* laid it down: " It is necessary that everyone should have half a shekel to pay for himself. Therefore when he comes to the exchange to change a shekel for two half-shekels he is obliged to allow the money-changer some gain." The word for this discount was *kollubos* and the money-changers are called *kollubistai*. This word *kollubos* produced. the comedy character name Kollybos in Greek and Collybus in Latin, which meant much the same as Shylock in English.

What enraged Jesus was that pilgrims to the Passover who could ill afford it, were being fleeced at an exorbitant rate by the money-changers. It was a rampant and shameless social injustice—and what was worse, it was being done in the name of religion.

Besides the money-changers there were also the sellers of oxen and sheep and doves. Frequently a visit to the Temple meant a sacrifice. Many a pilgrim would wish to make thank-offering for a favourable journey to the Holy City; and most acts and events in life had their appropriate sacrifice. It might therefore seem to be a natural and helpful thing that the victims for the sacrifices could be bought in the Temple court. It might well have been so. But the law was that any animal offered in sacrifice must be perfect and unblemished. The Temple authorities had appointed inspectors (*mumcheh*) to examine the victims which were to be offered. The fee for inspection was 1p. If a worshipper bought a victim outside the Temple, it was to all intents and purposes certain that it would be rejected after examination. Again that might not have mattered much, but a pair of doves could cost as little as 4p outside the Temple, and as much as 75p inside. Here again was bare-faced extortion at the expense of poor and humble pilgrims, who were practically blackmailed into buying their victims from the Temple booths if they wished to sacrifice at all—once more a glaring social injustice aggravated by the fact that it was perpetrated in the name of pure religion.

It was that which moved Jesus to flaming anger. We are told that he took cords and made a whip. Jerome thinks that the very sight of Jesus made the whip unnecessary. " A certain fiery and starry light shone from his eyes, and the majesty of the Godhead gleamed in his face." Just because Jesus loved God, he loved God's children, and it was impossible for him to stand passively by while the worshippers of Jerusalem were treated in this way.

THE ANGER OF JESUS

John 2: 12–16 (*continued*)

WE have seen that it was the exploitation of the pilgrims by conscienceless men which moved Jesus to immediate wrath; but there were deep things behind the cleansing of the Temple. Let us see if we can penetrate to the even deeper reasons why Jesus took this drastic step.

No two of the evangelists give Jesus's words in precisely the same way. They all remembered their own version. It is only by putting all the accounts together that we get a true picture of what Jesus said. So then let us set down the different ways in which the writers report the words of Jesus. Matthew gives them as: " My house shall be called a house of prayer, but you make it a den of robbers " (*Matthew* 21: 13). Mark has it: " My house shall be called a house of prayer for all the nations. But you have made it a den of robbers " (*Mark* 11: 17). Luke has it: " My house shall be a house of prayer; but you have made it a den of robbers " (*Luke* 19: 46). John has it: " Take these things away; you shall not make my Father's house a house of trade " (*John* 2: 16).

There were at least three reasons why Jesus acted as he did, and why anger was in his heart.

(i) He acted as he did because God's house was being desecrated. In the Temple there was worship without reverence. Reverence is an instinctive thing. Edward Seago, the artist, tells how he took two gipsy children on a visit to a cathedral in England. They were wild enough children at ordinary times. But from the moment they came into the cathedral they were strangely quiet; all the way home they were unusually solemn; and it was not until the evening that they returned to their normal boisterousness. Instinctive reverence was in their un-instructed hearts.

Worship without reverence can be a terrible thing. It may be worship which is formalized and pushed through anyhow; the most dignified prayers on earth can be read like a passage from an auctioneer's catalogue. It may be worship which does not realize the holiness of God, and which sounds as if, in H. H. Farmer's phrase, the worshipper was " pally with the Deity." It may be worship in which leader or congregation are completely unprepared. It may be the use of the house of God for purposes and in a way where reverence and the true function of God's house are forgotten. In that court of God's house at Jerusalem there would be arguments about prices, disputes about coins that were worn and thin, the clatter of the market place. That particular form of irreverence may not be common now, but there are other ways of offering an irreverent worship to God.

(ii) Jesus acted as he did in order to show that the whole paraphernalia of animal sacrifice was completely irrelevant. For centuries the prophets had been saying exactly that. " What to me is the multitude of your sacrifices? says the Lord; I have had enough of burnt offerings of rams and the fat of fed beasts; I do not delight in the blood of bulls, or of lambs, or of goats.... Bring no more vain offerings " (*Isaiah* 1: 11–17). " For in the day that I brought them out of the land of Egypt, I did not speak to your fathers or command them concerning burnt offerings and sacrifices " (*Jeremiah* 7: 22). " With their flocks and herds they shall go to seek the Lord, but they will not find him " (*Hosea* 5: 6). " They love sacrifice; they sacrifice flesh and eat it; but the Lord has no delight in them " (*Hosea* 8:

13). " For thou hast no delight in sacrifice; were I to give a burnt offering, thou wouldst not be pleased " (*Psalm* 51: 16). There was a chorus of prophetic voices telling men of the sheer irrelevancy of the burnt offerings and the animal sacrifices which smoked continuously upon the altar at Jerusalem. Jesus acted as he did to show that no sacrifice of any animal can ever put a man right with God.

We are not totally free from this very tendency today. True, we will not offer animal sacrifice to God. But we can identify his service with the installation of stained glass windows, the obtaining of a more sonorous organ, the lavishing of money on stone and lime and carved wood, while real worship is far away. It is not that these things are to be condemned—far from it. They are often—thank God—the lovely offerings of the loving heart. When they are aids to true devotion they are God-blessed things; but when they are substitutes for true devotion they make God sick at heart.

(iii) There is still another reason why Jesus acted as he did. Mark has a curious little addition which none of the other gospels has: " My house shall be called the house of prayer for all the nations " (*Mark* 11: 17). The Temple consisted of a series of courts leading into the Temple proper and to the Holy Place. There was first the Court of the Gentiles, then the Court of the Women, then the Court of the Israelites, then the Court of the Priests. All this buying and selling was going on in the Court of the Gentiles which was the only place into which a Gentile might come. Beyond that point, access to him was barred. So then if there was a Gentile whose heart God had touched, he might come into the Court of the Gentiles to mediate and pray and distantly touch God. The Court of the Gentiles was the only place of prayer he knew.

The Temple authorities and the Jewish traders were making the Court of the Gentiles into an uproar and a rabble where no man could pray. The lowing of the oxen, the bleating of the sheep, the cooing of the doves, the shouts of the hucksters, the rattle of the coins, the voices raised in bargaining disputes—all these combined to make the Court of the Gentiles a place where no man could worship. The conduct in the Temple court shut out the seeking Gentile from the presence of God. It may well be that this was most in Jesus's mind; it may well be that Mark alone preserved the little phrase which means so much. Jesus was moved to the depths of his heart because seeking men were being shut out from the presence of God.

Is there anything in our church life—a snobbishness, an exclusiveness, a coldness, a lack of welcome, a tendency to make the congregation into a closed club, an arrogance, a fastidiousness—which keeps the seeking stranger out? Let us remember the wrath of Jesus against those who made it difficult and even impossible for the seeking stranger to make contact with God.

THE NEW TEMPLE

John 2: 17–22

His disciples remembered that there is a scripture which stands written: " For zeal for your house has consumed me." Then the Jews demanded of him: " What sign do you show us to justify your acting in this way? " Jesus answered: " Destroy this Temple and in three days I will raise it up." Then the Jews said: " It has taken forty-six years to build the Temple so far, and are you going to raise it up in three days? " But he was speaking about the temple of his body. So when he was raised from the dead, his disciples remembered that he had said this, and they believed on the scripture and on the word which Jesus spoke.

IT was quite certain that an act like the cleansing of the Temple would produce an immediate reaction in those who saw it happening. It was not the kind of thing that anyone could look at with complete indifference. It was much too staggering for that.

Here we have two reactions. First, there is the reaction of the disciples which was to remember the words of *Psalm* 69: 9. The point is that this Psalm was taken to refer to the Messiah. When the Messiah came he would be burned up with a zeal for the house of God. When this verse leapt into their minds, it meant the conviction that Jesus was the Messiah seized the minds of the disciples even more deeply and more definitely. This action befitted none but the Messiah, and they were surer than ever that Jesus was in fact the Anointed One of God.

Second, there is the reaction of the Jews, a very natural one. They asked what right Jesus had to act like that and demanded that he should at once prove his credentials by some sign. The point is this. They acknowledged the act of Jesus to be that of one who thereby claimed to be the Messiah. It was always expected that when the Messiah came he would confirm his claims by doing amazing things. False Messiahs did in fact arise and promise to cleave the waters of Jordan in two or make the walls of the city collapse at a word. The popular idea of the Messiah was connected with wonders. So the Jews said: " By this act of yours you have publicly claimed to be the Messiah. Now show us some wonder which will prove your claim."

Jesus's reply constitutes the great problem of this passage. What did he really say? And what did he really mean? It is always to be remembered that verses 21 and 22 are John's interpretation written long afterwards. He was inevitably reading into the passage ideas which were the product of seventy years of thinking about and experience of the Risen Christ. As Irenaeus said long ago: " No prophecy is fully understood until after the fulfilment of it." But what did Jesus originally say and what did he originally mean?

There is no possible doubt that Jesus spoke words which were very like these, words which could be maliciously twisted into a destructive claim. When Jesus was on trial, the false witness borne against him was: " This fellow said, I am able to destroy the temple of God, and to build it in three days " (*Matthew* 26: 61). The charge levelled against Stephen was: " We have heard him say that this Jesus of Nazareth will destroy this place, and will change the customs which Moses delivered to us " (*Acts* 6: 14).

We must remember two things and we must put them together. First, Jesus certainly never said he would destroy the material Temple and then rebuild it. Jesus in fact looked for the end of the Temple. He said to the woman of Samaria that the day was coming when men would worship God neither in Mount Gerizim, nor in Jerusalem, but in spirit and in truth (*John* 4: 21). Second, the cleansing of the Temple, as we have seen, was a dramatic way of showing that the whole Temple worship with its ritual and its sacrifice was irrelevant and could do nothing to lead men to God. It is clear that Jesus did expect that the Temple would pass away; that he had come to render its worship unnecessary and obsolete; and that therefore he would never suggest that he would rebuild it.

We must now turn to Mark. As so often, we find the little extra suggestive and illuminating phrase there. As Mark relates the charge against Jesus, it ran: " I will destroy this Temple that is made with hands, and in three days I will build another *not made with hands* " (*Mark* 14: 58). What Jesus really meant was that his coming had put an end to all this man-made, man-arranged way of worshipping God and put in its place a spiritual worship; that he put an end to all this business of animal sacrifice and priestly ritual and put in its place a direct approach to the Spirit of God which did not need an elaborate man-made Temple and a ritual of incense and sacrifice offered by the hands of men. The threat of Jesus was: " Your Temple worship, your elaborate ritual, your lavish animal sacrifices are at an end, because I have come." The promise of Jesus was: " I will give you a way to come to God without all this human elaboration and human ritual. I have come to destroy this Temple in Jerusalem and to make the whole earth the Temple where men can know the presence of the living God."

The Jews saw that. It was in 19 B.C. that Herod had begun to build that wondrous Temple; it was not until A.D. 64 that the building was finally finished. It was forty-six years since it had been started; it was to be another twenty before it was ended. Jesus shattered the Jews by telling them that all its magnificence and splendour and all the money and skill that had been lavished on it were completely irrelevant; that he had come to show men a way to come to God without any Temple at all.

That must be what Jesus actually said; but in the years to come John saw far more than that in Jesus's saying. He saw in it nothing less than a prophecy of the Resurrection; *and John was right*. He was right for this basic reason, that the whole round earth could never become the temple of the living God until Jesus was released from the body and was everywhere present; and until he was with men everywhere, even to the end of the world.

It is the presence of the living, risen Christ which makes the whole world into the Temple of God. So John says that when they remembered, they saw in this a promise of the Resurrection. They did not see that at the time; they could not; it was only their own experience of the living Christ which one day showed them the true depth of what Jesus said.

Finally John says that " they believed the scripture." What scripture? John means that scripture which haunted the early church—" ... or let thy godly one see the Pit " (*Psalm* 16: 10). Peter quoted it at Pentecost (*Acts* 2: 31); Paul quoted it at Antioch (*Acts* 13: 35). It expressed the confidence of the church in the power of God and in the Resurrection of Jesus Christ.

We have here the tremendous truth that our contact with God, our entry into his presence, on our approach to him is not dependent on anything that men's hands can build or men's minds devise. In the street, in the home, at business, on the hills, on the open road, in church we have our inner temple, the presence of the Risen Christ for ever with us throughout all the world.

THE SEARCHER OF THE HEARTS OF MEN

John 2: 23–25

> When he was in Jerusalem, at the Passover, at the Feast, many believed in his name, as they saw the signs which he did; but Jesus himself would not entrust himself to them, because he knew them all, and because he had no need that anyone should testify to him what man is like, for he well knew what was in human nature.

JOHN does not relate the story of any wonder that Jesus did in Jerusalem at the Passover season; but Jesus did do wonders there; and there were many who, when they saw his powers, believed in him. The question John is answering here is—if there were many who believed in Jerusalem right at the beginning, why did Jesus not there and then set up his standard and openly declare himself?

The answer is that Jesus knew human nature only too well. He knew that there were many to whom he was only a nine-days' wonder. He knew that there were many who were attracted only by the sensational things he did. He knew that there were none who understood the way that he had chosen. He knew that there were many who would have followed him while he continued to produce miracles and wonders and signs, but who, if he had begun to talk to them about service and self-denial, if he had begun to talk to them about self-surrender to the will of God, if he had begun to talk to them about a cross and about carrying a cross, would have stared at him with blank incomprehension and left him on the spot.

It is a great characteristic of Jesus that he did not want followers unless they clearly knew and definitely accepted what was involved in following him. He refused—in the modern phrase—to cash in on a moment's popularity. If he had entrusted himself to the mob in Jerusalem, they would have declared him Messiah there and then and would have waited for the kind of material action they expected the Messiah to take. But Jesus was a leader who refused to ask men ever to accept him until they understood what accepting meant. He insisted that a man should know what he was doing.

Jesus knew human nature. He knew the fickleness and instability of the heart of man. He knew that a man can be swept away in a moment of emotion, and then back out when he discovers what decision really means. He knew how human nature hungers for sensations. He wanted not a crowd of men cheering they knew not what, but a small company who knew what they were doing and who were prepared to follow to the end.

There is one thing we must note in this passage, for we shall have occasion to mark it again and again. When John speaks of Jesus's miracles he calls them *signs*. The New Testament uses three different words for the wonderful works of God and of Jesus, and each has something to tell us about what a miracle really is.

(i) It uses the word *teras*. *Teras* simply means a marvellous thing. It is a word with no moral significance at all. A conjuring trick might be a *teras*. A *teras* was simply an astonishing happening which left a man gasping with surprise. The New Testament never uses this word alone of the works of God or of Jesus.

(ii) It uses the word *dunamis*. *Dunamis* literally means *power*; it is the word from which *dynamite* comes. It can be used of any kind of extraordinary power. It can be used of the power of growth, of the powers of nature, of the power of a drug, of the power of a man's genius. It always has the meaning of an effective power which does things and which any man can recognize. (iii) It uses the word *sēmeion*. *Sēmeion* means a *sign*. This is John's favourite word. To him a miracle was not simply an astonishing happening; it was not simply a deed of power; it was a sign. That is to say, it told men something about the person who did it; it revealed something of his character; it laid bare something of his nature; it was an action through which it was possible to understand better and more fully the character of the person who did it. To John the supreme thing about the miracles of Jesus was that *they told men something about the nature and the character of God*. The power of Jesus was used to heal the sick, to feed the hungry, to comfort the sorrowing; and the fact that Jesus used his power in that way was proof that God cared for the sorrows and the needs and the pains of men. To John the miracles were signs of the love of God.

In any miracle, then, there are three things. There is the wonder which leaves men dazzled, astonished, aghast. There is the power which is effective, which can deal with and mend a broken body, an unhinged mind, a bruised heart, which can do things. There is the sign which tells us of the love in the heart of the God who does such things for men.

THE MAN WHO CAME BY NIGHT

John 3: 1–6

> There was a man who was one of the Pharisees who was called Nicodemus, a ruler of the Jews. He came to Jesus by night and said to him: " Rabbi, we know that you are a teacher who has come from God, for no one can do the signs which you do unless God is with him." Jesus answered him: " This is the truth I tell you—unless a man is reborn from above, he cannot see the kingdom of God." Nicodemus said to him: " How can a man be born when he is old? Surely he cannot enter into his mother's womb a second time and be born? " Jesus answered: " This is the truth I tell you—unless a man is born of water and the Spirit, he cannot enter into the kingdom of God. That which is born from the flesh is flesh, and that which is born of the Spirit is spirit."

FOR the most part we see Jesus surrounded by the ordinary people, but here we see him in contact with one of the aristocracy of Jerusalem. There are certain things that we know about Nicodemus.

(i) Nicodemus must have been wealthy. When Jesus died Nicodemus brought for his body " a mixture of myrrh and aloes about an hundred pound weight " (*John* 19: 39), and only a wealthy man could have brought that.

(ii) Nicodemus was a Pharisee. In many ways the Pharisees were the best people in the whole country. There were never more than 6,000 of them; they were what was known as a *chaburah*, or brotherhood. They entered into this brotherhood by taking a pledge in front of three witnesses that they would spend all their lives observing every detail of the scribal law.

What exactly did that mean? To the Jew the Law was the most sacred thing in all the world. The Law was the first five books of the Old Testament. They believed it to be the perfect word of God. To add one word to it or to take one word away from it was a deadly sin. Now if the Law is the perfect and complete word of God, that must mean that it contained everything a man need know for the living of a good life, if not explicitly, then implicitly. If it was not there in so many words, it must be possible to deduce it. The Law as it stood consisted of great, wide, noble principles which a man had to work out for himself. But for the later Jews that was not enough. They said: " The Law is complete; it contains everything necessary for the living of a good life; therefore in the Law there must be a regulation to govern every possible incident in every possible moment for every possible man." So they set to to extract from the great principles of the law an infinite number of rules and regulations to govern every conceivable situation in life. In other words they changed the law of the great principles into the legalism of by-laws and regulations.

The best example of what they did is to be seen in the Sabbath law. In the Bible itself we are simply told that we must remember the Sabbath day to keep it holy and that on that day no work must be done, either by a man or by his servants or his animals. Not content with that, the later Jews spent hour after hour and generation after generation defining what work is and listing the things that may and may not be done on the Sabbath day. The *Mishnah* is the codified scribal law. The scribes spent their lives working out these rules and regulations. In the *Mishnah* the section on the Sabbath extends to no fewer than twenty-four chapters. The *Talmud* is the explanatory commentary on the *Mishnah*, and in the Jerusalem *Talmud* the section explaining the Sabbath law runs to sixty-four and a half columns; and in the Babylonian *Talmud* it runs to one hundred and fifty-six double folio pages. And we are told about a rabbi who spent two and a half years in studying one of the twenty-four chapters of the *Mishnah*.

The kind of thing they did was this. To tie a knot on the Sabbath was to work; but a knot had to be defined. " The following are the knots the making of which renders a man guilty; the knot of camel drivers and that of sailors; and as one is guilty by reason of tying them, so also of untying them." On the other hand knots which could be tied or untied with one hand were quite legal. Further, " a woman may tie up a slit in her shift and the strings of her cap and those of her girdle, the straps of shoes or sandals, of skins of wine and oil." Now see what happened. Suppose a man wished to let down a bucket into a well to draw water on the Sabbath day. He could not tie a rope to it, for a knot on a rope was illegal on the Sabbath; but he could tie it to a woman's girdle and let it down, for a knot in a girdle was quite legal. That was the kind of thing which to the scribes and Pharisees was a matter of life and death; that was religion; that to them was pleasing and serving God.

Take the case of journeying on the Sabbath. *Exodus* 16: 29 says: " Remain every man of you in his place; let no man go out of his place on the seventh day." A Sabbath day's journey was therefore limited to two thousand cubits, that is, one thousand yards. But, if a rope was tied across the end of a street, the whole street became one house and a man could go a thousand yards beyond the end of the street. Or, if a man deposited enough food for one meal on Friday evening at any given place, that place technically became his house and he could go a thousand yards beyond it on the Sabbath day. The rules and regulations and the evasions piled up by the hundred and the thousand.

Take the case of carrying a burden. *Jeremiah* 17: 21–24 said: " Take heed for the sake of your lives and do not bear a burden on the Sabbath day." So a burden had to be defined. It was defined as " food equal in weight to a dried fig, enough wine for mixing in a goblet, milk enough for one swallow, honey enough to put upon a wound, oil enough to anoint a small member, water enough to moisten an eye-salve," and so on and on. It had then to be settled whether or not on the Sabbath a woman could wear a brooch, a man could wear a wooden leg or dentures; or would it be carrying a burden to do so? Could a chair or even a child be lifted? And so on and on the discussions and the regulations went.

It was the *scribes* who worked out these regulations; it was the *Pharisees* who dedicated their lives to keeping them.

Obviously, however misguided a man might be, he must be desperately in earnest if he proposed to undertake obedience to every one of the thousands of rules. That is precisely what the Pharisees did. The name *Pharisee* means *the Separated One*; and the Pharisees were those who had separated themselves from all ordinary life in order to keep every detail of the law of the scribes.

Nicodemus was a Pharisee, and it is astonishing that a man who regarded goodness in that light and who had given himself to that kind of life in the conviction that he was pleasing God should wish to talk to Jesus at all.

(iii) Nicodemus was a ruler of the Jews. The word is *archōn*. This is to say that he was a member of the Sanhedrin. The Sanhedrin was a court of seventy members and was the supreme court of the Jews. Of course under the Romans its powers were more limited than once they had been; but they were still extensive. In particular the Sanhedrin had religious jurisdiction over every Jew in the world; and one of its duties was to examine and deal with anyone suspected of being a false prophet. Again it is amazing that Nicodemus should come to Jesus at all.

(iv) It may well be that Nicodemus belonged to a distinguished Jewish family. Away back in 63 B.C. when the Romans and the Jews had been at war, Aristobulus, the Jewish leader, sent a certain Nicodemus as his ambassador to Pompey, the Roman Emperor. Much later in the terrible last days of Jerusalem, the man who negotiated the surrender of the garrison was a certain Gorion, who was the son either of Nicomedes or Nicodemus. It may well be that both these men belonged to the same family as our Nicodemus, and that it was one of the most distinguished families in Jerusalem. If that is true it is amazing that this Jewish aristocrat should come to this homeless prophet who had been the carpenter of Nazareth that he might talk to him about his soul.

It was by night that Nicodemus came to Jesus. There were probably two reasons for that.

(i) It may have been a sign of caution. Nicodemus quite

frankly may not have wished to commit himself by coming to Jesus by day. We must not condemn him. The wonder is that with his background, he came to Jesus at all. It was infinitely better to come at night than not at all. It is a miracle of grace that Nicodemus overcame his prejudices and his upbringing and his whole view of life enough to come to Jesus.

(ii) But there may be another reason. The rabbis declared that the best time to study the law was at night when a man was undisturbed. Throughout the day Jesus was surrounded by crowds of people all the time. It may well be that Nicodemus came to Jesus by night because he wanted an absolutely private and completely undisturbed time with Jesus.

Nicodemus was a puzzled man, a man with many honours and yet with something lacking in his life. He came to Jesus for a talk so that somehow in the darkness of the night he might find light.

THE MAN WHO CAME BY NIGHT

John 3: 1–6 (*continued*)

WHEN John relates conversations that Jesus had with enquirers, he has a way of following a certain scheme. We see that scheme very clearly here. The enquirer says something (verse 2). Jesus answers in a saying that is hard to understand (verse 3). That saying is misunderstood by the enquirer (verse 4). Jesus answers with a saying that is even more difficult to understand (verse 5). And then there follows a discourse and an explanation. John uses this method in order that we may see men thinking things out for themselves and so that we may do the same.

When Nicodemus came to Jesus, he said that no one could help being impressed with the signs and wonders that he did. Jesus's answer was that it was not the signs and the wonders that were really important; the important thing was such a change in a man's inner life that it could only be described as a new birth.

When Jesus said that a man must be *born anew* Nicodemus misunderstood him, and the misunderstanding came from the fact that the word which the Revised Standard Version translates *anew*, the Greek word *anōthen*, has three different meanings. (i) It can mean *from the beginning, completely radically*. (ii) It can mean *again*, in the sense of *for the second time*. (iii) It can mean *from above*, and, therefore, *from God*. It is not possible for us to get all these meanings into any English word; and yet all three of them are in the phrase *born anew*. To be born anew is to undergo such a radical change that it is like a new birth; it is to have something happen to the soul which can only be described as being born all over again; and the whole process is not a human achievement, because it comes from the grace and power of God.

When we read the story, it looks at first sight as if Nicodemus took the word *anew* in only the second sense, and with a crude literalism. How can anyone, he said, enter again into his mother's womb and be born a second time when he is already an old man? But there is more to Nicodemus's answer than that. In his heart there was a great unsatisfied longing. It is as if he said with infinite, wistful yearning: " You talk about being born anew; you talk about this radical, fundamental change which is so necessary. I know that it is *necessary*; but in my experience it is *impossible*. There is nothing I would like more; but you might as well tell me, a full grown man, to enter into my mother's womb and be born all over again." It is not the *desirability* of this change that Nicodemus questioned; that he knew only too well; it is the *possibility*. Nicodemus is up against the eternal problem, the problem of the man who wants to be changed and who cannot change himself.

This phrase *born anew*, this idea of *rebirth*, runs all through the New Testament. Peter speaks of being born anew by God's great mercy (1 *Peter* 1: 3); he talks about being *born anew* not of perishable seed, but of imperishable (1 *Peter* 1: 22, 23). James speaks of God bringing us forth by the word of truth (*James* 1: 18). The Letter *to Titus* speaks of *the washing of regeneration* (*Titus* 3: 5). Sometimes this same idea is spoken of as a death followed by a resurrection or a re-creation. Paul speaks of the Christian as dying with Christ and then rising to life anew (*Romans* 6: 1–11). He speaks of those who have lately come into the Christian faith as *babes in Christ* (1 *Corinthians* 3: 1, 2). If any man is in Christ it is as if he had been *created* all over again (2 *Corinthians* 5: 17). In Christ there is a new creation (*Galatians* 6: 15). The new man is *created* after God in righteousness (*Ephesians* 4: 22–24). The person who is at the first beginnings of the Christian faith is a child (*Hebrews* 5: 12–14). All over the New Testament this idea of *rebirth*, *re-creation* occurs.

Now this was not an idea which was in the least strange to the people who heard it in New Testament times. The Jew knew all about rebirth. When a man from another faith became a Jew and had been accepted into Judaism by prayer and sacrifice and baptism, he was regarded as being *reborn*. " A proselyte who embraces Judaism," said the rabbis, " is like a new-born child." So radical was the change that the sins he had committed before his reception were all done away with, for now he was a different person. It was even theoretically argued that such a man could marry his own mother or his own sister, because he was a completely new man, and all the old connections were broken and destroyed. The Jew knew the idea of rebirth.

The Greek also knew the idea of rebirth and knew it well. By far the most real religion of the Greeks at this time was the faith of the mystery religions. The mystery religions were all founded on the story of some suffering and dying and rising god. This story was played out as a passion play. The initiate had a long course of preparation, instruction, asceticism and fasting. The drama was then played out with gorgeous music, marvellous ritual, incense and everything to play upon the emotions. As it was played out, the worshipper's aim was to become one with the god in such a way that he passed through the god's sufferings and shared the god's triumph and the god's divine life. The mystery religions offered mystic union with some god. When that union was achieved the initiate was, in the language of the Mysteries, *a twice-born*. The Hermetic Mysteries had as part of their basic belief: " There can be no salvation without regeneration." Apuleius, who went through initiation, said that he underwent " a voluntary death," and that thereby he attained " his spiritual birthday," and was " as it were reborn." Many of the Mystery initiations took place at midnight when the day dies and is reborn. In the Phrygian, the initiate, after his initiation, was fed with milk as if he was a new-born babe.

The ancient world knew all about rebirth and regeneration. It longed for it and searched for it everywhere. The most famous of all Mystery ceremonies was the *taurobolium*. The candidate was put into a pit. On the top of the pit there was a lattice-work cover. On the cover a bull was slain by having its throat cut. The blood poured down and the initiate lifted up his head and bathed himself in the blood; and when he came out of the pit he was *renatus in aeternum*, reborn for all eternity. When Christianity came to the world with a message of rebirth, it came with precisely that for which all the world was seeking.

What, then, does this rebirth mean for us? In the New Testament, and especially in the Fourth Gospel, there are four closely inter-related ideas. There is the idea of rebirth; there is the idea of the kingdom of heaven, into which a man cannot enter unless he is reborn; there is the idea of sonship of God; and there is the idea of eternal life. This idea of being reborn is not something which is peculiar to the thought of the Fourth Gospel. In *Matthew* we have the same great truth put more simply and more vividly: " Unless you turn and become like children, you will never enter the kingdom of heaven " (*Matthew* 18: 3). All these ideas have a common thought behind them.

BORN AGAIN

John 3: 1–6 (*continued*)

LET us start with the *kingdom of heaven*. What does it mean? We get our best definition of it from the Lord's Prayer. There are two petitions side by side:

> Thy Kingdom come:
> Thy will be done in earth as it is in heaven.

It is characteristic of Jewish style to say things twice, the
second way explaining and amplifying the first. Any verse of
the Psalms will show us this Jewish habit of what is technically
known as parallelism:

> The Lord of hosts is with us:
> The God of Jacob is our refuge (*Psalm* 46: 7).
>
> For I know my transgressions:
> And my sin is ever before me (*Psalm* 51: 3).
>
> He makes me lie down in green pastures:
> He leads me beside still waters (*Psalm* 23: 2).

Let us apply that principle to these two petitions in the Lord's
Prayer. The second petition amplifies and explains the first; we
then arrive at the definition: *the kingdom of heaven is a society
where God's will is as perfectly done on earth as it is in heaven.*
To be in the kingdom of heaven is therefore to lead a life in
which we have willingly submitted everything to the will of
God; it is to have arrived at a stage when we perfectly and
completely accept the will of God.

Now let us take *sonship.* In one sense sonship is a tremendous *privilege.* To those who believe there is given the
power to become sons (*John* 1: 12). But the very essence of
sonship is necessarily *obedience.* " He who has commandments,
and keeps them, he it is who loves me " (*John* 14: 21). The
essence of sonship is love; and the essence of love is obedience.
We cannot with any reality say that we love a person and then
do things which hurt and grieve that person's heart. Sonship is
a privilege, but a privilege which is entered into only when full
obedience is given. So then to be a son of God and to be in the
kingdom are one and the same thing. The son of God and the
citizen of the kingdom are both people who have completely
and willingly accepted the will of God.

Now let us take *eternal life.* It is far better to speak of *eternal*
life than to speak of *everlasting* life. The main idea behind
eternal life is not simply that of duration. It is quite clear that a

life which went on for ever could just as easily be hell as heaven. The idea behind eternal life is the idea of a certain quality of life. What kind? There is only one person who can properly be described by this adjective eternal (*aiōnios*) and that one person is God. Eternal life is the kind of life that God lives; it is God's life. To enter into eternal life is to enter into possession of that kind of life which is the life of God. It is to be lifted up above merely human, transient things into that joy and peace which belong only to God. Clearly a man can enter into this close fellowship with God only when he renders to him that love, that reverence, that devotion, that obedience which truly bring him into fellowship with him.

Here then we have three great kindred conceptions, entry into the kingdom of heaven, sonship of God and eternal life; and all are dependent on and are the products of perfect obedience to the will of God. It is just here that the idea of being *reborn* comes in. It is what links all these three conceptions together. It is quite clear that, as we are and in our own strength, we are quite unable to render to God this perfect obedience; it is only when God's grace enters into us and takes possession of us and changes us that we can give to him the reverence and the devotion we ought to give. It is through Jesus Christ that we are reborn; it is when he enters into possession of our hearts and lives that the change comes.

When that happens we are born of *water and the Spirit*. There are two thoughts there. *Water* is the symbol of cleansing. When Jesus takes possession of our lives, when we love him with all our heart, the sins of the past are forgiven and forgotten. *The Spirit* is the symbol of *power*. When Jesus takes possession of our lives it is not only that the past is forgotten and forgiven; if that were all, we might well proceed to make the same mess of life all over again; but into life there enters a new power which enables us to be what by ourselves we could never be and to do what by ourselves we could never do. Water and the Spirit stand for the cleansing and the strengthening power of Christ, which wipes out the past and gives victory in the future.

Finally, in this passage, John lays down a great law. That which is born of the flesh is flesh and that which is born of the Spirit is spirit. A man by himself is flesh and his power is limited to what the flesh can do. By himself he cannot be other than defeated and frustrated; that we know only too well; it is the universal fact of human experience. But the very essence of the Spirit is power and life which are beyond human power and human life; and when the Spirit takes possession of us, the defeated life of human nature becomes the victorious life of God.

To be born again is to be changed in such a way that it can be described only as rebirth and re-creation. The change comes when we love Jesus and allow him into our hearts. Then we are forgiven for the past and armed by the Spirit for the future; then we can truly accept the will of God. And then we become citizens of the kingdom; then we become sons of God; then we enter into eternal life, which is the very life of God.

THE DUTY TO KNOW AND THE RIGHT TO SPEAK

John 3: 7–13

Do not be surprised that I said to you: " You must be reborn from above. The wind blows where it will, and you hear the sound of it, but you do not know whence it comes and whither it goes. So is every one that is born of the Spirit." Nicodemus answered: " How can these things happen? " Jesus answered: " Are you the man whom everyone regards as the teacher of Israel, and you do not understand these things? This is the truth I tell you—we speak what we know, and we bear witness to what we have seen; but you do not receive our witness. If I have spoken to you of earthly things and you do not believe me, how will you believe me if I speak to you about heavenly things." No one has gone up to heaven, except he who came down from heaven, I mean, the Son of Man, who is in heaven.

There are two kinds of misunderstanding. There is the mis-understanding of the man who misunderstands because he has not yet reached a stage of knowledge and of experience at which he is able to grasp the truth. When a man is in that state our duty is to do all that we can to explain things to him so that he will be able to grasp the knowledge which is being offered to him. There is also the misunderstanding of the man who is unwilling to understand; there is a failure to see which comes from the refusal to see. A man can deliberately shut his mind to truth which he does not wish to accept.

Nicodemus was like that. The teaching about a new birth from God should not have been strange to him. Ezekiel, for instance, had spoken repeatedly about the new heart that must be created in a man. " Cast away from you all the trans-gressions, which you have committed against me, and get yourselves a new heart and a new spirit! Why will you die, O house of Israel? " (*Ezekiel* 18: 31). " A new heart I will give you, and a new spirit I will put within you " (*Ezekiel* 36: 26). Nicodemus was an expert in scripture and again and again the prophets had spoken of that very experience of which Jesus was speaking. If a man does not wish to be reborn, he will deliberately misunderstand what rebirth means. If a man does not wish to be changed, he will deliberately shut his eyes and his mind and his heart to the power which can change him. In the last analysis what is the matter with so many of us is simply the fact that, when Jesus Christ comes with his offer to change us and re-create us, we more or less say: " No thank you: I am quite satisfied with myself as I am, and I don't want to be changed."

Nicodemus was driven back on another defence. In effect he said: " This rebirth about which you talk may be possible; but I can't understand how it works." The answer of Jesus depends for its point on the fact that the Greek word for *spirit*, *pneuma*, has two meanings. It is the word for *spirit*, but it is also the regular word for *wind*. The same is true of the Hebrew word *ruach*; it too means both *spirit* and *wind*. So Jesus said to Nicodemus: " You can hear and see and feel the *wind* (*pneuma*)); *but you do not know where it comes from or where it* is going to. You may not understand how and why the wind

blows; but you can see what it does. You may not understand
where a gale came from or where it is going to, but you can see
the trail of flattened fields and uprooted trees that it leaves
behind it. There are many things about the wind you may not
understand; but its effect is plain for all to see." He went on,
" the *Spirit* (*pneuma*) is exactly the same. You may not know
how the Spirit works; but you can see the effect of the Spirit in
human lives."

Jesus said: " This is no theoretical thing of which we are
speaking. We are talking of what we have actually seen. We can
point to man after man who has been re-born by the power of
the Spirit." Dr. John Hutton used to tell of a workman who had
been a drunken reprobate and was converted. His work-mates
did their best to make him feel a fool. " Surely," they said to
him, " you can't believe in miracles and things like that. Surely,
for instance, you don't believe that Jesus turned water into
wine." " I don't know," the man answered, " whether he turned
water into wine when he was in Palestine, but I do know that in
my own house and home he has turned beer into furniture! "

There are any number of things in this world which we use
every day without knowing how they work. Comparatively few
of us know how electricity or radio or television works; but we
do not deny that they exist because of that. Many of us drive a
motor car with only the haziest notion of what goes on below
its bonnet; but our lack of understanding does not prevent us
using and enjoying the benefits which a motor car confers. We
may not understand how the Spirit works; but the effect of the
Spirit on the lives of men is there for all to see. The unanswerable argument for Christianity is the Christian life. No man can
disregard a faith which is able to make bad men good.

Jesus said to Nicodemus: " I have tried to make things
simple for you; I have used simple human pictures taken from
everyday life; and you have not understood. How can you ever
expect to understand the deep things, if even the simple things
are beyond you? " There is a warning here for every one of us.
It is easy to sit in discussion groups, to sit in a study and to
read books, it is easy to discuss the intellectual truth of

Christianity; but the essential thing is to experience the power of Christianity. And it is fatally easy to start at the wrong end and to think of Christianity as something to be discussed, not as something to be experienced. It is certainly important to have an intellectual grasp of the orb of Christian truth; but it is still more important to have a vital experience of the power of Jesus Christ. When a man undergoes treatment from a doctor, when he has to have an operation, when he is given some medicine to take, he does not need to know the anatomy of the human body, the scientific effect of the anaesthetic, the way in which the drug works on his body, in order to be cured. Ninety-nine men out of every hundred accept the cure without being able to say how it was brought about. There is a sense in which Christianity is like that. At its heart there is a mystery, but it is not the mystery of intellectual appreciation; it is the mystery of redemption.

In reading the Fourth Gospel there is the difficulty of knowing when the words of Jesus stop and the words of the writer of the gospel begin. John has thought so long about the words of Jesus that insensibly he glides from them to his own thoughts about them. Almost certainly the last words of this passage are the words of John. It is as if someone asked: " What right has Jesus to say these things? What guarantee do we have that they are true? " John's answer is simple and profound. " Jesus," he says, " came down from heaven to tell us the truth of God. And, when he had companied with men and died for them, he returned to his glory." It was John's contention that Jesus's right to speak came from the fact that he knew God personally, that he had come direct from the secrets of heaven to earth, that what he said to men was most literally God's own truth, for Jesus was and is the embodied mind of God.

THE UPLIFTED CHRIST

John 3: 14, 15

> And as Moses lifted up the serpent in the wilderness, so the Son of Man must be lifted up, that every one who believes in him may have eternal life.

JOHN goes back to a strange Old Testament story which is told in *Numbers* 21: 4-9. On their journey through the wilderness the people of Israel murmured and complained and regretted that they had ever left Egypt. To punish them God sent a plague of deadly, fiery serpents; the people repented and cried for mercy. God instructed Moses to make an image of a serpent and to hold it up in the midst of the camp; and those who looked upon the serpent were healed. That story much impressed the Israelites. They told how in later times that brazen serpent became an idol and in the days of Hezekiah had to be destroyed because people were worshipping it (2 *Kings* 18: 4). The Jews themselves were always a little puzzled by this incident in view of the fact that they were absolutely forbidden to make graven images. The rabbis explained it this way: " It was not the serpent that gave life. So long as Moses lifted up the serpent, they believed on him who had commanded Moses to act thus. It was God who healed them." The healing power lay not in the brazen serpent; it was only a symbol to turn their thoughts to God; and when they did that they were healed.

John took that old story and used it as a kind of parable of Jesus. He says: " The serpent was lifted up; men looked at it; their thoughts were turned to God; and by the power of that God in whom they trusted they were healed. Even so Jesus must be lifted up; and when men turn their thoughts to him, and believe in him, they too will find eternal life."

There is a wonderfully suggestive thing here The verb *to lift up* is *hupsoun*. The strange thing is that it is used of Jesus in two senses. It is used of his being *lifted up upon the Cross*; and it is used of his being *lifted up into glory* at the time of his ascension

into heaven. It is used of the Cross in *John* 8: 28; 12: 32. It is used
of Jesus's ascension into glory in *Acts* 2: 33; 5: 31; *Philippians* 2:
9. There was a double lifting up in Jesus's life—the lifting on the
Cross and the lifting into glory. And the two are inextricably
connected. The one could not have happened without the other.
For Jesus the Cross was the way to glory; had he refused it, had
he evaded it, had he taken steps to escape it, as he might so easily
have done, there would have been no glory for him. It is the same
for us. We can, if we like, choose the easy way; we can, if we like,
refuse the cross that every Christian is called to bear; but if we do,
we lose the glory. It is an unalterable law of life that if there is no
cross, there is no crown.

In this passage we have two expressions whose meaning we
must face. It will not be possible to extract all their meaning,
because they both mean more than ever we can discover; but we
must try to grasp at least something of it.

(i) There is the phrase which speaks of *believing in Jesus*. It
means at least three things.

(*a*) It means believing with all our hearts that God is as Jesus
declared him to be. It means believing that God loves us, that God
cares for us, that God wants nothing more than to forgive us. It
was not easy for a Jew to believe that. He looked on God as one
who imposed his laws upon his people and punished them if they
broke them. He looked on God as a judge and on man as a
criminal at his judgment seat. He looked on God as one who
demanded sacrifices and offerings; to get into his presence man
had to pay the price laid down. It was hard to think of God not as
a judge waiting to exact penalty, not as a task-master waiting to
pounce, but as a Father who longed for nothing so much as to
have his erring children come back home. It cost the life and the
death of Jesus to tell men that. And we cannot begin to be
Christians until with all our hearts we believe that.

(*b*) How can we be sure that Jesus knew what he was talking
about? What guarantee is there that his wonderful good news
is true? Here we come upon the second article in belief. We
must believe that Jesus is the Son of God, that in him is the
mind of God, that he knew God so well, was so close to God,

was so one with God, that he could tell us the absolute truth about him.

(c) But belief has a third element. We believe that God is a loving Father because we believe that Jesus is the Son of God and that therefore what he says about God is true. Then comes this third element. We must stake everything on the fact that what Jesus says is true. Whatever he says we must do; whenever he commands we must obey. When he tells us to cast ourselves unreservedly on the mercy of God we must do so. We must take Jesus at his word. Every smallest action in life must be done in unquestioning obedience to him.

So then belief in Jesus has these three elements—belief that God is our loving Father, belief that Jesus is the son of God and therefore tells us the truth about God and life, and unswerving and unquestioning obedience to Jesus.

(ii) The second great phrase is *eternal life*. We have already seen that eternal life is the very life of God himself. But let us ask this: if we possess eternal life, what do we have? If we enter into eternal life, what is it like? To have eternal life envelops every relationship in life with peace.

(a) It gives us peace with God. We are no longer cringing before a tyrannical king or seeking to hide from an austere judge. We are at home with our Father.

(b) It gives us peace with men. If we have been forgiven we must be forgiving. It enables us to see men as God sees them. It makes us and all men into one great family joined in love.

(c) It gives us peace with life. If God is Father, God is working all things together for good. Lessing used to say that if he had one question to ask the Sphinx, who knew everything, it would be:" Is this a friendly universe? " When we believe that God is Father, we also believe that such a father's hand will never cause his child a needless tear. We may not understand life any better, but we will not resent life any longer.

(d) It gives us peace with ourselves. In the last analysis a man is more afraid of himself than of anything else. He knows his own weakness; he knows the force of his own temptations; he knows his own tasks and the demands of his own life. But now he knows

that he is facing it all with God. It is not he who lives but Christ
who lives in him. There is a peace founded on strength in his life.

(*e*) It makes him certain that the deepest peace on earth is only
a shadow of the ultimate peace which is to come. It gives him a
hope and a goal to which he travels. It gives him a life of glorious
wonder here and yet, at the same time, a life in which the best is
yet to be.

THE LOVE OF GOD

John 3: 16

> For God so loved the world that he gave his only Son so that
> every one who believes in him should not perish but have
> everlasting life.

All great men have had their favourite texts; but this has been
called " Everybody's text." Herein for every simple heart is the
very essence of the gospel. This text tells us certain great things.

(i) It tells us that the initiative in all salvation lies with God.
Sometimes Christianity is presented in such a way that it
sounds as if God had to be pacified, as if he had to be
persuaded to forgive. Sometimes men speak as if they would
draw a picture of a stern, angry, unforgiving God and a gentle,
loving, forgiving Jesus. Sometimes men present the Christian
message in such a way that it sounds as if Jesus did something
which changed the attitude of God to men from condemnation
to forgiveness. But this text tells us that it was with God that it
all started. It was God who sent his Son, and he sent him
because he loved men. At the back of everything is the love of
God.

(ii) It tells us that the mainspring of God's being is love. It is
easy to think of God as looking at men in their heedlessness and
their disobedience and their rebellion and saying: " I'll break
them: I'll discipline them and punish them and scourge them
until they come back." It is easy to think of God as seeking the
allegiance of men in order to satisfy his own desire for power

and for what we might call a completely subject universe. The tremendous thing about this text is that it shows us God acting not for his own sake, but for ours, not to satisfy his desire for power, not to bring a universe to heel, but to satisfy his love. God is not like an absolute monarch who treats each man as a subject to be reduced to abject obedience. God is the Father who cannot be happy until his wandering children have come home. God does not smash men into submission; he yearns over them and woos them into love.

(iii) It tells us of the width of the love of God. It was *the world* that God so loved. It was not a nation; it was not the good people; it was not only the people who loved him; it was the world. The unlovable and the unlovely, the lonely who have no one else to love them, the man who loves God and the man who never thinks of him, the man who rests in the love of God and the man who spurns it—all are included in this vast inclusive love of God. As Augustine had it: " God loves each one of us as if there was only one of us to love."

LOVE AND JUDGMENT

John 3: 17–21

> For God did not send his son into the world to condemn the world, but that the world might be saved through him. He who believes in him is not condemned; but he who does not believe already stands condemned. And this is the reason of this condemnation—the light came into the world and men loved the darkness rather than the light, for their deeds were evil. Every one of whose deeds are depraved hates the light, and does not come to the light, but his deeds stand convicted. But he who puts the truth into action comes to the light, that his deeds may be made plain for all to see, because they are done in God.

Here we are faced with one othe apparent paradoxes of the Fourth Gospel—the paradox of love and judgment. We have just been thinking of the love of God, and now suddenly we are confronted with judgment and condemnation and conviction.

John has just said that it was because God so loved the world that he sent his Son into the world. Later he will go on to show us Jesus saying: " For judgment I came into this world " (*John* 9: 39). How can both things be true?

It is quite possible to offer a man an experience in nothing but love and for that experience to turn out a judgment. It is quite possible to offer a man an experience which is meant to do nothing but bring joy and bliss and yet for that experience to turn out a judgment. Suppose we love great music and get nearer to God in the midst of the surge and thunder of a great symphony than anywhere else. Suppose we have a friend who does not know anything about such music and we wish to introduce him to this great experience, to share it with him, and give him this contact with the invisible beauty which we ourselves enjoy. We have no aim other than to give our friend the happiness of a great new experience. We take him to a symphony concert; and in a very short time he is fidgeting and gazing around the hall, extremely bored. That friend has passed judgment on himself that he has no music in his soul. The experience designed to bring him new happiness has become only a judgment.

This always happens when we confront a man with greatness. We may take him to see some great masterpiece of art; we may take him to listen to a prince of preachers; we may give him a great book to read; we may take him to gaze upon some beauty. His reaction is a judgment; if he finds no beauty and no thrill we know that he has a blind spot in his soul. A visitor was being shown round an art gallery by one of the attendants. In that gallery there were certain masterpieces beyond all price, possessions of eternal beauty and unquestioned genius. At the end of the tour the visitor said: " Well, I don't think much of your old pictures." The attendant answered quietly: " Sir, I would remind you that these pictures are no longer on trial, but those who look at them are." All that the man's reaction had done was to show his own pitiable blindness.

This is so with regard to Jesus. If, when a man is confronted with Jesus, his soul responds to that wonder and beauty, he is on the way to salvation. But if, when he is confronted with Jesus, he sees nothing lovely, he stands condemned. His reaction has condemned him. God sent Jesus in love. He sent him for that man's salvation; but that which was sent in love has become a condemnation. It is not God who has condemned the man; God only loved him; the man has condemned himself.

The man who reacts in hostility to Jesus has loved the darkness rather than the light. The terrible thing about a really good person is that he always has a certain unconscious element of condemnation in him. It is when we compare ourselves with him that we see ourselves as we are. Alcibiades, the spoilt Athenian man of genius, was a companion of Socrates and every now and again he used to break out: " Socrates, I hate you, for every time I meet you, you let me see what I am." The man who is engaged on an evil task does not want a flood of light shed on it and him; but the man engaged on an honourable task does not fear the light.

Once an architect came to Plato and offered for a certain sum of money to build him a house into none of whose rooms it would be possible to see. Plato said: " I will give you double the money to build a house into whose every room everyone can see." It is only the evil-doer who does not wish to see himself and who does not wish anyone else to see him. Such a man will inevitably hate Jesus Christ, for Christ will show him what he is and that is the last thing that he wants to see. It is the concealing darkness that he loves and not the revealing light.

By his reaction to Jesus Christ, a man stands revealed and his soul laid bare. If he regards Christ with love, even with wistful yearning, for him there is hope; but if in Christ he sees nothing attractive he has condemned himself. He who was sent in love has become to him judgment.

A MAN WITHOUT ENVY

John 3: 22–30

After these things Jesus and his disciples went to the district of Judaea. He spent some time there with them, and he was baptizing; and John was baptizing at Ainon, near Salem, because there was much water there. The people kept coming to him and being baptized, for John had not yet been thrown into prison. A discussion arose between some of John's disciples and a Jew about the matter of cleansing. So they came to John and said to him: " Rabbi, look now! The man who was with you on the other side of Jordan, the man to whom you bore your witness, is baptizing and they are all going to him." John answered: " A man can receive only what is given to him from heaven. You yourselves can testify that I said, ' I am not the Anointed One of God,' but, ' I have been sent before him.' He who has the bride is the bridegroom. But the friend of the bridegroom who stands and listens for him, rejoices at the sound of the voice of the bridegroom. So, then, my joy is complete. He must increase, but I must decrease."

WE have already seen that part of the aim of the writer of the Fourth Gospel is to ensure that John the Baptist received his proper place as the forerunner of Jesus, but no higher place than that. There were those who were still ready to call John master and lord; the writer of the Fourth Gospel wishes to show that John had a high place, but that the highest place was reserved for Jesus alone; and he also wishes to show that John himself had never any other idea than that Jesus was supreme. To that end he shows us the ministry of John and the ministry of Jesus overlapping. The synoptic gospels are different: *Mark* 1: 14 tells us that it was *after* John was put into prison that Jesus began his ministry. We need not argue which account is historically correct; but the likelihood is that the Fourth Gospel makes the two ministries overlap so that by contrast the supremacy of Jesus may be clearly shown.

One thing is certain—this passage shows us the loveliness of the humility of John the Baptist. It was clear that men were leaving John for Jesus. John's disciples were worried. They did not like to see their master take second place. They did not like to see him abandoned while the crowds flocked out to hear and see this new teacher.

In answer to their complaints, it would have been very easy for John to feel injured, neglected and unjustifiably forgotten. Sometimes a friend's sympathy can be the worst possible thing for us. It can make us feel sorry for ourselves and encourage us to think that we have not had a fair deal. But John had a mind above that. He told his disciples three things.

(i) He told them that he had never expected anything else. He told them that in point of fact he had assured them that his was not the leading place, but that he was merely sent as the herald, the forerunner and the preparer for the greater one to come. It would ease life a great deal if more people were prepared to play the subordinate role. So many people look for great things to do. John was not like that. He knew well that God had given him a subordinate task. It would save us a lot of resentment and heartbreak if we realized that there are certain things which are not for us, and if we accepted with all our hearts and did with all our might the work that God has given us to do. To do a secondary task *for God* makes it a great task. As Mrs. Browning had it: " All service ranks the same with God." Any 'ask done for God is necessarily great.

(ii) He told them that no man could receive more than God gave him. If the new teacher was winning more followers it was not because he was stealing them from John, but because God was giving them to him. There was a certain American minister called Dr. Spence; once he was popular and his church was full; but as the years passed his people drifted away. To the church across the road came a new young minister who was attracting the crowds. One evening in Dr. Spence's church there was a very small gathering. The doctor looked at the little flock. " Where have all the people gone? " he asked. There was an embarrassed silence; then one of his office-bearers said: " I think they have gone to the church across the street to hear the new minister." Dr. Spence was silent for a moment; then he smiled. " Well, then," he said, " I think we ought to follow them." And he descended from his pulpit and led his people across the road. What jealousies, what heartburnings, what resentfulness we might escape, if we would only remember that someone else's success is given to him by God, and were prepared to accept God's verdict and God's choice.

(iii) Finally, John used a very vivid picture which every Jew would recognize, for it was part of the heritage of Jewish thought. He called Jesus the bridegroom and himself the friend of the bridegroom. One of the great pictures of the Old Testament is of Israel as the bride of God and God as the bridegroom of Israel. The union between God and Israel was so close that it could be likened only to a wedding. When Israel went after strange gods it was as if she were guilty of infidelity to the marriage bond (*Exodus* 34: 15 cp. *Deuteronomy* 31: 16; *Psalm* 73: 27; *Isaiah* 54: 5). The New Testament took this picture over and spoke of the church as the bride of Christ (2 *Corinthians* 11: 2; *Ephesians* 5: 22–32). It was this picture that was in John's mind. Jesus had come from God; he was the Son of God, Israel was his rightful bride and he was Israel's bridegroom. But one place John did claim for himself, that of the friend of the bridegroom.

The friend of the bridegroom, the *shoshben*, had a unique place at a Jewish wedding. He acted as the liaison between the bride and the bridegroom; he arranged the wedding; he took out the invitations; he presided at the wedding feast. He brought the bride and the bridegroom together. And he had one special duty. It was his duty to guard the bridal chamber and to let no false lover in. He would open the door only when in the dark he heard the bridegroom's voice and recognized it. When he heard the bridegroom's voice he let him in and went away rejoicing, for his task was completed and the lovers were together. He did not grudge the bridegroom the bride. He knew that his only task had been to bring bride and bridegroom together. And when that task was done he willingly and gladly faded out of the centre of the picture.

John's task had been to bring Israel and Jesus together; to arrange the marriage between Christ the bridegroom and Israel the bride. That task completed he was happy to fade into obscurity for his work was done. It was not with envy that he said that Jesus must increase and he must decrease; it was with joy. It may be that sometimes we would do well to remember that it is not to ourselves we must try to attach people; it is to Jesus Christ. It is not for ourselves we seek the loyalty of men; it is for him.

THE ONE FROM HEAVEN

John 3: 31–36

> He who comes from above is above all. He who is from the earth is from the earth and speaks from the earth. He who comes from heaven is above all. It is to what he has seen and heard that he bears witness; and no one receives his witness. He who has received his witness sets his seal on the fact that God is true. He whom God sent speaks the words of God, for he does not partially measure out the Spirit upon him. The Father loves the Son and has given all things into his hand. He who believes in the Son has eternal life. He who does not believe in the Son will not see life, but the wrath of God rests upon him.

As we have seen before, one of the difficulties in the Fourth Gospel is to know when the characters are speaking and when John is adding his own commentary. These verses may be the words of John the Baptist; but more likely they are the witness and the comment of John the evangelist.

John begins by asserting the supremacy of Jesus. If we want information, we have to go to the person who possesses that

information. If we want information about a family, we will get
it at first hand only from a member of that family. If we want
information about a town we will get it at first hand only from
someone who comes from that town. So, then, if we want
information about God, we will get it only from the Son of
God; and if we want information about heaven and heaven's
life, we will get it only from him who comes from heaven. When
Jesus speaks about God and about the heavenly things, says
John, it is no carried story, no second-hand tale, no information
from a secondary source; he tells us that which he himself has
seen and heard. To put it very simply, because Jesus alone
knows God, he alone can give us the facts about God, and these
facts are the gospel.

It is John's grief that so few accept the message that Jesus
brought; but when a man does accept it, he attests the fact that
in his belief the word of God is true. In the ancient world, if a
man wished to give his full approval to a document, such as a
will or an agreement or a constitution, he affixed his seal to the
foot of it. The seal was the sign that he agreed with this and
regarded it as binding and true. So when a man accepts the
message of Jesus, he affirms and attests that he believes what
God says is true.

John goes on: we can believe what Jesus says, because on
him God poured out the Spirit in full measure, keeping nothing
back. Even the Jews themselves said that the prophets received
from God *a certain measure of the Spirit*. The full measure of
the Spirit was reserved for God's own chosen one. Now, in
Hebrew thought the Spirit of God had two functions—first, the
Spirit revealed God's truth to men; and, second, the Spirit
enabled men to recognize and understand that truth when
it came to them. So to say that the Spirit was on Jesus in
the completest possible way is to say that he perfectly knew
and perfectly understood the truth of God. To put that in
another way—to listen to Jesus is to listen to the very voice of
God.

Finally, John again sets before men the eternal choice—life
or death. All through history this choice had been set before

Israel. *Deuteronomy* records the words of Moses: " See, I have
set before you this day life and good, death and evil. . . . I call
heaven and earth to witness against you this day, that I have set
before you life and death, blessing and curse; therefore choose
life, that you and your descendants may live " (*Deuteronomy*
30: 15–20). The challenge was reiterated by Joshua: " Choose
this day whom you will serve " (*Joshua* 24: 15). It has been said
that all life concentrates upon a man at the crossroads. Once
again John returns to his favourite thought. What matters is a
man's reaction to Christ. If that reaction be love and longing,
that man will know life. If it be indifference or hostility, that
man will know death. It is not that God sends his wrath upon
him; it is that he brings that wrath upon himself.

BREAKING DOWN THE BARRIERS

John 4: 1–9

So when the Lord learned that the Pharisees had heard that Jesus
was making and baptizing more disciples than John (although it
was not Jesus himself who was in the habit of baptizing but his
disciples), he quitted Judaea and went away again to Galilee. Now
he had to pass through Samaria. He came to a town of Samaria,
called Sychar, which is near the piece of ground which Jacob gave
to Joseph, his son, and Jacob's well was there. So Jesus, tired from
the journey, was sitting by the well just as he was. It was about
midday. There came a woman of Samaria to draw water. Jesus
said to her: " Give me to drink." For his disciples had gone away
into the town to buy provisions. So the Samaritan woman said to
him: " How is it that you who are a Jew ask a drink from me, a
Samaritan woman? " (For there is no familiarity between Jews
and Samaritans.)

FIRST of all, let us set the scene of this incident. Palestine is only
120 miles long from north to south. But within that 120 miles

there were in the time of Jesus three definite divisions of
territory. In the extreme north lay Galilee; in the extreme south
lay Judaea; and in between lay Samaria. Jesus did not wish
at this stage in his ministry to be involved in a controversy about
baptism; so he decided to quit Judaea for the time being and
transfer his operations to Galilee. There was a centuries-old
feud between the Jews and the Samaritans, the cause of
which we will shortly see. But the quickest way from Judaea
to Galilee lay through Samaria. Using that route, the journey
could be done in three days. The alternative route was to cross
the Jordan, go up the eastern side of the river to avoid Samaria,
recross the Jordan north of Samaria and then enter Galilee.
This was a route which took twice as long. So then Jesus had
to pass through Samaria if he wished to take the shortest route
to Galilee.

On the way they came to the town of Sychar. Just short of
Sychar the road to Samaria forks. The one branch goes
north-east to Scythopolis; the other goes west to Nablus and
then north to Engannim. At the fork of the road there stands to
this day the well known as Jacob's well.

This was an area which had many Jewish memories attached
to it. There was a piece of ground there which had been bought
by Jacob (*Genesis* 33: 18, 19). Jacob, on his deathbed, had
bequeathed that ground to Joseph (*Genesis* 48: 22). And, on
Joseph's death in Egypt, his body had been taken back to
Palestine and buried there (*Joshua* 24: 32). So around this area
there gathered many Jewish memories.

The well itself was more than 100 feet deep. It is not a
springing well of water; it is a well into which the water
percolates and gathers. But clearly it was a well so deep that no
one could gain water from it unless he had something with
which to draw the water.

When Jesus and his little band came to the fork in the road
Jesus sat down to rest, for he was tired with the journey. It was
midday. The Jewish day runs from 6 a.m. to 6 p.m. and the
sixth hour is twelve o'clock midday. So the heat was at its
greatest, and Jesus was weary and thirsty from travelling. His

disciples went on ahead to buy some food in the Samaritan town. Something must have been beginning to happen to them. Before they had met Jesus it is entirely unlikely that they would have even thought of buying food in any Samaritan town. Little by little, perhaps even unconsciously, the barriers were going down.

As Jesus sat there, there came to the well a Samaritan woman. Why she should come to that well is something of a mystery, for it was more than half-a-mile from Sychar where she must have stayed and there was water there. May it be that she was so much of a moral outcast that the women even drove her away from the village well and she had to come here to draw water? Jesus asked her to give him a drink. She turned in astonishment. " I am a Samaritan," she said. " You are a Jew. How is it that you ask a drink from me? " And then John explains to the Greeks for whom he is writing that there was no kind of come and go at all between the Jews and the Samaritans.

Now it is certain that all we have here is the briefest possible report of what must have been a long conversation. Clearly there was much more to this meeting than is recorded here. If we may use an analogy, this is like the minutes of a committee meeting where we have only the salient points of the discussion recorded. I think that the Samaritan woman must have unburdened her soul to this stranger. How else could Jesus have known of her tangled domestic affairs? For one of the very few times in her life she had found one with kindness in his eyes instead of critical superiority; and she opened her heart.

Few stories in the Gospel record show us so much about the character of Jesus.

(i) It shows us the reality of his humanity. Jesus was weary with the journey, and he sat by the side of the well exhausted. It is very significant that John who stresses the sheer deity of Jesus Christ more than any other of the gospel writers also stresses his humanity to the full. John does not show us a figure freed from the tiredness and the struggle of our humanity. He shows us one for whom life was an effort as it is for us; he shows us one who also was tired and had to go on.

(ii) It shows us the warmth of his sympathy. From an ordinary religious leader, from one of the orthodox church leaders of the day the Samaritan woman would have fled in embarrassment. She would have avoided such a one. If by any unlikely chance he had spoken to her she would have met him with an ashamed and even a hostile silence. But it seemed the most natural thing in the world to talk to Jesus. She had at last met someone who was not a critic but a friend, one who did not condemn but who understood.

(iii) It shows us Jesus as the breaker down of barriers. The quarrel between the Jews and the Samaritans was an old, old story. Away back about 720 B.C. the Assyrians had invaded the northern kingdom of Samaria and had captured and sub-jugated it. They did what conquerors often did in those days—they transported practically the whole population to Media (2 *Kings* 17: 6). Into the district the Assyrians brought other people—from Babylon, from Cuthah, from Ava, from Hamath and from Sepharvaim (2 *Kings* 17: 24). Now it is not possible to transport a whole people. Some of the people of the northern kingdom were left. Almost inevitably they began to inter-marry with the incoming foreigners; and thereby they committed what to the Jew was an unforgivable crime. They lost their racial purity. In a strict Jewish household even to this day if a son or a daughter marries a Gentile, his or her funeral service is carried out. Such a person is dead in the eyes of orthodox Judaism. So then the great majority of the inhabitants of Samaria were carried away to Media. They never came back but were assimilated into the country into which they were taken. They are the lost ten tribes. Those who remained in the country inter-married with the incoming strangers and lost their right to be called Jews at all.

In course of time a like invasion and a like defeat happened to the southern kingdom, whose capital was Jerusalem. Its inhabitants also were carried off to Babylon; but they did not lose their identity; they remained stubbornly and unalterably

Jewish. In time there came the days of Ezra and Nehemiah and the exiles returned to Jerusalem by the grace of the Persian king. Their immediate task was to repair and rebuild the shattered Temple. The Samaritans came and offered their help in this sacred task. They were contemptuously told that their help was not wanted. They had lost their Jewish heritage and they had no right to share in the rebuilding of the house of God. Smarting under this repulse, they turned bitterly against the Jews of Jerusalem. It was about 450 B.C. when that quarrel took place, and it was as bitter as ever in the days of Jesus.

It had further been embittered when the renegade Jew, Manasseh, married a daughter of the Samaritan Sanballat (*Nehemiah* 13: 28) and proceeded to found a rival temple on Mount Gerizim which was in the centre of the Samaritan territory. Still later in the Maccabean days, in 129 B.C., John Hyrcanus, the Jewish general and leader, led an attack against Samaria and sacked and destroyed the temple on Mount Gerizim. Between Jews and Samaritans there was an embittered hatred. The Jews contemptuously called them Chuthites or Cuthaeans after one of the peoples whom the Assyrians had settled there. The Jewish Rabbis said: " Let no man eat of the bread of the Cuthaeans, for he who eats their bread is as he who eats swine's flesh." *Ecclesiasticus* depicts God as saying: " With two nations is my soul vexed, and the third is no nation; they that sit upon the mountain of Samaria, and the Philistines, and that foolish people that dwell in Sichem " (*Ecclesiasticus* 50: 25, 26). Sichem or Shechem was one of the most famous of Samaritan cities. The hatred was returned with interest. It is told that Rabbi Jochanan was passing through Samaria on his way to Jerusalem to pray. He passed by Mount Gerizim. A Samaritan saw him, and asked him: " Where are you going? " " I am going to Jerusalem," he said, " to pray." The Samaritan answered: " Would it not be better for you to pray in this holy mountain (Mount Gerizim) than in that accursed house? " Pilgrims from Galilee to Jerusalem had to pass through Samaria, if, as we have seen, they travelled by the quickest way; and the Samaritans delighted to hinder them.

The Jewish-Samaritan quarrel was more than 400 years old. But it smouldered as resentfully and as bitterly as ever. It was small wonder that the Samaritan woman was astonished that Jesus, a Jew, should speak to her, a Samaritan.

(iv) But there was still another way in which Jesus was taking down the barriers. The Samaritan was a woman. The strict Rabbis forbade a Rabbi to greet a woman in public. A Rabbi might not even speak to his own wife or daughter or sister in public. There were even Pharisees who were called " the bruised and bleeding Pharisees " because they shut their eyes when they saw a woman on the street and so walked into walls and houses! For a Rabbi to be seen speaking to a woman in public was the end of his reputation—and yet Jesus spoke to this woman. Not only was she a woman; she was also a woman of notorious character. No decent man, let alone a Rabbi, would have been seen in her company, or even exchanging a word with her—and yet Jesus spoke to her.

To a Jew this was an amazing story. Here was the Son of God, tired and weary and thirsty. Here was the holiest of men, listening with understanding to a sorry story. Here was Jesus breaking through the barriers of nationality and orthodox Jewish custom. Here is the beginning of the universality of the gospel; here is God so loving the world, not in theory, but in action.

THE LIVING WATER

John 4: 10–15

Jesus answered her: " If you knew the free gift that God is offering you, and if you knew who is speaking to you, and if you knew who was saying to you: ' Give me to drink,' you would have asked him, and he would have given you living water." The woman said to him: " Sir, you have no bucket to draw with and the well is deep. Where does this living water that you have come from? Are you greater than our father Jacob who gave us the well, and who himself drank from it with his children and his cattle? " Jesus answered her: " Everyone who drinks of this water will thirst again; but whoever drinks of the water that I will give him will never thirst again for ever. But the water that I will give him will become a well of water within him, springing up to give him life eternal." The woman said to him: " Sir, give me this water, so that I will not thirst, and so that I will not have to come here to draw water."

WE have to note that this conversation with the Samaritan woman follows exactly the same pattern as the conversation with Nicodemus. Jesus makes a statement. The statement is taken in the wrong sense. Jesus remakes the statement in an even more vivid way. It is still misunderstood; and then Jesus compels the person with whom he is speaking to discover and to face the truth for herself. That was Jesus's usual way of teaching; and it was a most effective way, for, as someone has said: " There are certain truths which a man cannot *accept*; he must *discover* them for himself."

Just as Nicodemus did, the woman took the words of Jesus quite literally when she was meant to understand them spiritually. It was *living* water of which Jesus spoke. In ordinary language to the Jew *living* water was *running* water. It was the water of the running stream in contradistinction to the water of the stagnant cistern or pool. This well, as we have seen, was not a springing well, but a well into which the water percolated from the subsoil. To the Jew, *running*, *living* water from the stream was always better. So the woman is saying: " You are offering me pure stream water. Where are you going to get it? "

She goes on to speak of " our father Jacob." The Jews would, of course, have strenuously denied that Jacob was the father of the Samaritans, but it was part of the Samaritan claim that they were descended from Joseph, the son of Jacob, by way of Ephraim and Manasseh. The woman is in effect saying to Jesus: " This is blasphemous talk. Jacob, our great ancestor, when he came here, had to dig this well to gain water for his family and his cattle. Are you claiming to be able to get fresh, running stream water? If you are, you are claiming to be wiser and more powerful than Jacob. That is a claim that no one has any right to make."

When people were on a journey they usually carried with them a bucket made from the skin of some beast so that they could draw water from any well at which they halted. No doubt Jesus's band had such a bucket; and no doubt the disciples had taken it into the town with them. The woman saw that Jesus did not possess such a traveller's leathern bucket, and so again she says in effect: " You need not talk about drawing water and giving it to me. I can see for myself that you have not a bucket with which to draw water." H. B. Tristram begins his book entitled *Eastern Customs in Bible Lands* with this personal experience. He was sitting beside a well in Palestine beside the scene of the inn which figures in the story of the Good Samaritan. " An Arab woman came down from the hills above to draw water; she unfolded and opened her goatskin bottle, and then untwined a cord, and attached it to a very small leathern bucket which she carried, by means of which she slowly filled her skin, fastened its mouth, placed it on her shoulder, and bucket in hand, climbed the mountain. I thought of the woman of Samaria at Jacob's well, when an Arab footman, toiling up the steep path from Jericho, heated and wearied with his journey, turned aside to the well, knelt and peered wistfully down. But he had ' nothing to draw with and the well was deep.' He lapped a little moisture from the water spilt by the woman who had preceded him, and, disappointed, passed on." It was just that that the woman was thinking of when she said that Jesus had nothing wherewith to draw water from the depths of the well.

But the Jews had another way of using the word *water*. They often spoke of the *thirst* of the soul for God; and they often spoke of quenching that thirst with *living water*. Jesus was not using terms that were bound to be misunderstood; he was using terms that anyone with spiritual insight should have understood. In the *Revelation* that promise is: " To the thirsty I will give water without price from the fountain of the water of life " (*Revelation* 21: 6). The Lamb is to lead them to springs of living waters (*Revelation* 7: 17). The promise was that the chosen people would draw water with joy from the wells of salvation (*Isaiah* 12: 3). The Psalmist spoke of his soul being thirsty for the living God (*Psalm* 42: 1). God's promise was: " I will pour water on the thirsty land " (*Isaiah* 44: 3). The summons was that every one who was thirsty should come to the waters and freely drink (*Isaiah* 55: 1). Jeremiah's complaint was that the people had forsaken God who was the fountain of living waters and had hewed themselves out broken cisterns which could hold no water (*Jeremiah* 2: 13). Ezekiel had had his vision of the river of life (*Ezekiel* 47: 1–12). In the new world there would be a cleansing fountain opened (*Zechariah* 13: 1). The waters would go forth from Jerusalem (*Zechariah* 14: 8).

Sometimes the Rabbis identified this living water with the wisdom of the Law; sometimes they identified it with nothing less than the Holy Spirit of God. All Jewish pictorial religious language was full of this idea of the thirst of the soul which could be quenched only with the living water which was the gift of God. But the woman chose to understand this with an almost crude literalism. She was blind because she would not see.

Jesus went on to make a still more startling statement that he could give her living water which would banish her thirst for ever. The point is that again the woman took this literally; but in point of fact it was nothing less than a Messianic claim. In the prophetic vision of the age to come, the age of God, the promise was: " They shall not hunger or thirst " (*Isaiah* 49: 10). It was with God and none other that the living fountain of the all-quenching water existed. " With thee is the fountain of life," the Psalmist had cried (*Psalm* 36: 9). It is from the very throne of God that the river of life is to flow (*Revelation* 22: 1). It is the Lord who is the fountain of living water (*Jeremiah* 17: 13). It is in the Messianic age that the parched ground is to become a pool and the thirsty ground springs of water (*Isaiah* 35: 7). When Jesus spoke about bringing to men the water which quenches thirst for ever, he was doing no less than stating that he he was the Anointed One of God who was to bring in the new age.

Again the woman did not see it. And I think that this time she spoke with a jest, as if humouring one who was a little mad.

" Give me this water," she said, " so that I will never be thirsty
again and will not have to walk to the well day after day." She was
jesting with a kind of humouring contempt about eternal things.

At the heart of all this there is the fundamental truth that
in the human heart there is a thirst for something that only
Jesus Christ can satisfy. Sinclair Lewis in one of his books
draws a picture of a respectable little business man who kicked
over the traces. He is talking to the girl he loves. She says to
him: " On the surface we seem quite different; but deep down
we are fundamentally the same. We are both desperately
unhappy about something—and we don't know what it is." In
every man there is this nameless unsatisfied longing; this vague
discontent; this something lacking; this frustration.

In *Sorrell and Son* Warwick Deeping tells of a conversation
between Sorrell and his son. The boy is talking about life. He
says that it is like groping in an enchanted fog. The fog breaks
for a moment; you see the moon or a girl's face; you think you
want the moon or the face; and then the fog comes down again;
and leaves you groping for something, you don't quite know
what. Wordsworth, in the *Ode on the Intimations of Immorta-
lity*, speaks of,

> " Those obstinate questionings
> Of sense and outward things,
> Fallings from us, vanishings;
> Blank misgivings of a creature
> Moving about in worlds not realized."

Augustine talks about " our hearts being restless till they find
rest in thee."

Part of the human situation is that we cannot find happiness
out of the things that the human situation has to offer. As
Browning had it:

> " Just when we're safest, there's a sunset touch,
> A fancy from a flower-bell, someone's death,
> A chorus ending from Euripides—
> And that's enough for fifty hopes and fears
> As old and new at once as Nature's self.
> To rap and knock and enter in our soul."

We are never safe from the longing for eternity which God has put in man's soul. There is a thirst which only Jesus Christ can satisfy.

FACING THE TRUTH

John 4: 15–21

> The woman said to him: " Sir, give me this water, so that I will not thirst, and so that I will not have to come here to draw water." Jesus said to her: " Go, call your husband, and come back here." The woman answered: " I have not got a husband." Jesus said to her: " You spoke well when you said, ' I have not got a husband.' For you have had five husbands, and the one you now have is not your husband. This is the truth that you have told." The woman said to him: " Sir, I see that you are a prophet. Our fathers worshipped in this mountain and you say Jerusalem is the place where we ought to worship." Jesus said: " Woman, believe me, the hour is coming when you will worship the Father neither in this mountain nor in Jerusalem."

WE have seen how the woman jestingly asked Jesus to give her the living water in order that she should not thirst again and might be spared the tiring journey to the well. Suddenly and stabbingly Jesus brought her to her senses. The time for verbal by-play was past; the time for jesting was over. " Go," said Jesus, " and fetch your husband and come back with him." The woman stiffened as if a sudden pain had caught her; she recoiled as if hit by a sudden shock; she grew white as one who had seen a sudden apparition; and so indeed she had, for *she had suddenly caught sight of herself.*

She was suddenly compelled to face herself and the looseness and immorality and total inadequacy of her life. There are two revelations in Christianity: the revelation of God and the revelation of ourselves. No man ever really sees himself until he sees himself in the presence of Christ; and then he is appalled at the sight. There is another way of putting it—Christianity begins with a sense of sin. It begins with the sudden realization that life as we are living it will not do. We awake to ourselves and we awake to our need of God.

Some people have held, because of this mention of the five husbands, that this story is not an actual incident but an allegory. We have seen that, when the original people of Samaria were exiled and transported to Media, people from five other places were brought in. These five different people brought in their own gods (2 *Kings* 17: 29); and it has been held that the woman stands for Samaria and the five husbands for the five false gods to whom the Samaritans, as it were, married themselves. The sixth husband stands for the true God, but, they worship him, not truly, but in ignorance; and therefore they are not married to him at all. It may be that there is a reminder of this Samaritan infidelity to God in the story; but it is far too vivid to be a manufactured allegory. It reads too much like life.

Someone has said that prophecy is criticism based on hope. A prophet points out to a man or a nation what is wrong; but he does so not to push them into despair but to point the way to cure and to amendment and to rightness of life. So Jesus began by revealing to this woman her own sinful state; but goes on to tell her of the true worship in which our souls can meet God.

The woman's question comes strangely to us. She says, and she is obviously troubled when she says it: " Our fathers say that we ought to worship here on Mount Gerizim; you say that we ought to worship in Jerusalem; what am I to do? " The Samaritans adjusted history to suit themselves. They taught that it was on Mount Gerizim that Abraham had been willing to sacrifice Isaac; they taught that it was there that Melchizedek had appeared to Abraham; they declared that it was on Mount Gerizim that Moses had first entered an altar and sacrificed to God when the people entered the promised land, although in fact it was on Mount Ebal that was done (*Deuteronomy* 27: 4). They tampered with the text of scripture and with history to glorify Mount Gerizim. The woman had been brought up to regard Mount Gerizim as the most sacred spot in the world and to despise Jerusalem. What was in her mind was this. She was

saying to herself: " I am a sinner before God; I must offer to
God an offering for my sin; I must take that offering to the
house of God to put myself right with him; where am I going to
take it? " To her, as to all her contemporaries, the only cure for
sin was sacrifice. Her great problem was, where was that
sacrifice to be made? By this time she is not arguing about the
respective merits of the Temple on Mount Gerizim and the
Temple on Mount Zion. All she wants to know is: Where can I
find God?

Jesus's answer was that the day of the old man-made
rivalries was coming to an end; and the time was on the way
when men would find God everywhere. It had been Zephaniah's
vision that men shall worship God " each in his place "
(*Zephaniah* 2: 11). It was Malachi's dream that in every place
incense would be offered as a pure offering to the name of God
(*Malachi* 1: 11). Jesus's answer to the woman was that she did
not need to go anywhere special to find God, neither to Mount
Gerizim nor to Mount Zion. She did not need to offer sacrifice
in some special place; true worship finds God in every
place.

THE TRUE WORSHIP

John 4: 22–26

" You do not know what you are worshipping. We do know what
we worship, because the world's salvation has its origin among
the Jews. But the hour is coming—the hour is now here—when
the real worshippers will worship the Father in spirit and in truth;
for it is worshippers like that that the Father is looking for. God is
Spirit; and those who worship him must worship him in spirit and
in truth." The woman said to him: " I know that the Messiah, he
who is called Christ, is coming. When he has come he will
announce all things to us." Jesus said to her: " I who am speaking
to you am he."

JESUS had told the Samaritan woman that the old rivalries were
on the way out, that the day was coming when controversy

about the respective merits of Mount Gerizim and Mount Zion would be an irrelevancy, that he who truly sought God would find him anywhere. For all that Jesus still stressed the fact that the Jewish nation had a unique place in God's plan and revelation.

The Samaritans worshipped in ignorance, he said. There was one sense in which that was factually true. The Samaritans accepted only the Pentateuch, the first five books of the Old Testament. They rejected all the rest of the Old Testament. They had therefore rejected all the great messages of the prophets and all the supreme devotion of the Psalms. They had in fact a truncated religion because they had a truncated Bible; they had rejected the knowledge that was open to them and that they might have had. Further, the Jewish Rabbis had always charged the Samaritans with a merely superstitious worship of the true God. They always said that the Samaritan worship was founded not on love and knowledge, but on ignorance and fear. As we have seen, when the foreign peoples were brought in to dwell in Samaria, they brought their own gods with them (2 *Kings* 17: 29). We are told that a priest from Bethel came and told them how they should fear the Lord (2 *Kings* 17: 28). But all the probability is that they merely added Jehovah to their list of gods because they were superstitiously afraid to leave him out. After all he was the God of the land in which they were living and it might be dangerous not to include him in their worship.

In a false worship we may detect three faults.

(i) A false worship is a selective worship. It chooses what it wishes to know about God and omits the rest. The Samaritans took as much of scripture as they wished and paid no attention to the rest. One of the most dangerous things in the world is a one-sided religion. It is very easy for a man to accept and hold such parts of God's truth as suit him and to disregard the remainder. We have seen, for instance, how certain thinkers and churchmen and politicians justify *apartheid* and racial segregation by appeal to certain parts of scripture, while they conveniently forget the far greater parts which forbid it.

A minister in a great city organized a petition to help a man who had been condemned for a certain crime. It seemed to him that this was a case where Christian mercy ought to operate. His telephone bell rang, and a woman's voice said to him: " I am astonished that you, a minister, should be lending your weight to this petition for mercy." " Why should you be surprised? " he asked. The voice said: " I suppose you know your Bible." " I hope so," he said. " Then," said the voice, " are you not aware that the Bible says, ' An eye for an eye and a tooth for a tooth '? " Here was a woman who took the part of the Bible which suited her argument and forgot the great merciful teaching of Jesus in the Sermon on the Mount.

We would do well to remember that, although no man will ever grasp the whole orb of truth, it is total truth that we should aim at, not the snatching at fragments which happen to suit ourselves and our own position.

(ii) A false worship is an ignorant worship. Worship ought to be the approach to God of the whole man. A man has a mind and he has a duty to exercise it. Religion may begin with an emotional response; but the time comes when that emotional response has to be thought out. E. F. Scott said that religion is far more than merely the strenuous exercise of the intellect, but that nonetheless a very great part of religious failure is due to nothing other than intellectual sloth. To fail to think things out is in itself a sin. In the last analysis, religion is never safe until a man can tell, not only what he believes, but why he believes it. Religion is hope, but it is hope with reason behind it (1 *Peter* 3: 15).

(ii) A false worship is a superstitious worship. It is a worship given, not out of a sense of need nor out of any real desire, but basically because a man feels that it might be dangerous not to give it. Many a person will refuse to walk beneath a ladder; many a person will have a pleased feeling when a black cat crosses his path; many a person will pick up a pin with the idea that good luck will follow; many a person will have an uncomfortable feeling when he is one of thirteen sitting at a table. He does not believe in these superstitions, but he has the feeling that there might be something in them and he had better play safe. There are many people whose religion is founded on a kind of vague fear of what might happen if they leave God out of the reckoning. But real religion is founded not on fear but on the love of God and gratitude for what God has done. Too much religion is a kind of superstitious ritual to avert the possible wrath of the unpredictable gods.

Jesus pointed to the true worship. God, he said, is spirit. Immediately a man grasps that, a new flood-light breaks over him. If God is spirit, God is not confined to *things*; and therefore idol worship is not only an irrelevancy, it is an insult to the very nature of God. If God is spirit, God is not confined to *places*; and therefore to limit the worship of God to Jerusalem or to any other spot is to set a limit to that which by its nature overpasses all limits. If God is spirit, a man's gifts to God must be gifts of the spirit. Animal sacrifices and all man-made things become inadequate. The only gifts that befit the nature of God are the gifts of the spirit—love, loyalty, obedience, devotion.

A man's spirit is the highest part of him. That is the part which lasts when the physical part has vanished. That is the part which dreams the dreams and sees the visions which, because of the weakness and faultiness of the body, may never be carried out. It is the spirit of a man which is the source of his highest dreams and thoughts and ideals and desires. The true worship is when man, through his spirit, attains to friendship and intimacy with God. Genuine worship does not consist in coming to a certain place nor in going through a certain ritual or liturgy nor even in bringing certain gifts. True worship is when the spirit, the immortal and invisible part of man, speaks to and meets with God, himself immortal and invisible.

This passage closes with a great declaration. There had opened before this Samaritan woman a vista which bewildered and staggered her. Here were things beyond her understanding, things full of wonder. All that she could say was: " When the Messiah, the Christ, the Anointed One of God comes, then we will know all about it." Jesus said to her: " I who am speaking to you am he." It is as if Jesus said this is not a dream of the truth; this *is* the truth itself.

SHARING THE WONDER

John 4: 27–30

> Upon this his disciples came up; and they were in a state of amazement that he was talking to a woman; but no one said: " What are you looking for? " or, " Why are you talking to her? " So the woman left her water-pot, and went away to the town and said to the people: " Come and see a man who told me all things that I have done! Can this be the Anointed One of God? " They came out of the town and were coming to him.

THERE is little wonder that the disciples were in a state of bewildered amazement when they returned from their errand to the town of Sychar and found Jesus talking to the Samaritan woman. We have already seen the Jewish idea of women. The Rabbinic precept ran: " Let no one talk with a woman in the street, no, not with his own wife." The Rabbis so despised women and so thought them incapable of receiving any real teaching that they said: " Better that the words of the law should be burned than deliver to women." They had a saying: " Each time that a man prolongs converse with a woman he causes evil to himself, and desists from the law, and in the end inherits Gehinnom." By Rabbinic standards Jesus could hardly have done a more shatteringly unconventional thing than to talk to this woman. Here is Jesus taking the barriers down.

There follows a curiously revealing touch. It is the kind which could hardly have come from anyone except from one who had actually shared in this scene. However staggered the disciples might be, it did not occur to them to ask the woman what she was looking for or to ask Jesus why he was talking to her. They were beginning to know him; and they had already arrived at the conclusion that, however surprising his actions

were, they were not to be questioned. A man has taken a great
step to real discipleship when he learns to say: " It is not for me
to question the actions and the demands of Jesus. My prejudices and my conventions must go down before them."

By this time the woman was on her way back to the village
without her water-pot. The fact that she left her water-pot
showed two things. It showed that she was in a hurry to share
this extraordinary experience, and it showed that she never
dreamed of doing anything else but come back. Her whole
action has much to tell us of real Christian experience.

(i) Her experience began with being compelled to face herself
and to see herself as she was. The same thing happened to
Peter. After the draft of fishes, when Peter suddenly discovered
something of the majesty of Jesus, all he could say was:
" Depart from me; for I am a sinful man, O Lord " (*Luke* 5: 8).
Our Christian experience will often begin with a humiliating
wave of self-disgust. It usually happens that the last thing a man
sees is himself. And it often happens that the first thing Christ
does for a man is to compel him to do what he has spent his life
refusing to do—look at himself.

(ii) The Samaritan woman was staggered by Christ's ability
to see into her inmost being. She was amazed at his intimate
knowledge of the human heart, and of her heart in particular.
The Psalmist was awed by that same thought. " Thou dis-
cernest my thoughts from afar. . . . Even before a word is on my
tongue, lo, O Lord, thou knowest it altogether " (*Psalm* 139:
1–4). It is told that once a small girl heard a sermon by C. H.
Spurgeon, and whispered to her mother at the end of it:
" Mother, how does he know what goes on in our house? "
There are no wrappings and disguises which are proof against
the gaze of Christ. It is his power to see into the depths of the
human heart. It is not that he sees only the evil there; he sees
also the sleeping hero in the soul of every man. He is like the
surgeon who sees the diseased thing, but who also sees the
health which will follow when the evil thing is taken away.

(iii) The first instinct of the Samaritan woman was to share
her discovery. Having found this amazing person, she was

compelled to share her find with others. The Christian life is based on the twin pillars of discovery and communication. No discovery is complete until the desire to share it fills our hearts; and we cannot communicate Christ to others until we have discovered him for ourselves. First to find, then to tell, are the two great steps of the Christian life.

(iv) This very desire to tell others of her discovery killed in this woman the feeling of shame. She was no doubt an outcast; she was no doubt a byword; the very fact that she was drawing water from this distant well shows how she avoided her neighbours and how they avoided her. But now she ran to tell them of her discovery. A person may have some trouble which he is embarrassed to mention and which he tries to keep secret, but once he is cured he is often so filled with wonder and gratitude that he tells everyone about it. A man may hide his sin; but once he discovers Jesus Christ as Saviour, his first instinct is to say to men: " Look at what I was and look at what I am; this is what Christ has done for me."

THE MOST SATISFYING FOOD

John 4: 31–34

> Meanwhile his disciples asked him: " Rabbi! Eat something! " " I have food," he said to them, " of which you do not know." " Surely," his disciples kept saying to each other, " someone can't have given him something to eat? " " My food," said Jesus to them, " is to do the will of him who sent me and to complete his work."

THIS passage follows the normal pattern of the conversations of the Fourth Gospel. Jesus says something which is misunderstood. He says something which has a spiritual meaning. It is at first taken with an uncomprehending literalism and then slowly he unfolds the meaning until it is grasped and realized. It is exactly the same as Jesus did when he talked to Nicodemus about being born again, and when he talked to the woman about the water which quenched the thirst of the heart for ever.

By this time the disciples had come back with food, and they asked Jesus to eat. They had left him so tired and exhausted that they were worried that he did not seem to want to eat any of the provisions which they had brought back. It is strange how a great task can lift a man above and beyond bodily needs. All his life Wilberforce, who freed the slaves, was a little, insignificant, ailing creature. When he rose to address the House of Commons, the members at first used to smile at this queer little figure; but as the fire and the power came from the man, they used to crowd the benches whenever he rose to speak. As it was put: " The little minnow became a whale." His message, his task, the flame of truth and the dynamic of power conquered his physical weakness. There is a picture of John Knox preaching in his old age. He was a done old man; he was so weak that he had to be half lifted up the pulpit steps and left supporting himself on the book-board; but before he had long begun his sermon the voice had regained its old trumpet-call and he was like " to ding the pulpit into blads (to knock the pulpit into splinters) and leap out of it." The message filled the man with a kind of supernatural strength.

Jesus's answer to his disciples was that he had food of which they knew nothing. In their simplicity they wondered if some-one had brought him food to eat. Then he told them: " My food is to do the will of him who sent me."

The great keynote of Jesus's life is submission to the will of God. His uniqueness lies in the very fact that he was the only person who ever was or who ever will be perfectly obedient to God's will. It can be truly said that Jesus is the only person in all the world who never did what he liked but always what God liked.

He was God-sent. Again and again the Fourth Gospel speaks of Jesus being *sent* by God. There are two Greek words used in the Fourth Gospel for this sending. There is *apostellein* which is used seventeen times and *pempein* which is used twenty-seven times. That is to say, no fewer than forty-four times the Fourth Gospel speaks, or shows us Jesus speaking, about his being sent by God. Jesus was one who was under orders. He was God's man.

Then once Jesus had come, again and again he spoke of the work that was given him to do. In *John* 5: 36 he speaks of the works which his Father has given him to do. In 17: 4 his only claim is that he has finished the work his Father gave him to do. When he speaks of taking up and laying down his life, of living and of dying, he says: " This commandment have I received of my Father " (10: 18). He speaks continually, as he speaks here, of *the will of God*. " I have come down from heaven," he says, " not to do my own will, but the will of him who sent me " (6: 38). " I always do," he says, " what is pleasing to him " (8: 29). In 14: 23 he lays it down, out of his personal experience and on his personal example, that the only proof of love lies in the keeping of the commandments of the one a man claims to love. This obedience of Jesus was not as it is with us, a spasmodic thing. It was the very essence and being, the mainspring and the core, the dynamic and the moving power of his life.

It is his great desire that we should be as he was.

(i) To do the will of God is the only way to peace. There can be no peace when we are at variance with the king of the universe.

(ii) To do the will of God is the only way to happiness. There can be no happiness when we set our human ignorance against the divine wisdom of God.

(iii) To do the will of God is the only way to power. When we go our own way, we have nothing to call on but our own power, and therefore collapse is inevitable. When we go God's way, we go in his power, and therefore victory is secure.

THE SOWER, THE HARVEST AND THE REAPERS

John 4: 35–38

" Are you not in the habit of saying: ' Four months, and the harvest will come '? Look you! I say to you, lift up your eyes and look at the fields, because they are already white for the harvesting. The harvester receives his reward and stores up fruit which makes for eternal life, so that he who sows and he who harvests may rejoice together. In this the saying is true—one sows and another harvests. I have sent you to harvest a crop which your labour did not produce. Others have laboured, and you have entered into their labours."

ALL this that was happening in Samaria had given Jesus a vision of a world to be harvested for God. When he said: " Four months, and the harvest will come," we are not to think that he was speaking of the actual time of year that it was in Samaria at that time. If that were so, it would have been somewhere round about January. There would have been no exhausting heat; and there would have been no scarcity of water. One would not have needed a well to find water; it would have been the rainy season, and there would have been plenty of water.

What Jesus is doing is quoting a proverb. The Jews had a sixfold division of the agricultural year. Each division was held to last two months—seedtime, winter, spring, harvest, summer and the season of extreme heat. Jesus is saying: " You have got a proverb; if you sow the seed, you must wait for at least four months before you can hope to begin to reap the harvest." Then Jesus looked up. Sychar is in the midst of a region that is still famous for its corn. Agricultural land was very limited in stony, rocky Palestine; practically nowhere else in the country could a man look up and see the waving fields of golden corn. Jesus swept his gaze and his hand round. " Look," he said, " the fields are white and ready for the harvest. They took four months to grow; but in Samaria there is a harvest for the reaping *now*."

For once, it is the *contrast* between nature and grace of which Jesus is thinking. In the ordinary harvest men sowed and waited; in Samaria things had happened with such divine suddenness that the word was sown and on the spot the harvest waited. H. V. Morton has a specially interesting suggestion about the fields white for the harvest. He himself was sitting at this very spot where Jacob's well is. As he sat, he saw the people come out from the village and start to climb the hill.

They came in little batches; and they were all wearing white robes and the white robes stood out against the ground and the sky. It may well be that just at this moment the people started to flock out to Jesus in response to the woman's story. As they streamed out in their white robes across the fields, perhaps Jesus said: " Look at the fields! See them now! They are white to the harvest! " The white-robed crowd was the harvest which he was eager to reap for God.

Jesus went on to show that the incredible had happened. The sower and the harvester could rejoice at the same time. Here was something no man might expect. To the Jew sowing was a sad and a laborious time; it was harvest which was the time of joy. " May those who sow in tears reap with shouts of joy! He that goes forth weeping, bearing the seed for sowing, shall come home with shouts of joy, bringing his sheaves with him " (*Psalm* 136: 5, 6).

There is something else hidden below the surface here. The Jews had their dreams of the golden age, the age to come, the age of God, when the world would be God's world, when sin and sorrow would be done away with and God would reign supreme. Amos paints his picture of it: " Behold the days are coming, saith the Lord, when the ploughman shall overtake the reaper, and the treader of grapes him who sows the seed " (*Amos* 9: 13). " Your threshing shall last the time of vintage, and the vintage shall last the time for sowing " (*Leviticus* 26: 5). It was the dream of that golden age that sowing and reaping, planting and harvesting, would follow hard upon the heels of each other. There would be such fertility that the old days of waiting would be at an end. We can see what Jesus is gently doing here. His words are nothing less than a claim that with him the golden age has dawned; God's time is here; the time when the word is spoken and the seed is sown and the harvest waits.

There was another side to that— and Jesus knew it. " There is another proverb," he said, " and it too is true—one sows and another harvests." Then he went on to make two applications of that.

(*a*) He told his disciples that they would reap a crop which had been produced not by their labour. He meant that *he* was sowing the seed, that in his Cross, above all, the seed of the love and the power of God would be sown, and that the day would come when the disciples would go out into the world and reap the harvest that his life and death had sown.

(*b*) He told his disciples that the day would come when *they* would sow and others would reap. There would be a time when the Christian Church sent out its evangelists; they would never see the harvest; some of them would die as martyrs, but the blood of the martyrs would be the seed of the church. It is as if he said: " Some day you will labour and you will see nothing for it. Some day you will sow and you will pass from the scene before the harvest is reaped. Never fear! Never be discouraged! The sowing is not in vain; the seed is not wasted! Others will see the harvest which it was not given to you to see."

So in this passage there are two things.

(i) There is *the reminder of an opportunity*. The harvest waits to be reaped for God. There come times in history when men are curiously and strangely sensitive to God. What a tragedy it is if Christ's Church at such a time fails to reap Christ's harvest!

(ii) There is *the reminder of a challenge*. It is given to many a man to sow but not to reap. Many a ministry succeeds, not by its own force and merits, but because of some saintly man who lived and preached and died and left an influence which was greater in his absence than in his presence. Many a man has to work and never sees the results of his labours. I was once taken round an estate which was famous for its rhododendrons. Its owner loved their acres and knew them all by name. He showed me certain seedlings which would take twenty-five years to flower. He was nearly seventy-five and would never see their beauty—*but someone would*. No work for Christ and no great undertaking ever fail. If we do not see the result of our labours, others will. There is no room for despair in the Christian life.

THE SAVIOUR OF THE WORLD

John 4: 39–42

> Many of the Samaritans from that city believed on him, because
> of the woman's story, for she testified: " He told me all things that
> I have done." So when the Samaritans came to him, they asked
> him to stay amongst them, and he stayed there two days. And
> many more believed when they heard his word, and they said to
> the woman: " No longer do we believe because of your talk. We
> ourselves have listened to him, and we know that this is really the
> Saviour of the World."

IN the events which happened at Samaria we have the pattern
by which the gospel so often spreads. In the rise of belief among
the Samaritans there were three stages.

(i) There was introduction. The Samaritans were introduced
to Christ by the woman. Here we see full-displayed God's
need of us. Paul said: " How are they to hear without a
preacher? " (*Romans* 10: 14). The word of God must be
transmitted by man to man. God cannot deliver his message
to those who have never heard it unless there is someone to
deliver it.

> " He has no hands but our hands
>   To do his work today:
> He has no feet but our feet
>   To lead men in his way:
> He has no voice but our voice
>   To tell men how he died:
> He has no help but our help
>   To lead them to his side."

It is at once our precious privilege and our terrible responsibility to bring men to Christ. The introduction cannot be made
unless there is a man to make it.

Further, that introduction is made on the strength of personal witness. The cry of the Samaritan woman was: " Look
what he has done for me and to me." It was not to a theory that

she called her neighbours; it was to a dynamic and changing power. The church can expand until the kingdoms of the world become the kingdoms of the Lord only when men and women themselves experience the power of Christ, and then transmit that experience to others.

(ii) There was nearer intimacy and growing knowledge. Once the Samaritans had been introduced to Christ, they sought his company. They asked him to stay with them that they might learn of him and come to know him better. It is true that a man must be introduced to Christ, but it is equally true that once he has been introduced he must himself go on to live in the presence of Christ. No man can go through an experience for another man. Others may lead us to the friendship of Christ, but we must claim and enjoy that friendship ourselves.

(iii) There came discovery and surrender. The Samaritans discovered in Christ the Saviour of the world. It is not likely that they themselves put it exactly that way. John was writing years afterwards, and was putting the discovery of the Samaritans into his own words, words which enshrine a life-time's living with and thinking about Jesus Christ. It is only in John that we find this tremendous title. We find it here and in 1 *John* 4: 14. To him it was the title *par excellence* for Christ.

John did not invent the title. In the Old Testament God had often been called the God of salvation, the Saviour, the saving God. Many of the Greek gods had acquired this title. At the time John was writing the Roman Emperor was invested with the title Saviour of the World. It is as if John said: " All that you have dreamed of has at last in Jesus come true."

We do well to remember this title. Jesus was not simply a *prophet*, who came with a message in words from God. He was not simply an *expert psychologist* with an uncanny faculty for seeing into the human mind. True, he showed that very skill in the case of the Samaritan woman, but he showed more than that. He was not simply *an example*. He did not come simply to show men the way in which life ought to be lived. A great example can be merely heart-breaking and frustrating when we find ourselves powerless to follow it.

Jesus was *Saviour.* He rescued men from the evil and hopeless situation in which they found themselves; he broke the chains that bound them to the past and gave them a power which enabled them to meet the future. The Samaritan woman is in fact the great example of his saving power. The town where she stayed would no doubt have labelled her a character beyond reformation; and she herself would no doubt have agreed that a respectable life was beyond her. But Jesus came and doubly rescued her; he enabled her to break away from the past and he opened a new future to her. There is no title adequate to describe Jesus except Saviour of the World.

THE UNANSWERABLE ARGUMENT

John 4: 43–45

> Two days after Jesus left there and went to Galilee. Jesus himself declared that a prophet has no honour in his own country. But when he came into Galilee, the Galilaeans welcomed him, because they had seen all that he had done at Jerusalem at the Feast, for they too had gone to the Feast.

ALL three synoptic gospels tell of the saying of Jesus that a prophet has no honour in his own country (*Mark* 6: 4; *Matthew* 13: 57; *Luke* 4: 24). It was an ancient proverb with much the same meaning as our own " familiarity breeds contempt." But John introduces it in a very strange place. The other gospels introduce it on occasions when Jesus was rejected by his own countrymen; John introduces it on an occasion when he was accepted.

It may be that John is reading the mind of Jesus. We have already seen that Jesus had left Judaea and set out for Galilee to avoid the controversy that an increasing publicity was bringing to him. The hour of conflict had not yet come (*John* 4: 1–4). It may be that his astonishing success in Samaria had actually surprised him; his words about the astonishing harvest have the ring of glad surprise about them. It may well be that Jesus set out for Galilee hoping to find rest and retirement there, because he did not expect those of his native country to respond to him. And it may be that exactly the same happened in Galilee as happened in Samaria, that against all expectations there was a surge of response to his teaching. We must either explain the saying in this way or assume that somehow it has crept into the wrong place.

However that may be, this passage and the one before give us the unanswerable argument for Christ. The Samaritans believed in Jesus, not because of someone else's story but because they themselves had heard him speak things whose like they had never heard. The Galilaeans believed in him, not because someone had told them about him but because they had seen him do in Jerusalem things whose like they had never seen. The words he spoke and the deeds he did were arguments to which there was no answer.

Here we have one of the great truths of the Christian life. *The only real argument for Christianity is a Christian experience.* It may be that sometimes we have to argue with people until the intellectual barriers which they have erected are battered down and the citadel of their mind capitulates. But in the great majority of cases the only persuasion we can use is to say: " I know what Jesus is like and I know what Jesus can do. All that I can ask you to do is to try him yourself and to see what happens." Effective Christian evangelism really begins when we can say: " I know what Christ has done for me," and go on to say: " Try him, and see what he can do for you."

Here again tremendous personal responsibility is laid upon us. No one is likely to attempt the experience unless our own lives show its value. There is little use in telling people that Christ will bring them joy and peace and power, if our own lives are gloomy, worried and defeated. Men will be persuaded to try the experiment only when they see that for us it has ended in an experience which is much to be desired.

A COURTIER'S FAITH

John 4: 46–54

So again he came to Cana in Galilee, where he had made the water into wine. Now there was a certain courtier whose son was ill in Capernaum. When this man heard that Jesus had come from Judaea into Galilee, he went to him and asked him to come down and heal his son, for he was going to die. Jesus said to him: " Unless you see signs and wonders you will never believe." The courtier said to him: " Sir, come down before my little lad dies." Jesus said to him: " Go your way! Your son lives! " The man believed the word which Jesus spoke to him, and started on his way home. While he was still on the way down, his slaves met him and said: " Your son lives! " So he asked them at what hour his condition had improved. They told him: " Yesterday, at one o'clock in the afternoon, the fever left him." The father knew that that was the hour at which Jesus said to him: " Your son lives! " And he and his whole household believed.

This is the second sign which Jesus did after he had come from Judaea into Galilee.

MOST of the commentators think this is another version of the story of the healing of the centurion's servant told in *Matthew* 8: 5–13 and *Luke* 7: 1–10; but there are differences which justify us in treating it as quite independent. Certain things about the conduct of this courtier are an example to all men.

(i) *Here is a courtier who came to a carpenter*. The Greek is *basilikos* which could even mean that he was a petty king; but it is used for a royal official and he was a man of high standing at the court of Herod. Jesus on the other hand had no greater status than that of the village carpenter of Nazareth. Further, Jesus was in Cana and this man lived in Capernaum, almost twenty miles away. That is why he took so long to get back home.

There could be no more improbable scene in the world than an important court official hastening twenty miles to beg a favour from a village carpenter. First and foremost, this courtier swallowed his pride. He was in need, and neither convention nor custom stopped him bringing his need to Christ. His action would cause a sensation but he did not care what people said so long as he obtained the help he so much wanted. If we want the help which Christ can give we must be humble enough to swallow our pride and not care what any man may say.

(ii) *Here is a courtier who refused to be discouraged.* Jesus met him with the at first sight bleak statement that people would not believe unless they were supplied with signs and wonders. It may well be that Jesus aimed that saying, not so much at the courtier himself, as at the crowd that must have gathered to see the outcome of this sensational happening. They would be there all agape to see what would happen.

But Jesus had a way of making sure that a person was in earnest. He did that to the Syro-Phoenician woman (*Matthew* 15: 21–28). If the man had turned irritably and petulantly away; if he had been too proud to accept a rebuke; if he had given up despairingly on the spot—Jesus would have known that his faith was not real. A man must be in earnest before the help of Christ can come to him.

(iii) *Here was a courtier who had faith.* It must have been hard for him to turn away and go home with Jesus's assurance that his little lad would live. Nowadays men are beginning to realize the power of thought and of telepathy in such a way that no one would reject this miracle simply because it was wrought at a distance; but it must have been difficult for the courtier. Yet he had faith enough to turn and walk back that twenty mile road with nothing but Jesus's assurance to comfort his heart.

It is of the very essence of faith that we should believe that what Jesus says is true. So often we have a kind of vague, wistful longing that the promises of Jesus should be true. The only way really to enter into them is to believe in them with the clutching intensity of a drowning man. If Jesus says a thing, it is not a case of " It *may* be true "; it is a case of " It *must* be true."

(iv) *Here was a courtier who surrendered.* He was not a man who got out of Christ what he wanted and then went away to forget. He and all his household believed. That would not be easy for him, for the idea of Jesus as the Anointed One of God must have cut across all his preconceived notions. Nor would it be easy at the court of Herod to profess faith in Jesus. He would have mockery and laughter to endure; and no doubt there would be those who thought that he had gone slightly mad.

But this courtier was a man who faced and accepted the facts. He had seen what Jesus could do; he had experienced it; and there was nothing left for it but surrender. He had begun with a sense of desperate need; that need had been supplied; and his sense of need had turned into an overmastering love. That must always be the story of the Christian life.

Most New Testament scholars think that at this point in the Fourth Gospel the chapters have somehow become misplaced. The hold that chapter 6 should come *before* chapter 5. The reason is this. Chapter 4 finishes with Jesus in Galilee (*John* 4: 54). Chapter 5 begins with Jesus in Jerusalem. Chapter 6 again shows us Jesus in Galilee. Chapter 7 begins with the implication that Jesus had just come into Galilee because of the opposition which he met in Jerusalem. The changes between Jerusalem and Galilee become very difficult to follow. On the other hand chapter 4 (4: 54) ends: " This the second sign that Jesus did, when he had come from Judaea to Galilee." Chapter 6 begins (6: 1): " After this thing Jesus went to the other side of the Sea of Galilee," which would be a natural sequence. Chapter 5 then shows us Jesus going to Jerusalem for a Feast and meeting with very serious trouble with the Jewish authorities. We are in fact told that from that time they began to persecute him (5: 10). Then chapter 7 begins by saying that Jesus went about in Galilee and " would not go about in Judea, because the Jews sought to kill him " (7: 1).

Here we have not altered the order; but we must note that to take chapter 6 before chapter 5 does give an easier and more natural order of events.

MAN'S HELPLESSNESS AND CHRIST'S POWER

John 5: 1–9

> After this there was a Feast of the Jews, and Jesus went up to
> Jerusalem. In Jerusalem, near the sheepgate, there is a bathing-
> pool with five porches, which is called in Hebrew Bethzatha. In
> these porches there lay a crowd of people who were ill and blind
> and lame and whose limbs were withered (waiting expectantly for
> the moving of the water. For an angel of the Lord came down into
> the pool every now and then and disturbed the water; so the first
> person to go in after the disturbing of the water regained his
> health from any illness which had him in its grip). There was a
> man there who had been ill for thirty-eight years. When Jesus saw
> him lying there, and since he knew that he had already been there
> for a long time, he said to him: " Do you want to be made well? "
> The sick man answered: " Sir, I have no one to hurry me into the
> pool when the water is disturbed; so, while I am on the way,
> someone gets down before me." Jesus said to him: " Get up! Lift
> your bed! and walk! " And the man was made well, and he lifted
> up his bed and walked.

THERE were three Jewish feasts which were feasts of obliga-
tion—Passover, Pentecost and Tabernacles. Every adult male
Jew who lived within fifteen miles of Jerusalem was legally
bound to attend them. If we take chapter 6 before chapter 5 we
may think of this feast as Pentecost, because the events of
chapter 6 happened when the Passover was near (*John* 6: 4).
The Passover was in mid-April, and Pentecost was seven weeks
later. John always shows us Jesus attending the great feasts, for
Jesus did not disregard the obligations of Jewish worship. To
him it was not a duty but a delight to worship with his own
people.

When Jesus arrived in Jerusalem he was apparently alone;
there is no mention of his disciples. He found his way to a
famous pool. Its name was either *Bethesda*, which means
House of Mercy, or more likely, *Bethzatha* which means House
of the Olive. The better manuscripts all have the second name,

and we know from Josephus that there was a quarter of
Jerusalem actually known as Bethzatha. The word for *pool* is
kolumbēthron, which comes from the verb *kolumban, to dive*.
The pool was deep enough to swim in. The passage we have put
in brackets is not in any of the greatest and best manuscripts
and was probably added later as an explanation of what people
were doing at the pool. Beneath the pool was a subterranean
stream which every now and again bubbled up and disturbed
the waters. The belief was that the disturbance was caused by
an angel, and that the first person to get into the pool after the
troubling of the water would be healed from any illness from
which he was suffering.

To us this is mere superstition. But it was the kind of belief
which was spread all over the world in ancient days and which
still exists in certain places. People believed in all kinds of
spirits and demons. The air was thick with them; they had their
abodes in certain places; every tree, every river, every stream,
every hill, every pool had its resident spirit.

Further, ancient peoples were specially impressed with the
holiness of water and especially of rivers and springs. Water
was so precious and rivers in spate could be so powerful that it
is not surprising that they were so impressed. In the west we
may know water only as something which comes out of a tap;
but in the ancient world, as in many places still to-day, water
was the most valuable and potentially the most dangerous of all
things.

Sir J. G. Frazer in *Folk-lore in the Old Testament* (ii,
412-423) quotes many instances of this reverence for water.
Hesiod, the Greek poet, said that when a man was about to ford
a river, he should pray and wash his hands, for he who wades
through a stream with unwashed hands incurs the wrath of the
gods. When the Persian king Xerxes came to the Strymon in
Thrace his magicians offered white horses and went through
other ceremonies before the army ventured to cross. Lucullus,
the Roman general, offered a bull to the River Euphrates before
he crossed it. To this day in south-east Africa some of the
Bantu tribes believe that rivers are inhabited by malignant

spirits which must be propitiated by flinging a handful of corn or some other offering into the river before it is crossed. When anyone is drowned in a river he is said to be " called by the spirits." The Baganda in Central Africa would not try to rescue a man carried away by a river because they thought that the spirits had taken him. The people who waited for the pool in Jerusalem to be disturbed were children of their age believing the things of their age.

It may be that as Jesus walked around, the man of this story was pointed out to him as a most pitiable case, because his disability made it very unlikely, even impossible, that he would ever be the first to get into the pool after it had been troubled. He had no one to help him in, and Jesus was always the friend of the friendless, and the helper of the man who has no earthly help. He did not trouble to read the man a lecture on the useless superstition of waiting for the water to be moved. His one desire was to help and so he healed the man who had waited so long.

In this story we see very clearly the conditions under which the power of Jesus operated. He gave his orders to men and, in proportion as they tried to obey, power came to them.

(i) Jesus began by asking the man if he wanted to be cured. It was not so foolish a question as it may sound. The man had waited for thirty-eight years and it might well have been that hope had died and left behind a passive and dull despair. In his heart of hearts the man might be well content to remain an invalid for, if he was cured, he would have to shoulder all the burden of making a living. There are invalids for whom invalidism is not unpleasant, because someone else does all he working and all the worrying. But this man's response was immediate. He wanted to be healed, though he did not see how he ever could be since he had no one to help him.

The first essential towards receiving the power of Jesus is to have intense desire for it. Jesus says: " Do you really want to be changed? " If in our inmost hearts we are well content to stay as we are, there can be no change for us.

(ii) Jesus went on to tell the man to get up. It is as if he said to him: " Man, bend your will to it and you and I will do this thing together! " The power of God never dispenses with the effort of man. Nothing is truer than that we must realize our own helplessness; but in a very real sense it is true that miracles happen when our will and God's power co-operate to make them possible.

(iii) In effect Jesus was commanding the man to attempt the impossible. " Get up! " he said. His bed would simply be a light stretcher-like frame—the Greek is *krabbatos*, a colloquial word which really means a pallet—and Jesus told him to pick it up and carry it away. The man might well have said with a kind of injured resentment that for thirty-eight years his bed had been carrying him and there was not much sense in telling him to carry it. But he made the effort along with Christ—and the thing was done.

(iv) Here is the road to achievement. There are so many things in this world which defeat us. When we have intensity of desire and determination to make the effort, hopeless though it may seem, the power of Christ gets its opportunity, and with him we can conquer what for long has conquered us.

THE INNER MEANING

John 5: 1–9 (*continued*)

CERTAIN scholars think this passage is an allegory.

The *man* stands for the people of Israel. The *five porches* stand for the five books of the law. In the porches the people lay ill. The law could show a man his sin, but could never mend it; the law could uncover a man's weakness, but could never cure it. The law, like the porches, sheltered the sick soul but could never heal it. The *thirty-eight years* stand for the thirty-eight years in which the Jews wandered in the desert before they entered the promised land; or for the number of the centuries men had been waiting for the Messiah. The *stirring of the waters* stands for baptism. In point of fact in early Christian art a man is often depicted as rising from the baptismal waters carrying a bed upon his back.

It may well be that it is now possible to read all these meanings into this story; but it is highly unlikely that John wrote it as an allegory. It has the vivid stamp of factual truth. But we do well to remember that any Bible story has in it far more than fact. There are always deeper truths below the surface and even the simple stories are meant to leave us face to face with eternal things.

HEALING AND HATRED

John 5: 10–18

It was Sabbath on that day. So the Jews said to the man who had been cured: " It is Sabbath and you have no right to lift your bed." He answered them: " He who made me well, it was he who said to me: ' Lift your bed and walk! ' " They asked him: " Who is the fellow who said to you: ' Lift your bed and walk '? " The man who had been cured did not know who he was, for Jesus had slipped away, for there was a crowd in the place. Afterwards Jesus found him in the Temple and said to him: " Look now! You have been made well. Sin no more in case something worse happens to you! " The man went away and told the Jews that it was Jesus who had made him well. Because of this the Jews were out to persecute Jesus, because he had done these things on the Sabbath. But Jesus answered them: " My Father continues his work until now, and so do I continue mine." Because of this the Jews tried all the harder to find a way to kill him, because not only was he habitually breaking the Sabbath, but he also kept on saying that God was his own Father, thereby making himself equal with God.

A MAN had been healed from a disease which, humanly speaking, was incurable. We might expect this to be an occasion of universal joy and thanksgiving; but some met the whole business with bleak and black looks. The man who had been healed was walking through the streets carrying his bed; the orthodox Jews stopped him and reminded him that he was breaking the law by carrying a burden on the Sabbath day.

We have already seen what the Jews did with the law of God. It was a series of great wide principles which men were left to

apply and carry out but throughout the years the Jews had
made it into thousands of little rules and regulations. The law
simply said that the Sabbath day must be different from other
days and that on it neither a man nor his servants nor his
animals must work; the Jews set out thirty-nine different
classifications of work, one of which was that it consisted in
carrying a burden.

They founded particularly on two passages. Jeremiah had
said: " Thus saith the Lord: take heed for the sake of your lives,
and do not bear a burden on the Sabbath day or bring it in by
the gates of Jerusalem. And do not carry a burden out of your
houses on the Sabbath or do any work, but keep the Sabbath
day holy, as I commanded your fathers " (*Jeremiah* 17: 19–27).
Nehemiah had been worried at the work and the trading that
went on on the Sabbath day and had stationed servants at the
gates of Jerusalem to see that no burdens were carried in or out
on the Sabbath (*Nehemiah* 13: 15–19).

Nehemiah 13: 15 makes it perfectly clear that what was in
question was trading on the Sabbath as if it had been an
ordinary day. But the Rabbis of Jesus's day solemnly argued
that a man was sinning if he carried a needle in his robe on the
Sabbath. They even argued as to whether he could wear his
artificial teeth or his wooden leg. They were quite clear that any
kind of brooch could not be worn on the Sabbath. To them all
this petty detail was a matter of life and death—and certainly
this man was breaking the rabbinic law by carrying his bed on
the Sabbath day.

His defence was that the man who had healed him had told
him to do it, but he did not know his identity. Later Jesus met
him in the Temple; at once the man hastened to tell the
authorities that Jesus was the one in question. He was not
seeking to get Jesus into trouble, but the actual words of the law
were: " If anyone carries anything from a public place to a
private house on the Sabbath intentionally he is punishable by
death by stoning." He was simply trying to explain that it was
not his fault that he had broken the law.

So the authorities levelled their accusations against Jesus.

The verbs in verse 18 are *imperfect tense*, which describes repeated action in past time. Clearly this story is only a sample of what Jesus habitually did.

His defence was shattering. God did not stop working on the Sabbath day and neither did he. Any scholarly Jew would grasp its full force. Philo had said: " God never ceases doing, but as it is the property of fire to burn and snow to chill, so it is the property of God to do." Another writer said: " The sun shines; the rivers flow; the processes of birth and death go on on the Sabbath as on any other day; and that is the work of God." True, according to the creation story, God rested on the seventh day; but he rested from *creation*; his higher works of judgment and mercy and compassion and love still went on.

Jesus said: " Even on the Sabbath God's love and mercy and compassion act; *and so do mine.*" It was this last passage which shattered the Jews, for it meant nothing less than that the work of Jesus and the work of God were the same. It seemed that Jesus was putting himself on an equality with God. What Jesus really was saying we shall see in our next section; but at the moment we must note this—Jesus teaches that human need must always be helped; that there is no greater task than to relieve someone's pain and distress and that the Christian's compassion must be like God's—unceasing. Other work may be laid aside but the work of compassion never.

Another Jewish belief enters into this passage. When Jesus met the man in the Temple he told him to sin no more in case something worse might happen to him. To the Jew sin and suffering were inextricably connected. If a man suffered, necessarily he had sinned; nor could he ever be cured until his sin was forgiven. The Rabbis said: " The sick arises not from sickness, until his sins be forgiven." The man might argue that he had sinned and been forgiven and had, so to speak, got away with it; and he might go on to argue that, since he had found someone who could release him from the consequences of sin, he could very well go on sinning and escaping. There were those in the church who used their liberty as an excuse for the flesh (*Galatians* 5: 13). There were those who sinned in the confidence that grace would abound (*Romans* 6: 1–18). There have always been those who have used the love and the forgiveness and the grace of God as an excuse to sin. But we have only to think what God's forgiveness cost, we have only to look at the Cross of Calvary, to know that we must ever hate sin because every sin breaks again the heart of God.

THE TREMENDOUS CLAIMS

John 5: 19–29

This is the truth I tell you—the Son cannot do anything which proceeds from himself. He can only do what he sees the Father doing. In whatever way the Father acts, the Son likewise acts in the same way; for the Father loves the son and has shown him everything that he does. And he will show him greater works than these, so that you will be moved to wondering amazement. For, as the Father raises the dead and makes them alive, so also the Son makes alive those whom he wishes. Neither does the Father judge anyone, but he has given the whole process of judging to the Son, that all may honour the Son, as they honour the Father. He who does not honour the Son does not honour the Father who sent him.

This is the truth I tell you—he who listens to my word and believes on him who sent me has eternal life, and is not on the way to judgment, but he has crossed from death to life.

This is the truth I tell you—the hour is coming and now is when the dead will hear the voice of the Son of God, and, when they have heard, they will live. For, as the Father has life in himself, so he has given to the Son to have life in himself; and he has given him authority to exercise the process of judgment, because he is the Son of Man. Do not be astonished at this, for the hour is coming when everyone in the tombs will hear his voice, and will come forth; those who have done good will come out to a resurrection which will give them life, but those whose actions were base will come out to a resurrection which will issue in judgment.

HERE we come to the first of the long discourses of the Fourth
Gospel. When we read passages like this we must remember
that John is not seeking so much to give us the words that Jesus
spoke as the things which Jesus meant. He was writing
somewhere round about A.D. 100. For seventy years he had
thought about Jesus and the wonderful things which Jesus had
said. Many of these things he had not fully understood when he
had heard them. But more than half a century of thinking under
the guidance of the Holy Spirit had shown him deeper and
deeper meaning in the words of Jesus. And so he sets down for
us not only what Jesus said, but also what Jesus meant.

This passage is so important that we must first study it as a
whole and then take it in shorter sections.

First, then, let us look at it as a whole. We must try to think
not only how it sounds to us, but also how it sounded to the
Jews who heard it for the first time. They had a background of
thoughts and ideas, of theology and belief, of literature and
religion which is very far from our background; and, to
understand a passage like this, we must try to think ourselves
into the mind of a Jew who listened to it for the first time.

This is an amazing passage, because it is woven together of
thoughts and expressions which are all claims by Jesus to be the
promised Messiah. Many of these claims we do not now readily
see, but they would be crystal clear to the Jews and would leave
them aghast.

(i) The clearest claim is the statement that Jesus is the Son of
Man. We know how common that strange title is in the gospels.
It has a long history. It was born in *Daniel* 7: 1–14. The
Authorized Version mistranslates *the Son of Man* for *a* son of
man (*Daniel* 7: 13).

The point of the passage is this. *Daniel* was written in days
of terror and of persecution, and it is a vision of the glory which
will some day replace the suffering which the people are under-
going. In *Daniel* 7: 1–7 the seer describes the great heathen
empires which have held sway under the symbolism of beasts.
There is the lion with eagle's wings (7: 4), which stands for the
Babylonian Empire; the bear with the three ribs in his mouth,

as one devouring the carcase (7: 5), which stands for the Median Empire; the leopard with four wings and four heads (7: 6), which stands for the Persian Empire; the beast, great and terrible, with iron teeth and with ten horns (7:7), which stands for the Macedonian Empire. All these terrible powers will pass away and the power and the dominion will be given to one *like a son of man.* The meaning is that the Empires which have held sway have been so savage that they could be described only in terms of wild beasts; but into the world there is going to come a power so gentle and kind that it will be human and not bestial. In *Daniel* the phrase describes the kind of power which is going to rule the world.

Someone has to introduce and exercise that power; and the Jews took this title and gave it to the chosen one of God who some day would bring in the new age of gentleness and love and peace; and so they came to call the Messiah *Son of Man.* Between the Old and the New Testaments there arose a whole literature which dealt with the golden age which was to come.

One book which was specially influential was the *Book of Enoch* and in it there appears again and again a great figure called *That Son of Man,* who is waiting in heaven until God sends him to earth to bring in his kingdom and rule over it. So when Jesus called himself the Son of Man, he was doing nothing less than call himself the Messiah. Here was a claim so clear that it could not be misunderstood.

(ii) But not only is this claim to be God's Messiah made in so many words; in phrase after phrase it is implicit. The very miracle which had happened to the paralysed man was a sign that Jesus was Messiah. It was Isaiah's picture of the new age of God that " then shall the lame man leap like a hart " (*Isaiah* 35: 6). It was Jeremiah's vision that the blind and the lame would be gathered in (*Jeremiah* 31: 8, 9).

(iii) There is Jesus's repeated claim to raise the dead and to be their judge when they are raised. In the Old Testament God alone can raise the dead and alone has the right to judge. " I, even I, am he and there is no god beside me: I kill and I make alive " (*Deuteronomy* 32: 39). " The Lord kills and brings to

life " (1 *Samuel* 2: 6). When Naaman, the Syrian, came seeking
to be cured from leprosy, the king of Israel said in bewildered
despair: " Am I God to kill and to make alive? " (2 *Kings* 5: 6).
The function of killing and making alive belonged inalienably to
God. It is the same with judgment. " The judgment is God's "
(*Deuteronomy* 1: 17).

In later thought this function of resurrecting the dead and
then acting as judge became part of the duty of God's chosen
one when he brought in the new age of God. *Enoch* says of the
Son of Man: " The sum of judgment was committed to him "
(*Enoch* 69: 26, 27). Jesus in our passage speaks of those who
have done good being resurrected to life and of those who have
done evil being resurrected to death. *The Apocalypse of Baruch*
lays it down that when God's age comes: " The aspect of those
who now act wickedly shall become worse than it is, as they
shall suffer torment," whereas those who have trusted in the law
and acted upon it shall be clothed in beauty and in splendour
(*Baruch* 51: 1–4). *Enoch* has it that in that day: " The earth
shall be wholly rent asunder, and all that is on earth shall perish,
and there shall be judgment on all men " (*Enoch* 1: 5–7). *The
Testament of Benjamin* has it: " All men shall rise, some to the
exalted, and some to be humbled and put to shame."

For Jesus to speak like this was an act of the most
extraordinary and unique courage. He must have known well
that to make claims like this would sound the sheerest blasphemy to the orthodox Jewish leaders and was to court death.
The man who listened to words like this had only two alter-
natives—he must either accept Jesus as the Son of God or hate
him as a blasphemer.

We now go on to take this passage section by section.

THE FATHER AND THE SON

John 5: 19, 20

This is the truth I tell you—the Son cannot do anything which
proceeds from himself. He can only do what he sees the Father

doing. In whatever way the Father acts, the Son likewise acts in
the same way; for the Father loves the Son, and has shown him
everything that he does. And he will show him greater works than
these, so that you will be moved to wondering amazement.

THIS is the beginning of Jesus's answer to the Jews' charge that
he was making himself equal to God. He lays down three things
about his relationship with God.

(i) He lays down his *identity* with God. The salient truth
about Jesus is that in him we see God. If we wish to see how
God feels to men, if we wish to see how God reacts to sin, if we
wish to see how God regards the human situation, we must look
at Jesus. The mind of Jesus is the mind of God; the words of
Jesus are the words of God; the actions of Jesus are the actions
of God.

(ii) This identity is not so much based on equality as on
complete *obedience*. Jesus never did what he wanted to do but
always what God wanted him to do. It is because his will was
completely submitted to God's will that we see God in him.
Jesus is to God as we must be to Jesus.

(iii) This obedience is not based on submission to power; it is
based on *love*. The unity between Jesus and God is a unity of
love. We speak of two minds having only a single thought and
two hearts beating as one. In human terms that is a perfect
description of the relationship between Jesus and God. There is
such complete identity of mind and will and heart that Father
and Son are one.

But this passage has something still more to tell us about
Jesus.

(i) It tells us of his complete *confidence*. He is quite sure that
what men were seeing then was only a beginning. On purely
human grounds the one thing Jesus might reasonably expect
was death. The forces of Jewish orthodoxy were gathering
against him and the end was already sure. But Jesus was quite
certain that the future was in the hands of God and that men
could not stop what God had sent him to do.

(ii) It tells of his complete *fearlessness*. That he would be
misunderstood was certain. That his words would inflame the

minds of his hearers and endanger his own life was beyond argument. There was no human situation in which Jesus would lower his claims or adulterate the truth. He would make his claim and speak his truth no matter what men might threaten to do. To him it was much more important to be true to God than to fear men.

LIFE, JUDGMENT AND HONOUR

John 5: 21–23

> For as the Father raises the dead and makes them alive, so the Son also makes alive those whom he wishes. Neither does the Father judge anyone, but he has given the whole process of judging to the Son, that all may honour the Son, as they honour the Father. He who does not honour the Son does not honour the Father who sent him.

HERE we see three great functions which belong to Jesus Christ as the Son of God.

(i) He is *the giver of life*. John meant this in a double sense. He meant it *in time*. No man is fully alive until Jesus Christ enters into him and he enters into Jesus Christ. When we make the discovery of the realm of music or of literature or of art or of travel, we sometimes speak of a new world opening out to us. That man into whose life Jesus Christ has entered finds life made new. He himself is changed; his personal relationships are changed; his conception of work and duty and pleasure is changed; his relationship to God is changed. He meant it in *eternity*. After this life is ended, for the man who has accepted Jesus Christ there opens life still more full and still more wonderful; while for the man who has refused Jesus Christ, there comes that death which is separation from God. Jesus Christ gives life both in this world and the world to come.

(ii) He is *the bringer of judgment*. John says that God committed the whole process of judgment to Jesus Christ. What he means is this—a man's judgment depends on his reaction to

Jesus. If he finds in Jesus the one person to be loved and followed, he is on the way to life. If he sees in Jesus an enemy, he has condemned himself. Jesus is the touchstone by which all men are tested; reaction to him is the test by which all men are divided.

(iii) He is *the receiver of honour.* The most uplifting thing about the New Testament is its unquenchable hope and its unconquerable certainty. It tells the story of a crucified Christ and yet never has any doubt that at the end all men will be drawn to that crucified figure and that all men will know him and acknowledge him and love him. Amid persecution and disregard, in spite of smallness of numbers and poverty of influence, in the face of failure and disloyalty, the New Testament and the early church never doubted the ultimate triumph of Christ. When we are tempted to despair we would do well to remember that the salvation of men is the purpose of God and that nothing, in the end, can frustrate his will. The evil will of man may delay God's purpose; it cannot defeat it.

ACCEPTANCE MEANS LIFE

John 5:24

This is the truth I tell you—he who listens to my word and believes on him who sent me has eternal life, and is not on the way to judgment, but he has crossed from death to life.

JESUS says quite simply that to accept him is life; and to reject him is death. What does it mean to listen to Jesus's word and to believe in the Father who sent him? To put it at its briefest it means three things. (i) It means to believe that God is as Jesus says he is; that he is love; and so to enter into a new relationship with him in which fear is banished. (ii) It means to accept the way of life that Jesus offers us, however difficult it may be and whatever sacrifices it may involve, certain that to accept it is the ultimate way to peace and to happiness, and to refuse it the ultimate way to death and judgment. (iii) It means to accept the help that the Risen Christ gives and the guidance that the Holy Spirit offers, and so to find strength for all that the way of Christ involves.

When we do that we enter into three new relationships. (i) We enter into a new relationship with God. The judge becomes the father; the distant becomes the near; strangeness becomes intimacy and fear becomes love. (ii) We enter into a new relationship with our fellow men. Hatred becomes love; selfishness becomes service; and bitterness becomes forgiveness. (iii) We enter into a new relationship with ourselves. Weakness becomes strength; frustration becomes achievement; and tension becomes peace.

To accept the offer of Jesus Christ is to find life. Everyone in one sense may be said to be alive; but there are few who can be said to know life in the real sense of the term. When Grenfell was writing to a nursing sister about her decision to come out to Labrador to help in his work there, he told her that he could not offer her much money, but that if she came she would discover that in serving Christ and the people of the country she would have the time of her life. Browning describes the meeting of two people into whose hearts love had entered. She looked at him, he looked at her, and " suddenly life awoke." A modern novelist makes one character say to another: " I never knew what life was till I saw it in your eyes."

The person who accepts the way of Christ has passed from death to life. In this world life becomes new and thrilling; in the world to come eternal life with God becomes a certainty.

DEATH AND LIFE

John 5: 25–29

This is the truth I tell you—the hour is coming and now is when the dead will hear the voice of the Son of God, and, when they have heard, they will live. For, as the Father has life in himself, so he has given to the Son to have life in himself. And he has given him authority to exercise the process of judgment, because he is

the Son of Man. Do not be astonished at this, for the hour is
coming when everyone in the tombs will hear his voice and will
come forth; those who have done good will come out to a
resurrection which will give them life, but those whose actions
were base will come out to a resurrection which will issue in
judgment.

HERE the Messianic claims of Jesus stand out most clearly. He
is the Son of Man; he is the life-giver and the life-bringer; he
will raise the dead to life and, when they are raised, he will be
their judge.

In this passage John seems to use the word *dead* in two
senses.

(i) He uses it of those who are spiritually dead; to them Jesus
will bring new life. What does it mean?

(*a*) To be spiritually dead is to have stopped trying. It is to
have come to look on all faults as ineradicable and all virtues as
unattainable. But the Christian life cannot stand still; it must
either go on or slip back; and to stop trying is therefore to slip
back to death.

(*b*) To be spiritually dead is to *have stopped feeling*. There are
many people who at one time felt intensely in face of the sin and
the sorrow and the suffering of the world; but slowly they have
become insensitive. They can look at evil and feel no indigna-
tion; they can look at sorrow and suffering and feel no
answering sword of grief and pity pierce their heart. When
compassion goes the heart is dead.

(*c*) To be spiritually dead is *to have stopped thinking*. J.
Alexander Findlay tells of a saying of a friend of his—" When
you reach a conclusion you're dead." He meant that when a
man's mind becomes so shut that it can accept no new truth, he
is mentally and spiritually dead. The day when the desire to
learn leaves us, the day when new truth, new methods, new
thought become simply a disturbance with which we cannot be
bothered, is the day of our spiritual death.   (*d*) To be spiritually dead is *to have stopped repenting*. The day when a man can
sin in peace is the day of his spiritual death; and it is easy to
slip into that frame of mind. The first time we do a wrong thing,

we do it with fear and regret. If we do it a second time, it is easier to do it. If we do it a third time, it is easier yet. If we go on doing it, the time comes when we scarcely give it a thought. To avoid spiritual death a man must keep himself sensitive to sin by keeping himself sensitive to the presence of Jesus Christ. (ii) John also uses the word *dead* literally. Jesus teaches that the resurrection will come and that what happens to a man in the after-life is inextricably bound up with what he has done in this life. The awful importance of this life is that it determines eternity. All through it we are fitting or unfitting ourselves for the life to come, making ourselves fit or unfit for the presence of God. We choose either the way which leads to life or the way which leads to death.

THE ONLY TRUE JUDGMENT

John 5: 30

> I cannot do anything which originates in myself. As I hear, so I judge. But the judgment which I exercise is just, because I do not seek to do what I wish to do, but I seek to do what he who sent me wishes to do.

IN the preceding passage Jesus has claimed the right of judgment. It was not unnatural that men should ask by what right he proposed to judge others. His answer was that his judgment was true and final because he had no desire to do anything other than the will of God. His claim was that his judgment was the judgment of God.

It is very difficult for any man to judge another man fairly. If we will honestly examine ourselves we will see that many motives may affect our judgment. It may be rendered unfair by *injured pride*. It may be rendered blind by our *prejudices*. It may be made bitter by *jealousy*. It may be made arrogant by *contempt*. It may be made harsh by *intolerance*. It may be made condemnatory by *self-righteousness*. It may be affected by our *own self-conceit*. It may be based on *envy*. It may be vitiated by an insensitive or deliberate *ignorance*. Only a man whose heart is pure and whose motives are completely un-mixed can rightly judge another man—which means to say that no man can.

On the other hand the judgment of God is perfect.

God alone is *holy* and therefore he alone knows the standards by which all men must be judged. God alone is perfectly *loving* and his judgment alone is delivered in the charity in which all true judgment must be given. God alone has full *knowledge* and judgment can be perfect only when it takes into account *all* the circumstances. The claim of Jesus to judge is based on the claim that in him is the perfect mind of God. He does not judge with the inevitable mixture of human motives; he judges with the perfect holiness, the perfect love and the perfect sympathy of God.

WITNESS TO CHRIST

John 5: 31–36

> If I bear witness about myself, my witness need not be accepted as true; but it is Another who is bearing witness about me, and I know that the witness which he bears about me is true. You sent your envoys to John, and he bore witness to the truth; but the testimony which I receive is not from any man, but I say these things that you may be saved. He was the lamp which burns and shines. For a time you were pleased to take pleasure in his light. But I have a greater testimony than John's. The works which the Father granted to me to accomplish, the very works which I do, are evidence about me to prove that my Father has sent me.

ONCE again Jesus is answering the charges of his opponents. His opponents are demanding. " What evidence can you adduce that your claims are true? " Jesus argues in a way that the Rabbis would understand for he uses their own methods.

(i) He begins by admitting the universal principle that the unsupported evidence of one person cannot be taken as proof.

There must be at least two witnesses. " On the evidence of two witnesses or of three witnesses he that is to die shall be put to death; a person shall not be put to death on the evidence of one witness " (*Deuteronomy* 17: 6). " A single witness shall not prevail against a man for any crime or for any wrong in connection with any offence that he has committed; only on the evidence of two witnesses, or of three witnesses, shall a charge be sustained " (*Deuteronomy* 19: 15). When Paul threatens to come to the Corinthians with rebuke and discipline he says that all his charges will be confirmed by two or three witnesses (2 *Corinthians* 13: 1). Jesus says that when a Christian has a legitimate complaint against a brother he must take with him some others to confirm the charge (*Matthew* 18: 16). In the early church it was the rule that no charge against an elder was entertained unless it was supported by two or three witnesses (1 *Timothy* 5: 19). Jesus began by fully admitting the normal Jewish law of evidence.

Further, it was universally held that a man's evidence about himself could not be accepted. The *Mishnah* said: " A man is not worthy of belief when he is speaking about himself." Demosthenes, the great Greek orator, laid it down as a principle of justice: " The laws do not allow a man to give evidence on his own behalf." Ancient law well knew that self-interest had an effect on a man's statements about himself. So Jesus agrees that his own unsupported testimony to himself need not be true.

(ii) But there are other witnesses to him. He says that " Another " is his witness, meaning God. He will return to that, but for the moment he cites John the Baptist who had repeatedly borne witness to him (*John* 1: 19, 20, 26; 1: 29; 1: 35, 36). Then Jesus pays a tribute to John and issues a rebuke to the Jewish authorities.

He says that John was the lamp which burns and shines. That was the perfect tribute to him. (*a*) A lamp bears a borrowed light. It does not light itself; it is lit. (*b*) John had warmth, for his was not the cold message of the intellect but the burning message of the kindled heart. (*c*) John had light. The function of light is to guide, and John pointed men on the way to repentance and to God. (*d*) In the nature of things a lamp burns itself out; in giving light it consumes itself. John was to decrease while Jesus increased. The true witness burns himself out for God.

In paying tribute to John, Jesus rebukes the Jews. They were pleased to take pleasure in John for a time, but they never really took him seriously. They were, as one has put it, like " gnats dancing in the sunlight," or like children playing while the sun shone. John was a pleasant sensation, to be listened to as long as he said the things they liked, and to be abandoned whenever he became awkward. Many people listen to God's truth like that; they enjoy a sermon as a performance. A famous preacher tells how after he had preached a sombre sermon on judgment, he was greeted with the comment: " That sermon was sure cute! " God's truth is not a thing by which to be pleasantly titillated; it is often something to be received in the dust and ashes of humiliation and repentance.

But Jesus does not even plead John's evidence. He says it is not the human evidence of any fallible man he is going to adduce to support his claims.

(iii) So he adduces the witness of his works. He had done that when John sent from prison to ask if he was the Messiah. He had told John's enquiring envoys to go back and tell him what they saw happening (*Matthew* 11: 4; *Luke* 7: 22). But Jesus cites his works, not to point to himself but to point to the power of God working in him and through him. His supreme witness is God.

THE WITNESS OF GOD

John 5: 37–43

And the Father who sent me has borne witness about me. You have never heard his voice, nor have you ever seen his form. You do not have his word dwelling in you, because you do not believe in the One whom he sent. You search the scriptures, because you think that in them you have eternal life. It is they which bear witness about me, yet you refuse to come to me that you may have life. I receive no glory from men; but I know you and I know that you do not have the love of God in you. I came in the name of my Father and yet you do not receive me. If another comes in his own name, you will receive him.

THE early part of this section may be taken in two ways.

(i) It may be that it refers to the unseen witness of God in a man's heart. In his first letter John writes: " He who believes in the Son of God, has the testimony (of God) in himself " (1 *John* 5: 9, 10). The Jew would have insisted that no man can ever see God. Even in the giving of the Ten Commandments " you heard the sound of words, but saw no form; there was only a voice " (*Deuteronomy* 4: 12). So this may mean: " It is true that God is invisible; and so is his witness, for it is the response which rises in the human heart when a man is confronted with me." When we are confronted with Christ we see in him the altogether lovely and the altogether wise; that conviction is the witness of God in our hearts. The Stoics held that the highest kind of knowledge comes not by thought but by what they called " arresting impressions; " a conviction seizes a man like someone laying an arresting hand on his shoulder. It may be that Jesus here means that the conviction in our hearts of his supremacy is the witness of God within.

(ii) It may be that John is really meaning that God's witness to Christ is to be found in the scriptures. To the Jew the scriptures were all in all. " He who has acquired the words of the law has acquired eternal life." " He who has the Law has a cord of grace drawn around him in this world and in the world to come." " He who says that Moses wrote even one verse of the Law in his own knowledge is a despiser of God." " This is the book of the commandments of God and the Law that endureth for ever. All they that hold it fast are appointed to life, but such as leave it shall die " (1 *Baruch* 4: 1, 2). " If food which is your life but for an hour, requires a blessing before and after it be eaten, how much more does the Law, in which lies the world that is to be, require a blessing? " The Jew searched the Law and yet failed to recognize Christ when he came. What was wrong? The best Bible students in the world, people who meticulously and continuously read scripture, rejected Jesus. How could that happen?

One thing is clear—they read scripture in the wrong way.

(i) They read it with a shut mind. They read it not to search for God but to find arguments to support their own positions. They did not really love God; they loved their own ideas about him. Water has as much chance of getting into concrete as the word of God had of getting into their minds. They did not humbly learn a theology from scripture; they used scripture to defend a theology which they themselves had produced. There is still danger that we should use the Bible to prove our beliefs and not to test them.

(ii) They made a still bigger mistake—they regarded God as having given men a written revelation. The revelation of God is a revelation in history. It is not God speaking, but God acting. The Bible itself is not his revelation; it is *the record of* his revelation. But they worshipped the Bible's words.

There is only one proper way to read the Bible—to read it as all pointing to Jesus Christ. Then many of the things which puzzle us, and sometimes distress us, are clearly seen as stages on the way, a pointing forward to Jesus Christ, who *is* the supreme revelation and by whose light all other revelation is to be tested. The Jews worshipped a God who wrote rather than a God who acted and therefore when Christ came they did not recognize him. The function of the scriptures is not to give life, but to point to him who can.

There are two most revealing things here.

(i) In verse 34 Jesus had said the purpose of his words was " that you may be saved." Here he says: " I am not looking for any glory from man." That is to say: " I am not arguing like this because I want to win an argument. I am not talking like this because I want to score off you and win the applause of men. It is because I love you and want to save you."

There is something tremendous here. When people oppose us and we argue back, what is our main feeling? Wounded pride? The conceit that hates any kind of failure? Annoyance? A desire to cram our opinions down other people's throats because we think them fools? Jesus talked as he did only because he loved men. His voice might be stern, but in the

sternness there was still the accent of yearning love; his eyes
might flash fire, but the flame was the flame of love.

(ii) Jesus says: " If another comes in his own name, him you
will receive." The Jews had their succession of impostors
claiming to be the Messiah and every one had his following (cp.
Mark 13: 6, 22; *Matthew* 24: 5, 24). Why do men follow
impostors? Because they are " men whose claims correspond
with men's own desires." The impostors came promising
empires and victory and material prosperity; Jesus came offering a Cross. The characteristic of the impostor is the offer of
the easy way; Jesus offered men the hard way of God. The
impostors perished and Christ lives on.

THE ULTIMATE CONDEMNATION

John 5: 44–47

> How can you believe when you are out for the glory that you get
> from each other, and when you do not search for the glory which
> comes from the only God? Do not think that it is I who will
> accuse you to the Father. You have an accuser—it is Moses I
> mean—on whom you set your hopes. If you had believed in
> Moses, you would have believed in me, for he wrote about me.
> If you do not believe in his writings, how will you believe in my
> words?

THE scribes and Pharisees desired the praise of men. They
dressed in such a way that everyone would recognize them.
They prayed in such a way that everyone would see. They loved
the front seats in the Synagogue. They loved the deferential
greetings of men on the street. And just because of that they
could not hear the voice of God. Why? So long as a man
measures himself against his fellow men he will be well content.
But the point is not: " Am I as good as my neighbour?"
The point is: " Am I as good as God? " " What do I look
like to him? " So long as we judge ourselves by human com-
parisons there is plenty of room for self-satisfaction, and that

kills faith, for faith is born of the sense of need. But when we compare ourselves with Jesus Christ, we are humbled to the dust, and then faith is born, for there is nothing left to do but trust to the mercy of God.

Jesus finishes with a charge that would strike home. The Jews believed the books which they believed Moses had given them to be the very word of God. Jesus said: " If you had read these books aright, you would have seen that they all pointed to me." He went on: " You think that because you have Moses to be your mediator you are safe; but Moses is the very one who will condemn you. Maybe you could not be expected to listen to me, but you are bound to listen to the words of Moses to which you attach such value—and they all spoke of me."

Here is the great and threatening truth. What had been the greatest privilege of the Jews had become their greatest condemnation. No one could condemn a man who had never had a chance. But knowledge had been given to the Jews; and the knowledge they had failed to use had become their condemnation. Responsibility is always the other side of privilege.

THE LOAVES AND FISHES

John 6: 1–13

> After these things Jesus went away across the Sea of Galilee, that is, the Sea of Tiberias. A great crowd was following him, because they were watching the signs which he did on those who were ill. Jesus went up into the hill and he was sitting there with his disciples. The Passover, the Feast of the Jews, was near. When Jesus lifted up his eyes and saw that a great crowd was coming to him, he said to Philip: " Where are we to buy bread for these to eat? " He was testing Philip when he said this, for he himself knew what he was going to do. Philip answered him: " Seven pounds worth of bread is not enough to give each of them a little to eat." One of the disciples said to him—it was Andrew, Simon Peter's brother—" There is a lad here who has five barley loaves and two little fishes. But what use are they among so many? " Jesus said:

" Make the men sit down." There was much grass in the place. So the men sat down to the number of about five thousand. So Jesus took the loaves and gave thanks for them, and dividing them up among those who were reclining there. So too he gave them of the fishes, as much as they wished. When they were satisfied, he said to the disciples: " Collect the broken pieces that are left over, so that nothing may be wasted." So they collected them, and they filled twelve baskets with the broken pieces of the loaves which remained over after the people had eaten.

THERE were times when Jesus desired to withdraw from the crowds. He was under continuous strain and needed rest. Moreover, it was necessary that sometimes he should get his disciples alone to lead them into a deeper understanding of himself. In addition, he needed time for prayer. On this particular occasion it was wise to go away before a head-on collision with the authorities took place, for the time of the final conflict had not yet come.

From Capernaum to the other side of the Sea of Galilee was a distance of about four miles and Jesus set sail. The people had been watching with astonishment the things he did; it was easy to see the direction the boat was taking; and they hastened round the top of the lake by land. The River Jordan flows into the north end of the Sea of Galilee. Two miles up the river were the fords of Jordan. Near the fords was a village called Bethsaida Julias, to distinguish it from the other Bethsaida in Galilee, and it was for that place that Jesus was making (*Luke* 9: 10). Near Bethsaida Julias, almost on the lakeside, was a little plain where the grass always grew. It was to be the scene of a wondrous happening.

At first Jesus went up into the hill behind the plain and he was sitting there with his disciples. Then the crowd began to appear in droves. It was nine miles round the top of the lake and across the ford, and they had made the journey with all speed. We are told that the Feast of the Passover was near and there would be even bigger crowds on the roads at that time. Possibly many were on the way to Jerusalem by that route. Many Galilaean pilgrims travelled north and crossed the ford and went through Peraea, and then re-crossed the Jordan near Jericho. The way was longer but it avoided the territory of the hated and dangerous Samaritans. It is likely that the great crowd was swelled by detachments of pilgrims on their way to the Passover Feast.

At sight of the crowd Jesus's sympathy was kindled. They were hungry and tired, and they must be fed. Philip was the natural man to whom to turn, for he came from Bethsaida (*John* 1: 44) and would have local knowledge. Jesus asked him where food could be got. Philip's answer was despairing. He said that even if food could be got it would cost more than two hundred *denarii* to give this vast crowd even a little each. A *denarius* was worth about 4p and was the standard day's wage for a working man. Philip calculated that it would take more than six months' wages to begin to feed a crowd like this.

Then Andrew appeared on the scene. He had discovered a lad with five barley loaves and two little fishes. Quite likely the boy had brought them as a picnic lunch. Maybe he was out for the day, and as a boy might, had got attached himself to the crowd. Andrew, as usual, was bringing people to Jesus.

The boy had not much to bring. Barley bread was the cheapest of all bread and was held in contempt. There is a regulation in the *Mishnah* about the offering that a woman who has committed adultery must bring. She must, of course, bring a trespass offering. With all offerings a meat-offering was made, and the meat-offering consisted of flour and wine and oil intermixed. Ordinarily the flour used was made of wheat; but it was laid down that, in the case of an offering for adultery, the flour could be barley flour, for barley is the food of beasts and the woman's sin was the sin of a beast. Barley bread was the bread of the very poor.

The fishes would be no bigger than sardines. Pickled fish from Galilee were known all over the Roman Empire. In those days fresh fish was an unheard-of luxury, for there was no means of transporting it any distance and keeping it in an eatable condition. Small sardine-like fish swarmed in the Sea of Galilee. They were caught and pickled and made into a kind of savoury.

The boy had his little pickled fish to help the dry barley bread down.

Jesus told the disciples to make the people sit down. He took the loaves and the fishes and he blessed them. When he did that he was acting as father of the family. The grace he used would be the one that was used in every home: " Blessed art Thou, O Lord, our God, who causest to come forth bread from the earth." The people ate and were filled. Even the word that is used for *filled* (*chortazesthai*) is suggestive. Originally, in classical Greek, it was a word used for feeding animals with fodder. When used of people it meant that they were fed to repletion.

When the people had eaten their fill, Jesus bade his disciples gather up the fragments left. Why the fragments? At Jewish feasts the regular practice was to leave something for the servants. That which was left was called the *Peah*; and no doubt the people left their usual part for those who had served them with the meal.

Of the fragments twelve baskets were taken up. No doubt each of the disciples had his basket (*kophinos*). It was bottle-shaped and no Jew ever travelled without his. Twice Juvenal (3: 14; 6: 542) talks of " the Jew with his basket and his truss of hay." (The truss of hay was to use as a bed, for many of the Jews lived a gipsy life.) The Jew with his inseparable basket was a notorious figure. He carried it partly because he was character-istically acquisitive, and partly because he needed to carry his own food if he was going to observe the Jewish rules of cleanness and uncleanness. From the fragments each of the disciples filled his basket. And so the hungry crowd were fed and more than fed.

THE MEANING OF A MIRACLE

John 6: 1–13 (*continued*)

WE will never know exactly what happened on that grassy plain near Bethsaida Julias. We may look at in in three ways.

(*a*) We may regard it simply as a miracle in which Jesus multiplied loaves and fishes. Some may find that hard to conceive of; and some may find it hard to reconcile with the fact that that is just what Jesus refused to do at his temptations (*Matthew* 4: 3, 4). If we can believe in the sheer miraculous character of this miracle, then let us continue to do so. But if we are puzzled, there are two other explanations.

(*b*) It may be that this was really a sacramental meal. In the rest of the chapter the language of Jesus is exactly that of the Last Supper, when he speaks about eating his flesh and drinking his blood. It could be that at this meal it was but a morsel, like the sacrament, that each person received; and that the thrill and wonder of the presence of Jesus and the reality of God turned the sacramental crumb into something which richly nourished their hearts and souls—as happens at every Communion Table to this day.

(*c*) There may be another and very lovely explanation. It is scarcely to be thought that the crowd left on a nine-mile expedition without making any preparations at all. If there were pilgrims with them, they would certainly possess supplies for the way. But it may be that none would produce what he had, for he selfishly— and very humanly—wished to keep it all for himself. It may then be that Jesus, with that rare smile of his, produced the little store that he and his disciples had; with sunny faith he thanked God for it and shared it out. Moved by his example, everyone who had anything did the same; and in the end there was enough, and more than enough, for all.

It may be that this is a miracle in which the presence of Jesus turned a crowd of selfish men and women into a fellowship of sharers. It may be that this story represents the biggest miracle of all—one which changed not loaves and fishes, but men and women.

However that may be, there were certain people there without whom the miracle would not have been possible.

(i) There was Andrew. There is a contrast between Andrew and Philip. Philip was the man who said: " The situation is hopeless; nothing can be done." Andrew was the man who said:

" I'll see what I can do; and I'll trust Jesus to do the rest."

It was Andrew who brought that lad to Jesus, and by bringing him made the miracle possible. No one ever knows what will come out of it when we bring someone to Jesus. If a parent trains up his child in the knowledge and the love and the fear of God, no man can say what mighty things that child may some day do for God and for men. If a Sunday School teacher brings a child to Christ, no man knows what that child may some day do for Christ and his church.

There is a tale of an old German schoolmaster who, when he entered his class of boys in the morning, used to remove his cap and bow ceremoniously to them. One asked him why he did this. His answer was: " You never know what one of these boys may some day become." He was right—because one of them was Martin Luther.

Andrew did not know what he was doing when he brought that lad to Jesus that day, but he was providing material for a miracle. We never know what possibilities we are releasing when we bring someone to Jesus.

(ii) There was the boy. He had not much to offer but in what he had Jesus found the materials of a miracle. There would have been one great deed fewer in history if that boy had withheld his loaves and fishes.

Jesus needs what we can bring him. It may not be much but he needs it. It may well be that the world is denied miracle after miracle and triumph after triumph because we will not bring to Jesus what we have and what we are. If we would lay ourselves on the altar of his service, there is no saying what he could do with us and through us. We may be sorry and embarrassed that we have not more to bring—and rightly so; but that is no reason for failing to bring what we have. Little is always much in the hands of Christ.

THE RESPONSE OF THE MOB

John 6: 14, 15

> So when the men had seen the sign which he had done, they said:
> " Truly, this is the prophet who is to come into the world." So
> Jesus, aware that they were going to come and seize him to make
> him king, withdrew again to the mountain alone.

HERE we have the reaction of the mob. The Jews were waiting
for the prophet whom they believed Moses had promised to
them. " The Lord your God will raise up for you a prophet like
me from among you, from your brethren—him you shall heed "
(*Deuteronomy* 18: 15). In that moment at Bethsaida Julias they
were willing to accept Jesus as that prophet and to carry him to
power on a wave of popular acclaim. But it was not so very
long before another mob was clamouring: " Crucify him!
Crucify him! " Why was it at that moment that the mob
acclaimed Jesus?

For one thing, they were eager to support Jesus when he gave
them what they wanted. He had healed them and fed them; and
they would thereupon have made him their leader. There is such
a thing as a bought loyalty. There is such a thing as cupboard
love. Dr. Johnson, in one of his more cynical moments, defined
gratitude as " a lively sense of favours still to come."

The attitude of that mob disgusts us. But are we so very
different? When we want comfort in sorrow, when we want
strength in difficulty, when we want peace in turmoil, when we
want help in face of depression, there is no one so wonderful as
Jesus and we talk to him and walk with him and open our
hearts to him. But when he comes to us with some stern
demand for sacrifice, with some challenge to effort, with the
offer of some cross, we will have nothing to do with him. When
we examine our hearts, it may be that we will find that we too
love Jesus for what we can get out of him.

For another thing, they wished to use him for their own
purposes and to mould him to their own dreams. They were

waiting for the Messiah; but they visualized him in their own way. They looked for a Messiah who would be king and conqueror, who would set his foot upon the eagle's neck and drive the Romans from the land. They had seen what Jesus could do; and the thought in their minds was: " This man has power, marvellous power. If we can harness him and his power to our dreams, things will begin to happen." If they had been honest, they would have had to admit that they wished to make use of him.

Again, are we so very different? When we appeal to Christ, is it for strength to go on with our own schemes and ideas, or is it for humility and obedience to accept his plans and wishes? Is our prayer: " Lord, give me strength to do what you want me to do " or is it in reality: " Lord, give me strength to do what I want to do "?

That crowd of Jews would have followed Jesus at that moment because he was giving them what they wanted and they wished to use him for their own purposes. That attitude still lingers. We would like Christ's gifts without his Cross; we would like to use him instead of allowing him to use us.

A VERY PRESENT HELP IN
TIME OF TROUBLE

John 6: 16–21

When evening came, his disiples went down to the sea, and, when they had embarked upon a boat, they started across the sea to Capernaum. By this time darkness had come on, and Jesus had not yet come to them; and the sea was roused because a great wind was blowing. So, when they had rowed between three and four miles, they saw Jesus walking on the sea, and coming near the boat, and they were afraid. But he said to them: " It is I; don't be afraid." So they wished to take him on board the boat; and immediately the boat reached the land for which they were making.

THIS is one of the most wonderful stories in the Fourth Gospel, and it is all the more wonderful when we press behind the meaning of the Greek to find that it really describes not some extraordinary miracle, but a simple incident in which John found, in a way he never forgot, what Jesus was like.

Let us reconstruct the story. After the feeding of the five thousand and the attempt to make him king, Jesus slipped away to the hills alone. The day wore on. It came to the time which the Jews described as " the second evening," the time between the twilight and the dark. Jesus had still not arrived. We must not think that the disciples were forgetful or discourteous in leaving Jesus behind, for, as Mark tells the story, Jesus sent them on ahead (*Mark* 6: 45), while he persuaded the crowds to go home. Doubtless it was his intention to walk round the head of the lake while they rowed across and to rejoin them in Capernaum.

The disciples set sail. The wind got up, as it can in the narrow, land-locked lake; and the waters were whipped to foam. It was Passover time, and that was the time of the full moon (*John* 6: 4). Up on the hillside Jesus had prayed and communed with God; as he set out the silver moon made the scene almost like daylight; and down on the lake below he could see the boat and the rowers toiling at the oars, making heavy weather of it. So he came down.

We must remember two facts. At the north end the lake was no more than four miles across; and John tells us that the disciples had rowed between three and four miles; that is to say, they were very nearly at their journey's end. It is natural to suppose that in the wind they hugged the shore of the lake, seeking what shelter they might find. That is the first fact and now we come to the second. They saw Jesus, as the Authorized Version and Revised Standard Version have it, walking *on the sea*. The Greek is *epi tēs thalassēs* which is precisely the phrase used in *John* 21: 1, where it means—it has never been questioned—that Jesus was walking on the seashore. That is what the phrase means in our passage, too.

Jesus was walking *epi tēs thalassēs*, by the seashore. The toiling disciples looked up, and suddenly saw him. It was all so unexpected, they had been bent so long over their oars, that they were alarmed because they thought it was a spirit they were seeing. Then across the waters came that well-loved voice—" It is I; don't be afraid." They wanted him to come on board; the Greek most naturally means that their wish was not fulfilled. Why? Remember the breadth of the lake was four miles and they had rowed about that distance. The simple reason was that, before they could take Jesus on board, the boat grounded on the shingle, and they were there.

Here is just the kind of story that a fisherman like John would have loved and remembered. Every time he thought of it he would feel that night again, the grey silver of the moonlight, the rough oar against his hand, the flapping sail, the shriek of the wind, the sound of the surging water, the astonishingly unexpected appearance of Jesus, the sound of his voice across the waves and the crunch of the boat as it reached the Galilaean side.

As he remembered, John saw wonders which are still there for us.

(i) He saw that Jesus *watches*. Up on the hill Jesus had been watching them. He had not forgotten. He was not too busy with God to think of them. John suddenly realized that all the time they had pulled at the oars Jesus's loving look was on them.

When we are up against it Jesus watches. He does not make things easy for us. He lets us fight our own battles. Like a parent watching his son put up a splendid effort in some athletic contest, he is proud of us; or, like a parent watching his son let the side down, he is sad. Life is lived with the loving eye of Jesus upon us.

(ii) He saw that Jesus *comes*. Down from the hillside Jesus came to enable the disciples make the last pull that would reach safety.

He does not watch us with serene detachment; when strength is failing he comes with strength for the last effort which leads to victory.

(iii) He saw that Jesus *helps*. He watches, he comes and he helps. It is the wonder of the Christian life that there is nothing that we are left to do alone. Margaret Avery tells how there was a teacher in a little country school who had told this story to her children, and she must have told it well. Some short time afterwards there was a blizzard of wind and snow. When school finished, the teacher was helping the children home. Sometimes she had practically to drag them through the drifts. When they were all very nearly exhausted with the struggle, she overheard a little boy say, half to himself: " We could be doing with that chap Jesus here now." We could always be doing with Jesus and we never need to do without him.

(iv) He saw that *Jesus brings us to the haven.* It seemed to John, as he remembered it, that, as soon as Jesus arrived, the keel of the boat grated on the shingle—and they were there. As the Psalmist had it: " Then they were glad because they had quiet, and he brought them to their desired haven " (*Psalm* 107: 30). Somehow in the presence of Jesus the longest journey is shorter and the hardest battle easier.

One of the loveliest things in the Fourth Gospel is that John, the old fisherman turned evangelist, found all the wealth of Christ in the memory of a fisherman's story.

THE MISTAKEN SEARCH

John 6: 22–27

On the next day, the crowd which was still standing on the far side of the sea, saw that there had been only one boat, and that Jesus had not gone into the boat with his disciples, but that the disciples had gone away alone. But some boats from Tiberias put in near the place where they had eaten the bread, after the Lord had given thanks. So when they saw that Jesus was not there, nor his disciples either, they embarked on the boats, and came to Capernaum, looking for Jesus. When they had found him on the other side of the sea, they said to him: " Rabbi, when did you get here? " Jesus answered: " This is the truth I tell you—you are looking for me, not because you saw signs, but because you ate of the loaves until your stomachs were filled. Do not work for the food which perishes, but work for the food which lasts, and which gives eternal life, that food which the Son of Man will give you; for the Father—God—has set his seal upon him."

The crowd had lingered on the far side of the lake. In the time of Jesus people did not need to keep office-hours. They had time to wait until he came back to them. They waited because having seen that there was only one boat and that the disciples had gone off in it without Jesus, they deduced that he must still be somewhere near at hand. After they had waited for some time, they began to realize that he was not coming back. Into the bay came some little boats from Tiberias. No doubt they had taken shelter from the storm of the night. The waiting people embarked on them and made the crossing of the lake back to Capernaum.

Discovering to their surprise that Jesus was already there, they asked him when he had arrived. To that question Jesus simply did not reply. This was no time to talk of things like that; life was too short for pleasant gossip about journeys. He went straight to the heart of the matter. " You have seen," he said, " wonderful things. You have seen how God's grace enabled a crowd to be fed. Your thoughts ought to have been turned to the God who did these things; but instead all that you are thinking about is bread." It is as if Jesus said: " You cannot think about your souls for thinking of your stomachs."

" Men," as Chrysostom said, " are nailed to the things of this life." Here were people whose eyes never lifted beyond the ramparts of the world to the eternities beyond. Once Napoleon and an acquaintance were talking of life. It was dark; they walked to the window and looked out. There in the sky were distant stars, little more than pin-points of light. Napoleon, who had sharp eyes while his friend was dim-sighted, pointed to the sky: " Do you see these stars? " he asked. " No," his friend answered. " I can't see them." " That," said Napoleon, " is the difference between you and me." The man who is earthbound is living half a life. It is the man with vision, who looks at the horizon and sees the stars, who is truly alive.

Jesus put his command in one sentence. " Don't work for the food which perishes but for that which lasts for ever and gives eternal life." Long ago a prophet called Isaiah had asked: " Why do you spend your money for that which is not bread?

and your labour for that which does not satisfy? " (*Isaiah* 55: 2). There are two kinds of hunger. There is physical hunger which physical food can satisfy; but there is a spiritual hunger which that food can never satisfy. A man may be as rich as Croesus and still have an incompleteness in his life.

In the years just after A.D. 60 the luxury of Roman society was unparalleled. It was at this time that they served feasts of peacocks' brains and nightingales' tongues; that they cultivated the odd habit of taking emetics between courses so that the next might taste better; that meals costing thousands of pounds were commonplace. It was at this time that Pliny tells of a Roman lady who was married in a robe so richly jewelled and gilded that it cost the equivalent of £432,000. There was a reason for all this, and the reason was a deep dissatisfaction with life, a hunger that nothing could satisfy. They would try anything for a new thrill, because they were both appallingly rich and appallingly hungry. As Matthew Arnold wrote:

> " In his cool hall with haggard eyes,
>   The Roman noble lay;
> He drove abroad in furious guise
>   Along the Appian Way;
> He made a feast, drank fierce and fast;
>   He crowned his hair with flowers;
> *No easier nor no quicker passed*
>   The impracticable hours."

Jesus' point was that all that these Jews were interested in was physical satisfaction. They had received an unexpectedly free and lavish meal; and they wanted more. But there are other hungers which can be satisfied only by him. There is the hunger for truth—in him alone is the truth of God. There is the hunger for life—in him alone is life more abundant. There is the hunger for love—in him alone is the love that outlasts sin and death. Christ alone can satisfy the hunger of the human heart and soul.

Why is this so? There is a wealth of meaning in the phrase: " God has set his seal upon him." H. B. Tristram in *Eastern Customs in Bible Lands* has a most interesting section on seals in the ancient world. It was not the *signature*, but the *seal* that authenticated. In commercial and political documents it was the seal, imprinted with the signet ring, which made the document valid; it was the seal which authenticated a will; it was the seal on the mouth of a sack or a crate that guaranteed the contents. Tristram tells how on his own eastern journeys, when he made an agreement with his muleteers and his porters, they set the impression of their seal upon it to show that it was binding. Seals were made of pottery or metal or jewels. In the British Museum there are the seals of most of the Assyrian kings. The seal was fixed on clay and the clay attached to the document.

The Rabbis had a saying: " The seal of God is truth." " One day," says the *Talmud*, " the great synagogue (the assembly of the Jewish experts in the law) were weeping, praying and fasting together, when a little scroll fell from the firmament among them. They opened it and on it was only one word, *Ameth*, which means *truth*. ' That,' said the Rabbi, ' is the seal of God.' " *Ameth* is spelt with three Hebrew letters—*aleph*, which is the first letter of the alphabet, *min* the middle letter, and *tau* the last. The truth of God is the beginning, the middle and the end of life.

That is why Jesus can satisfy the eternal hunger. He is sealed by God, he is God's truth incarnate and it is God alone who can truly satisfy the hunger of the soul which he created.

THE ONLY TRUE WORK

John 6: 28, 29

> They said to him: " What are we to do to work the works of God? " Jesus answered: " This is the work of God, to believe in him whom he has sent."

When Jesus spoke about the works of God, the Jews immediately thought in terms of " good " works. It was their conviction that a man by living a good life could earn the favour of God. They held that men could be divided into three classes—those

who were good, those who were bad and those who were in
between, who, by doing one more good work, could be trans-
ferred to the category of the good. So when the Jews asked
Jesus about the work of God they expected him to lay down
lists of things to do. But that is not what Jesus says at all.

His Jesus is extremely compressed and we must expand it
and see what lies behind it. He said that God's work was to
believe in him whom he had sent. Paul would have put it this
way—the one work that God desires from man is *faith*. Now
what does faith mean? It means being in such a relationship
with God that we are his friends, not terrified of him any more
but knowing him as our Father and our friend and giving him
the trust and the obedience and the submission which naturally
arise from this new relationship. How does believing in Jesus tie
up with that? It is only because Jesus came to tell us that God is
our Father and loves us and wants nothing more than to
forgive, that the old distance and enmity are taken away and
the new relationship with him made possible.

But that new relationship issues in a certain kind of life. Now
we know what God is like, our lives must answer to that
knowledge. That answer will be in three directions, each of
which corresponds to what Jesus told us of God.

(i) God is love. Therefore in our lives there must be love and
service of others corresponding to the love and the service of
God, and forgiveness of others corresponding to his forgiveness
of God.

(ii) God is holiness. Therefore in our lives there must be
purity corresponding to the holiness of God.

(iii) God is wisdom. Therefore in our lives there must be
complete submission and trust corresponding to the wisdom of
God.

The essence of the Christian life is a new relationship to God,
a relationship offered by him and made possible by the
revelation which Jesus gave us of him, a relationship which
issues in that service, purity and trust which are the reflection of
God. This is the work which God wishes us and enables us to
perform.

THE DEMAND FOR A SIGN

John 6: 30–34

> They said to him: " What sign are you going to perform that we
> may see it and believe in you? What is your work? Our fathers ate
> the manna in the wilderness. As it stands written: ' He gave them
> bread from heaven to eat.' " Jesus said to them: " This is the truth
> I tell you—Moses did not give you bread from heaven, but my
> Father gives you the real bread from heaven. The bread of God
> is he who comes down from heaven, and gives life to the world."
> They said to him: " Sir, always give us that bread."

HERE the argument becomes specifically Jewish in its expression and assumptions and allusions. Jesus had just made a great
claim. The true work of God was to believe in him. " Very
well," said the Jews, " this is in effect a claim to be the Messiah.
Prove it."

Their minds were still on the feeding of the crowd and
inevitably that turned their thoughts to the manna in the
wilderness. They could hardly help connecting the two things.
The manna had always been regarded as the bread of God
(*Psalm* 78: 24; *Exodus* 16: 15); and there was a strong rabbinic
belief that when the Messiah came he would again give the
manna. The giving of the manna was held to be the supreme
work in the life of Moses and the Messiah was bound to surpass
it. " As was the first redeemer so was the final redeemer; as the
first redeemer caused the manna to fall from heaven, even so
shall the second redeemer cause the manna to fall." " Ye shall
not find the manna in this age, but ye shall find it in the age that
is to come." " For whom has the manna been prepared? For the
righteous in the age that is coming. Everyone who believes is
worthy and eateth of it." It was the belief that a pot of the
manna had been hidden in the ark in the first temple, and that,
when the temple was destroyed, Jeremiah had hidden it away
and would produce it again when the Messiah came. In other
words, the Jews were challenging Jesus to produce bread from

God in order to substantiate his claims. They did not regard the bread which had fed the five thousand as bread from God; it had begun in earthly loaves and issued in earthly loaves. The manna, they held, was a different thing and a real test.

Jesus's answer was twofold. First, he reminded them that it was not *Moses* who had given them the manna; it was *God*. Second, he told them that the manna was not really the bread of God; it was only the symbol of the bread of God. The bread of God was he who came down from heaven and gave men not simply satisfaction from physical hunger, but life. Jesus was claiming that the only real satisfaction was in him.

THE BREAD OF LIFE

John 6: 35–40

> Jesus said to them: " I a the bread of life. He who comes to me will never hunger, and he who believes in me will never thirst any more. But I tell you, though you have seen me, yet you do not believe in me. All that the Father gives me will come to me, because I came down from heaven, not to do my will, but to do the will of him who sent me. This is the will of him who sent me—that I should lose none of those he gave to me, but that I should raise them all up on the last day. This is the will of my Father, that everyone who believes on the Son, when he sees him, should have everlasting life. And I will raise him up on the last day."

THIS is one of the great passages of the Fourth Gospel, and indeed of the New Testament. In it there are two great lines of thought that we must try to analyse.

First, what did Jesus mean when he said: " I am the bread of life "? It is not enough to regard this as simply a beautiful and poetical phrase. Let us analyse it step by step. (i) Bread sustains life. It is that without which life cannot go on. (ii) But what is life? Clearly by life is meant something far more than mere physical existence. What is this new spiritual meaning of life?

(iii) Real life is the new relationship with God, that relationship of trust and obedience and love of which we have already thought. (iv) That relationship is made possible only by Jesus Christ. Apart from him no one can enter into it. (v) That is to say, without Jesus there may be existence, but not life. (vi) Therefore, if Jesus is the essential of life, he may be described as the bread of life. The hunger of the human situation is ended when we know Christ and through him know God. The restless soul is at rest; the hungry heart is satisfied.

Second, this passage opens out to us the stages of the Christian life. (i) We see Jesus. We see him in the pages of the New Testament, in the teaching of the church, sometimes even face to face. (ii) Having seen him, we come to him. We regard him not as some distant hero and pattern, not as a figure in a book, but as someone accessible. (iii) We believe in him. That is to say, we accept him as the final authority on God, on man, on life. That means that our coming is not a matter of mere interest, nor a meeting on equal terms; it is essentially a submission. (iv) This process gives us life. That is to say, it puts us into a new and lovely relationship with God, wherein he becomes an intimate friend; we are now at home with the one whom we feared or never knew. (v) The possibility of this is free and universal. The invitation is to all men. The bread of life is ours for the taking. (vi) The only way to that new relationship is through Jesus. Without him it never would have been possible; and apart from him it is still impossible. No searching of the human mind or longing of the human heart can fully find God apart from Jesus. (vii) At the back of the whole process is God. It is those whom God has given him who come to Christ. God not only provides the goal; he moves in the human heart to awaken desire for him; and he works in the human heart to take away the rebellion and the pride which would hinder the great submission. We could never even have sought him unless he had already found us. (vii) There remains that stubborn something which enables us to refuse the offer of God. In the last analysis, the one thing which defeats God is the defiance of the human heart. Life is there for the taking—or the refusing.

When we take, two things happen.

First, into life enters new satisfaction. The hunger and the thirst are gone. The human heart finds what it was searching for and life ceases to be mere existence and becomes a thing at once of thrill and of peace.

Second, even beyond life we are safe. Even on the last day when all things end we are still secure. As a great commentator said: " Christ brings us to the haven beyond which there is no danger."

The offer of Christ is life in time and life in eternity. That is the greatness and glory of which we cheat ourselves when we refuse his invitation.

THE FAILURE OF THE JEWS

John 6: 41–51

So the Jews kept murmuring about him, because he said: " I am the bread which came down from heaven." They kept saying: " Is this not Jesus, the son of Joseph, whose father and mother we know? How can he now say: ' I have come down from heaven '? " Jesus answered: " Stop murmuring to each other. No one can come to me except the Father who sent me draws him; and I will raise him up on the last day. It stands written in the prophets: ' And all will be taught by God.' Everyone who has listened and learned from my Father comes to me. Not that anyone has seen the Father, except he who is from God—*he* has seen the Father. This is the truth I tell you—he who believes has eternal life. I am the bread of life. Your fathers ate the manna in the wilderness, and died. This is the bread of life which comes down from heaven that a man may eat of him and not die. I am the bread of life which came down from heaven. If anyone eats of this bread he will live forever."

THIS passage shows the reasons why the Jews rejected Jesus, and in rejecting him, rejected eternal life.

(i) They judged things by human values and by external standards. Their reaction in face of the claim of Jesus was to produce the fact that he was a carpenter's son and that they had seen him grow up in Nazareth. They were unable to understand how one who was a tradesman and who came from a poor home could possibly be a special messenger from God.

T. E. Lawrence was a close personal friend of Thomas Hardy, the poet. In the days when Lawrence was serving as an aircraftman in the Royal Air Force he sometimes used to visit Hardy and his wife in his aircraftman's uniform. On one occasion his visit coincided with a visit of the Mayoress of Dorchester. She was bitterly affronted that she had to submit to meeting a common aircraftman, for she had no idea who he was. In French she said to Mrs. Hardy that never in all her born days had she had to sit down to tea with a private soldier. No one said anything: then Lawrence said in perfect French: " I beg your pardon, Madame, but can I be of any use as an interpreter? Mrs. Hardy knows no French." A snobbish and discourteous woman had made a shattering mistake because she judged by externals.

That is what the Jews did with Jesus. We must have a care that we never neglect a message from God because we despise or do not care for the messenger. A man would hardly refuse a cheque for £1,000 because it happened to be enclosed in an envelope which did not conform to the most aristocratic standards of notepaper. God has many messengers. His greatest message came through a Galilaean carpenter, and for that very reason the Jews disregarded it.

(ii) The Jews argued *with each other*. They were so taken up with their private arguments that it never struck them to refer the decision to God. They were exceedingly eager to let everyone know what they thought about the matter; but not in the least anxious to know what God thought. It might well be that sometimes in a court or committee, when every man is desirous of pushing his opinion down his neighbour's throat, we would be better to be quiet and ask God what he thinks and what he wants us to do. After all it does not matter so very much what we think; but what God thinks matters intensely; and we so seldom take steps to find it out.

(iii) The Jews listened, *but they did not learn.* There are different kinds of listening. There is the listening of criticism; there is the listening of resentment; there is the listening of superiority; there is the listening of indifference; there is the listening of the man who listens only because for the moment he cannot get the chance to speak. The only listening that is worth while is that which hears and learns; and that is the only way to listen to God.

(iv) The Jews resisted *the drawing of God.* Only those accept Jesus whom God draws to him. The word which John uses for *to draw* is *helkuein.* The word used in the Greek translation of the Hebrew when Jeremiah hears God say as the Authorized Version has it: " With loving-kindness have I drawn thee " (*Jeremiah* 31: 3). The interesting thing about the word is that it almost always implies some kind of resistance. It is the word for drawing a heavily laden net to the shore (*John* 21: 6, 11). It is used of Paul and Silas being dragged before the magistrates in Philippi (*Acts* 16: 19). It is the word for drawing a sword from the belt or from its scabbard (*John* 18: 10). Always there is this idea of resistance. God can draw men, but man's resistance can defeat God's pull.

Jesus is the bread of life; which means that he is the essential for life; therefore to refuse the invitation and command of Jesus is to miss life and to die. The Rabbis had a saying: " The generation in the wilderness have no part in the life to come." In the old story in *Numbers* the people who cravenly refused to brave the dangers of the promised land after the report of the scouts, were condemned to wander in the wilderness until they died. Because they would not accept the guidance of God they were for ever shut out from the promised land. The Rabbis believed that the fathers who died in the wilderness not only missed the promised land, but also missed the life to come. To refuse the offer of Jesus is to miss life in this world and in the world to come; whereas to accept his offer is to find real life in this world and glory in the world to come.

HIS BODY AND HIS BLOOD

John 6: 51–59

" The bread which I will give him is my flesh, which is given that the world may have life." So the Jews argued with each other. " How," they said, " can this man give us his flesh to eat? " Jesus said to them: " This is the truth I tell you—unless you eat the flesh of the Son of Man and drink his blood, you cannot possess eternal life within yourselves. He who eats my flesh and drinks my blood has eternal life, and I will raise him up on the last day. My flesh is the real food and my blood is the real drink. He who eats my flesh and drinks my blood remains in me and I in him. As the living Father has sent me, so I live through him; and he who eats me will live through me. This is the bread which came down from heaven. It is not a case of eating, as your fathers ate and died. He who eats this bread lives for ever." He said these things when he was teaching in the synagogue at Capernaum.

To most of us this is a very difficult passage. It speaks in language and moves in a world of ideas which are quite strange to us and which may seem even fantastic and grotesque. But to those who heard it first, it was moving among familiar ideas which went back to the very childhood of the race.

These ideas would be quite normal to anyone brought up in ancient sacrifice. The animal was very seldom burned entire. Usually only a token part was burned on the altar, although the whole animal was offered to the god. Part of the flesh was given to the priests as their perquisite; and part to the worshipper to make a feast for himself and his friends within the temple precincts. At that feast the god himself was held to be a guest. More, once the flesh had been offered to the god, it was held that he had entered into it; and therefore when the worshipper ate it he was literally eating the god. When people rose from such a feast they went out, as they believed, literally god-filled. We may think of it as idolatrous worship, we may think of it as a vast delusion; yet the fact remains these people went out quite certain that in them there was now the dynamic vitality of their god. To people used to that kind of experience a section like this presented no difficulties at all.

Further, in that ancient world the one live form of religion was to be found in the Mystery Religions. The one thing the Mystery Religions offered was communion and even identity with some god. The way it was done was this. All the Mystery Religions were essentially passion plays. They were stories of a god who had lived and suffered terribly and who died and rose again. The story was turned into a moving play. Before the initiate could see it, he had to undergo a long course of instruction in the inner meaning of the story. He had to undergo all kinds of ceremonial purifications. He had to pass through a long period of fasting and abstention from sexual relationships.

At the actual presentation of a passion play everything was designed to produce a highly emotional atmosphere. There was carefully calculated lighting, sensuous incense, exciting music, a wonderful liturgy; everything was designed to work up the initiate to a height of emotion and expectation that he had never experienced before. Call it hallucination if you like; call it a combination of hypnotism and self hypnotism. But something happened; and that something was identity with the god. As the carefully prepared initiate watched he became one with the god. He shared the sorrows and the griefs; he shared the death, and the resurrection. He and the god became for ever one; and he was safe in life and in death.

Some of the sayings and prayers of the Mystery Religions are very beautiful. In the Mysteries of Mithra the initiate prayed: " Abide with my soul; leave me not, that I may be initiated and that the holy spirit may dwell within me." In the Hermetic Mysteries the initiate said: " I know thee Hermes, and thou knowest me; *I am thou and thou art I.*" In the same Mysteries a prayer runs: " Come to me, Lord Hermes, as babes to mothers' wombs." In the Mysteries of Isis the worshipper said: " As truly as Osiris lives, so shall his followers live. As truly as Osiris is not dead, his followers shall die no more."

We must remember that those ancient people knew all about

the striving, the longing, the dreaming for identity with their god and for the bliss of taking him into themselves. They would not read phrases like eating Christ's body and drinking his blood with crude and shocked literalism. They would know something of that ineffable experience of union, closer than any earthly union, of which these words speak. This is language that the ancient world could understand—and so can we.

It may be well that we should remember that here John is doing what he so often does. He is not giving, or trying to give, the actual words of Jesus. He has been thinking for seventy years of what Jesus said; and now, led by the Holy Spirit, he is giving the *inner significance* of his words. It is not the words that he reports; that would merely have been a feat of memory. It is the essential meaning of the words; that is the guidance of the Holy Spirit.

HIS BODY AND HIS BLOOD

John 6: 51–59 (*continued*)

LET us see now if we can find out something of what Jesus meant and of what John understood from words like this. There are two ways in which we may take this passage.

(i) We may take it in a quite general sense. Jesus spoke about eating his flesh and drinking his blood.

Now the flesh of Jesus was his complete humanity. John in his First Letter lays it down almost passionately: " Every spirit that confesses that Jesus Christ has come in the flesh is of God; and every spirit which does not confess Jesus is not of God." In fact, the spirit which denies that Jesus is come in the flesh is of antichrist (1 *John* 4: 2, 3). John insisted that we must grasp and never let go the full humanity of Jesus, that he was bone of our bone and flesh of our flesh. What does this mean? Jesus, as we have seen again and again, was the mind of God become a person. This means that in Jesus we see God taking human life upon him, facing our human situation, struggling with our human problems, battling with our human temptations, working out our human relationships.

Therefore it is as if Jesus said: " Feed your heart, feed your mind, feed your soul on the thought of my manhood. When you are discouraged and in despair, when you are beaten to your knees and disgusted with life and living—remember *I* took that life of yours and these struggles of yours on me." Suddenly life and the flesh are clad with glory for they are touched with God. It was and is the great belief of the Greek Orthodox Christology that Jesus deified our flesh by taking it on himself. To eat Christ's body is to feed on the thought of his manhood until our own manhood is strengthened and cleansed and irradiated by his.

Jesus said we must drink his blood. In Jewish thought *the blood stands for the life*. It is easy to understand why. As the blood flows from a wound, life ebbs away; and to the Jew, *the blood belonged to God*. That is why to this day a true Jew will never eat any meat which has not been completely drained of blood. " Only you shall not eat flesh with its life, that is, its blood " (*Genesis* 9: 4). " Only you shall not eat its blood " (*Deuteronomy* 15: 23). Now see what Jesus is saying—" You must drink my blood—you must take my life into the very centre of your being—and that life of mine is the life which belongs to God." When Jesus said we must drink his blood he meant that we must take his life into the very core of our hearts.

What does that mean? Think of it this way. Here in a bookcase is a book which a man has never read. It may be the glory and the wonder of the tragedies of Shakespeare; but so long as it remains unread upon his bookshelves it is external to him. One day he takes it down and reads it. He is thrilled and fascinated and moved. The story sticks to him; the great lines remain in his memory; now when he wants to, he can take that wonder out from inside himself and remember it and think about it and feed his mind and his heart upon it. Once the book was outside him. Now it is inside him and he can feed upon it. It is that way with any great experience in life. It remains external until we take it within ourselves.

It is so with Jesus. So long as he remains a figure in a book he is external to us; but when he enters into our hearts we can feed upon the life and the strength and the dynamic vitality that he gives to us. Jesus said that we must drink his blood. He is saying: " You must stop thinking of me as a subject for theological debate; you must take me into you, and you must come into me; and then you will have real life." That is what Jesus meant when he spoke about us abiding in him and himself abiding in us.

When he told us to eat his flesh and drink his blood, he was telling us to feed our hearts and souls and minds on his humanity, and to revitalize our lives with his life until we are filled with the life of God.

(ii) But John meant more than that, and was thinking also of the Lord's Supper. He was saying: " If you want life, you must come and sit at that table where you eat that broken bread and drink that poured-out wine which somehow, in the grace of God, bring you into contact with the love and the life of Jesus Christ." But—and here is the sheer wonder of his point of view—*John has no account of the Last Supper*. He brings in his teaching about it, not in the narrative of the Upper Room, but in the story of a picnic meal on a hillside near Bethsaida Julias by the blue waters of the Sea of Galilee.

There is no doubt that John is saying that for the true Christian *every meal has become a sacrament*. It may well be that there were those who—if the phrase be allowed—were making too much of the Sacrament within the church, making a magic of it, implying that it was the only place where we might enter into the nearer presence of the Risen Christ. It is true that the Sacrament is a special appointment with God; but John held with all his heart that every meal in the humblest home, in the richest palace, beneath the canopy of the sky with only the grass for carpet was a sacrament. He refused to limit the presence of Christ to an ecclesiastical environment and a correctly liturgical service. He said: " At any meal you can find again that bread which speaks of the manhood of the Master, that wine which speaks of the blood which is life."

In John's thought the communion table and the dinner table and the picnic on the seashore or the hillside are all alike in that at all of them we may taste and touch and handle the bread and the wine which brings us Christ. Christianity would be a poor thing if Christ were confined to churches. It is John's belief that we can find him anywhere in a Christ-filled world. It is not that he belittles the Sacrament; but he expands it, so that we find Christ at his table in church, and then go out to find him everywhere where men and women meet together to enjoy the gifts of God.

THE ALL-IMPORTANT SPIRIT

John 6: 59–65

When they had heard this discourse many of his disciples said: " This word is hard! Who is able to listen to it? " Jesus well knew within himself that his disciples were murmuring about this; so he said to them: " Does this cause you to stumble? What then if you were to see the Son of Man ascending to where he formerly was? The life-giving power is the Spirit; the flesh is of no help. The words which I have spoken to you are spirit and life. But there are some who do not believe." For Jesus knew from the beginning who they were who did not believe, and who it was who was going to betray him. So that was why he often said: " No man can come to me, except it has been given to him by the Father to do so."

IT is little wonder that the disciples found the discourse of Jesus hard. The Greek word is *sklēros*, which means not *hard to understand*; but *hard to accept*. The disciples knew quite well that Jesus had been claiming to be the very life of God come down from heaven, and that no one could live this life or face eternity without submitting to him.

Here we come upon a truth that re-emerges in every age. Time and again it is not the intellectual difficulty which keeps men from becoming Christians; it is the height of Christ's moral demand. At the heart of all religion there must be mystery, for the simple reason that at that heart there is God.

In the nature of things man cannot ever fully understand God. Any honest thinker will accept that there must be mystery.

The real difficulty of Christianity is two-fold. It demands an act of surrender to Christ, an acceptance of him as the final authority; and it demands a moral standard of the highest level. The disciples were well aware that Jesus had claimed to be the very life and mind of God come down to earth; their difficulty was to accept that as true, with all its implications. To this day many a man refuses Christ, not because he puzzles intellect, but because he challenges his life.

Jesus goes on, not to try to prove his claim, but to state that some day events will prove it. What he is saying is this: " You find it difficult to believe that I am the bread, the essential of life, which *came down* from heaven. Well then, you will have no difficulty in accepting that claim when some day you see me *ascending back* to heaven." It is a forecast of the Ascension. It means that the Resurrection is the guarantee of the claims of Jesus. He was not one who lived nobly and died gallantly for a lost cause; he was the one whose claims were vindicated by the fact that he rose again.

Jesus goes on to say that the all-important thing is the life-giving power of the Spirit; the flesh is of no help. We can put that very simply in a way which will give us at least something of its meaning—the most important thing is the spirit in which any action is done. Someone has put it this way: " All human things are trivial if they exist for nothing beyond themselves." The real value of anything depends on its aim. If we eat simply for the sake of eating, we become gluttons, and it is likely to do us far more harm than good; if we eat to sustain life, to do our work better, to maintain the fitness of our body at its highest peak, food has a real significance. If a man spends a great deal of time on sport simply for the sake of sport, he is at least to some extent wasting his time. But if he spends that time in order to keep his body fit and thereby to do his work for God and men better, sport ceases to be trivial and becomes important. The things of the flesh all gain their value from the spirit in which they are done.

Jesus goes on: " My words are spirit and life." He alone can tell us what life is, put into us the spirit in which it must be lived, give us the strength so to live it. Life takes its value from its purpose and its goal. Christ alone can give us true purpose in life, and the power to work out that purpose against the constant opposition that comes from without and within.

Jesus was well aware that some would not only reject his offer but would reject it with hostility. No man can accept him unless he is moved by the Spirit of God to do so but to the end of the day a man can resist that Spirit. Such a man is shut out not by God, but by himself.

ATTITUDES TO CHRIST

John 6: 66–71

> After this many of his disciples turned back and would not walk with him any more. Jesus said to the Twelve: " Surely you too do not want to go away? " Simon Peter answered him: " Lord, to whom are we to go? You have the words of eternal life; and we have believed and we have come to know that you are the Holy One of God." Jesus answered them: " Did I not choose you twelve, and one of you is a devil? " He meant Judas, the son of Simon Iscariot, for he was going to betray him—and he was one of the Twelve.

HERE is a passage instinct with tragedy, for in it is the beginning of the end. There was a time when men came to Jesus in large numbers. When he was in Jerusalem at the Passover many saw his miracles and believed in his name (2: 23). So many came to be baptized by his disciples that the numbers were embarrassing (4: 1–3). In Samaria great things happened (4: 1, 39, 45). In Galilee the crowds flocked after him just the day before (6: 2). But the tone of things had changed; from now on there was a growing hatred which was going to culminate in the Cross. Already John launches us on the last act of the tragedy. It is circumstances like these which reveal men's hearts and show them in their true colours. In these circumstances there were three different attitudes to Jesus.

(i) There was *defection*. Some turned back and walked with him no more. They drifted away for various reasons.

Some saw quite clearly where Jesus was heading. It was not possible to challenge the authorities as he was doing and get away with it. He was heading for disaster and they were getting out in time. They were fair-weather followers. It has been said that the test of an army is how it fights when it is tired. Those who drifted away would have stuck by Jesus so long as his career was on the upward way, but at the first shadow of the Cross they left him.

Some shirked the challenge of Jesus. Fundamentally their point of view was that they had come to Jesus to get something from him; when it came to suffering *for* him and giving *to* him they quit. No one can give so much as Jesus, but if we come to him solely to get and never to give we will certainly turn back. The man who would follow Jesus must remember that in following him there is always a Cross.

(ii) There was *deterioration*. It is in Judas above all that we see this. Jesus must have seen in him a man whom he could use for his purposes. But Judas, who might have become the hero, became the villain; he who might have become a saint became a name of shame.

There is a terrible story about an artist who was painting the Last Supper. It was a great picture and it took him many years. As model for the face of Christ he used a young man with a face of transcendent loveliness and purity. Bit by bit the picture was filled in and one after another the disciples were painted. The day came when he needed a model for Judas whose face he had left to the last. He went out and searched in the lowest haunts of the city and in the dens of vice. At last he found a man with a face so depraved and vicious as matched his requirement. When the sittings were at an end the man said to the artist: " You painted me before." " Surely not," said the artist. " O yes," said the man, " I sat for your Christ." The years had brought terrible deterioration.

The years can be cruel. They can take away our ideals and our enthusiasms and our dreams and our loyalties. They can leave us with a life that has grown smaller and not bigger. They can leave us with a heart that is shrivelled instead of one expanded in the love of Christ. There can be a lost loveliness in life—God saves us from that!

(iii) There was *determination*. This is John's version of Peter's great confession at Caesarea Philippi (*Mark* 8: 27; *Matthew* 16: 13; *Luke* 9: 18). It was just such a situation as this that called out the loyalty of Peter's heart. To him the simple fact was that there was just no one else to go to. Jesus alone had the words of life.

Peter's loyalty was based on a personal relationship to Jesus Christ. There were many things he did not understand; he was just as bewildered and puzzled as anyone else. But there was something about Jesus for which he would willingly die. In the last analysis Christianity is not a philosophy which we accept, nor a theory to which we give allegiance. It is a personal response to Jesus Christ. It is the allegiance and the love which a man gives because his heart will not allow him to do anything else.

NOT MAN'S TIME BUT GOD'S

John 7: 1–9

After these things Jesus moved about in Galilee, for he did not wish to move about in Judaea, because the Jews were out to kill him. The festival of the Jews which is called the Festival of Tabernacles was near. So his brothers said to him: " Leave here and go down to Jerusalem so that your disciples will get the chance to see the works that you do. For no one goes on doing things in secret, when he wishes to draw public attention to himself. Since you can do these things, show yourself to the world." For even his brothers did not believe in him. So Jesus said to them: " The time of opportunity that I am looking for has not yet come; but your time is always ready. The world cannot hate you, but it hates me, because I bear witness about it that its deeds are evil. Go up to the festival yourselves. I am not yet going up to the festival, because my time has not yet come." When he had said these things to them he remained in Galilee.

THE Festival of Tabernacles fell at the end of September and the beginning of October. It was one of the obligatory festivals and every adult male Jew who lived within fifteen miles of Jerusalem was legally bound to attend it. But devout Jews from far outside the fifteen mile radius delighted to go to it. It lasted altogether for eight days. Later in this chapter we shall have occasion to deal more fully with it. When it came round, Jesus's brothers urged him to go to Jerusalem for it; but Jesus rejected their arguments and went in his own good time.

There is one unique thing in this passage which we must note. According to the Revised Standard Version (verse 7) Jesus says: " My time is not yet come." Jesus frequently spoke about his *time* or his *hour*. But here he uses a different word, and uses it for the only time. In the other passages (*John* 2: 4; 7: 30; 8: 20; 12: 27) the word that Jesus or John uses is *hōra*, which means the *destined hour of God*. Such a time or hour was not movable nor avoidable. It had to be accepted without argument and without alteration because it was the hour at which the plan of God had decided that something must happen. But in this passage the word is *kairos*, which characteristically means an *opportunity*; that is, the best time to do something, the moment when circumstances are most suitable, *the psychological moment*. Jesus is not saying here that the destined hour of God has not come but something much simpler. He is saying that that was not the moment which would give him the chance for which he was waiting.

That explains why Jesus later actually did go to Jerusalem. Many people have been troubled about the fact that he first told his brothers he would not go and then went. Schopenhauer, the German philosopher, actually said: " Jesus Christ did of set purpose utter a falsehood." Other people have argued that it means that Jesus said that he was not going up to the festival *publicly* but that did not preclude him from going *privately*. But

Jesus is saying simply: " If I go up with you just now I will not get the opportunity I am looking for. The time is not opportune." So he delayed his going until the middle of the festival, since to arrive with the crowds all assembled and expectant gave him a far better opportunity than to go at the very beginning. Jesus is choosing his time with careful prudence in order to get the most effective results.

From this passage we learn two things.

(i) It is impossible to force Jesus's hand. His brothers tried to force him into going to Jerusalem. It was what we might call a dare. They were quite right from the human point of view. Jesus's great miracles had been wrought in Galilee—the changing of the water into wine (*John* 2: 1ff); the healing of the nobleman's son (*John* 4: 46); the feeding of the five thousand (*John* 6: 1ff). The only miracle that he had wrought in Jerusalem was the curing of the impotent man at the pool (*John* 5: 1ff). It was not unnatural to tell Jesus to go to Jerusalem and let his supporters there see what he could do. The story makes it clear that the healing of the impotent man had been regarded far more as an act of Sabbath breaking than as a miracle. Further, if Jesus was ever to succeed in winning men, he could not hope to do so by hiding in a corner; he must act in such a way that everyone could see what he did. Still further, Jerusalem was the keypoint. The Galilaeans were notoriously hot-blooded and hot-headed. Anyone who wanted a following would have no difficulty in raising one in the excitable atmosphere of Galilee; but Jerusalem was a very different proposition. It was the acid test.

Jesus's brothers could have put up a good case for their insistence; but Jesus's hand is not to be forced. He does things, not in man's time, but in God's. Man's impatience of man must learn to wait on God's wisdom.

(ii) It is impossible to treat Jesus with indifference. It did not matter when his brothers went to Jerusalem, for no one would notice they were there and nothing whatever depended on their going. But Jesus's going was a very different thing. Why? Because his brothers were in tune with the world and they did not make it uncomfortable. But Jesus's coming is a condemnation of the world's way of life and a challenge to selfishness and lethargy. Jesus had to choose his moment, for when he arrives something happens.

REACTIONS TO JESUS

John 7: 10–13

> When his brothers had gone up to the festival, then he too went up, not openly, but, as it were, in secret. So the Jews searched for him at the festival, and kept saying: "Where is he?" And there was many a heated argument about him among the crowds. Some said: "He is a good man." But others said: "No; far from it; he is leading the people astray." But no one spoke about him openly because of their fear of the Jews.

JESUS chose his own moment and went to Jerusalem. Here we have the reactions of the people when they were confronted with him. Now one of the supreme interests of this chapter is the number of such reactions of which it tells; and we collect them all here.

(i) There was the reaction of his brothers (verses 1–5). It was really a reaction of half-amused and teasing contempt. They did not really believe in him; they were really egging him on, as you might egg on a precocious boy. We still meet that attitude of tolerant contempt to Christianity.

George Bernaños in *The Diary of a Country Priest* tells how the country priest used sometimes to be invited to dinner at the big aristocratic house of his parish. The owner would encourage him to speak and argue before his guests, but he did it with that half-amused, half-contemptuous tolerance with which he might encourage a child to show off or a dog to display his tricks. There are still people who forget that Christian faith is a matter of life and death.

(ii) There was the sheer hatred of the Pharisees and of the chief priests (verses 7, 19). They did not hate him for the same

reason, because in point of fact they hated each other. The
Pharisees hated him because he drove through their petty rules
and regulations. If he was right, they were wrong; and they
loved their own little system more than they loved God. The
Sadducees were a political party. They did not observe the
Pharisaic rules and regulations. Nearly all the priests were
Sadducees. They collaborated with their Roman masters, and
they had a very comfortable and even luxurious time. They did
not want a Messiah; for when he came their political set-up
would disintegrate and their comfort would be gone. They hated
Jesus because he interfered with the vested interests which were
dearer to them than God.

It is still possible for a man to love his own little system more
than he loves God, and to place his own vested interests above
the challenge of the adventurous and the sacrificial way.

(iii) Both these reactions issued in the consuming desire to
eliminate Jesus (verses 30, 32). When a man's ideals clash with
those of Christ, either he must submit or he must seek to
destroy him. Hitler would have no Christians about him, for the
Christian owed a higher loyalty than loyalty to the state. A man
is faced with a simple alternative if he allows Christ into his
orbit. He can either do what he likes or he can do what Christ
likes; and if he wishes to go on doing as he likes, he must
seek to eliminate Christ.

(iv) There was arrogant contempt (verses 15, 47–49). What
right had this man to come and lay down the law? Jesus had no
cultural background; he had no training in the rabbinic schools
and colleges. Surely no intelligent person was going to listen to
him? Here was the reaction of academic snobbery.

Many of the greatest poets and writers and evangelists have
had no technical qualifications at all. That is not for one
moment to say that study and culture and education are to be
despised and abandoned; but we must have a care never to
wave a man away and consign him to the company who do not
matter simply because he lacks the technical equipment of the
schools.

(v) There was the reaction of the crowd. This was twofold.

First, there was the reaction of *interest* (verse 11). The one thing impossible when Jesus really invades life is indifference. Apart from anything else, Jesus is the most interesting figure in the world. Second, there was the reaction of *discussion* (verses 12, 43). They talked about Jesus; they put forward their views about him; they debated about him. There is both value and danger here. The value is that nothing helps us clarify our own opinions like pitting them against someone else's. Mind sharpens mind as iron sharpens iron. The danger is that religion can so very easily come to be regarded as a matter for argument and debate and discussion, a series of fascinating questions, about which a man may talk for a lifetime—and do nothing. There is all the difference in the world between being an argumentative amateur theologian, willing to talk until the stars go out, and a truly religious person, who has passed from talking about Christ to knowing him.

VERDICTS ON JESUS

John 7: 10–13 (*continued*)

In this chapter there is a whole series of verdicts on Jesus.

(i) There is the verdict that he was a *good man* (verse 12). That verdict is true, but it is not the whole truth. It was Napoleon who made the famous remark: " I know men, and Jesus Christ is more than a man." Jesus was indeed truly man; but in him was the mind of God. When he speaks it is not one man speaking to another; if that were so we might argue about his commands. When he speaks it is God speaking to men; and Christianity means not arguing about his commands, but accepting them.

(ii) There is the verdict that he was a *prophet* (verse 40). That too is true. The prophet is the forth-teller of the will of God, the man who has lived so close to God that he knows his mind and purposes. That is true of Jesus; but there is this difference. The prophet says: " Thus saith the Lord." His authority is borrowed

and delegated. His message is not his own. Jesus says: " I say
unto you." He has the right to speak, not with a delegated
authority, but with his own.

(iii) There is the verdict that he was a *deluded madman*
(verse 20). It is true that either Jesus is the only completely sane
person in the world or he was mad. He chose a Cross when he
might have had power. He was the Suffering Servant when he
might have been the conquering king. He washed the feet of his
disciples when he might have had men kneeling at his own feet.
He came to serve when he could have subjected the world to
servitude. It is not common sense that the words of Jesus give
us, but uncommon sense. He turned the world's standards
upside down, because into a mad world he brought the supreme
sanity of God.

(iv) There is the verdict that he was a *seducer*. The Jewish
authorities saw in him one who was leading men away from
true religion. He was accused of every crime against religion in
the calendar—of being a Sabbath-breaker, of being a drunkard
and a glutton, of having the most disreputable friends, of
destroying orthodox religion. It is quite clear that, if we prefer
our idea of religion to his, he will certainly appear a seducer—
and it is one of the hardest things in the world for any man to
do to admit that he is wrong.

(v) There is the verdict that he was a *man of courage* (verse
26). No one could ever doubt his sheer courage. He had the
moral courage to defy convention and be different. He had the
physical courage that could bear the most terrible pain. He had
the courage to go on when his family abandoned him, and his
friends forsook him, and one of his own circle betrayed him.
Here we see him courageously entering Jerusalem when to enter
it was to enter the lions' den. He " feared God so much that he
never feared the face of any man."

(vi) There is the verdict that he had a *most dynamic
personality* (verse 46). The verdict of the officers who were sent
to arrest him and came back empty-handed was that never had
any man spoken like this. Julian Duguid tells how he once
voyaged on the same Atlantic liner as Sir Wilfred Grenfell, and

he says that when Grenfell came into a room you could tell it even if you had your back to him, for a wave of vitality emanated from him. When we think of how this Galilaean carpenter faced the highest in the land and dominated them until it was they who were on trial and not he, we are bound to admit that he was at least one of the supreme personalities in history. The picture of a gentle, anaemic Jesus will not do. From him flowed a power that sent those despatched to arrest him back in empty-handed bewilderment.

(vii) There is the verdict that he was the *Christ*, the Anointed One of God. Nothing less will do. It is the plain fact that Jesus does not fit into any of the available human categories; only the category of the divine will do.

Before we leave the general study of this chapter there are three other reactions to Jesus that we must note.

(i) There was the crowd's reaction of *fear* (verse 13). They talked about him but they were afraid to talk too loud. The word that John uses for their talking is an onomatopoetic word—that is, a word which imitates the sound of what it describes. It is the word *goggusmos* (two *g*'s in Greek are pronounced *ng*). The Authorized Version translates it *murmuring*; the Revised Standard Version, *muttering*. It indicates a kind of growling, discontented undertone. It is the word used for the grumbling of the children of Israel in the wilderness when they complained against Moses. They muttered the complaints they were afraid to utter out loud. Fear can keep a man from making a clarion call of his faith and can turn it into an indistinct mutter. The Christian should never be afraid to tell the world in ringing tones that he believes in Christ.

(ii) The reaction of a certain number of the crowd was *belief* (verse 31). These were the men and women who could not deny the evidence of their own eyes. They heard what Jesus said; they saw what he did; they were confronted with his dynamism; and they believed. If a man rids himself of prejudice and fear, he is bound in the end to finish in belief.

(iii) The reaction of Nicodemus was to *defend* Jesus (verse 50). In that council of the Jewish authorities his was the lone voice raised in defence. There lies the duty of every one of us. Ian Maclaren, author of *Beside the Bonnie Brier Bush*, used to tell students when they preached: " Speak a good word for Jesus Christ." We live today in a world which is hostile to Christianity in many ways and in many places, but the strange thing is that the world was never more ready to talk about Christ and to discuss religion. We live in a generation when every one of us can earn the royal title, " Defender of the Faith." It is the privilege that God has given us that we can all be advocates and defenders of Christ in face of the criticism —and sometimes the mockery—of men.

THE ULTIMATE AUTHORITY

John 7: 15–18

The Jews were amazed. " How," they said, " can this fellow read when he is quite uneducated? " " My teaching," said Jesus, " is not mine, but it belongs to him who sent me. If anyone is willing to do his will, he will understand whether my teaching derives from God, or whether I am speaking from no source beyond myself. The man who speaks from no other source beyond himself is out for his own glory. He who seeks the glory of him who sent him is true, and there is no wickedness in him."

WE have already had occasion to see that it is very likely that some parts of John's gospel have become misplaced. Maybe he never had time to put it fully in order; maybe the leaves on which it was written were finally assembled wrongly. This section and the one which follows form one of the clearest cases of misplacement. As these two passages come in here they hardly make sense for they have no connection with their context. It is almost certain that they should come after 5: 47. Chapter 5 tells of the healing of the impotent man at the healing pool. That miracle was done on the Sabbath and was regarded by the Jewish authorities as a breach of that day. In his defence Jesus cited the writings of Moses and said that if they really knew what these writings meant and really believed in them, they would also believe in him. The chapter finishes: " If you had believed in Moses, you would have believed in me, for he wrote about me. If you do not believe in his writings, how will you believe in my words? " (*John* 5: 47). If we go straight from there and read *John* 7: 15–24 it makes a clear connection. Jesus has just referred to the writing of Moses, and immediately the astonished Jewish leaders break in: " How can this fellow read when he is quite uneducated? " We will understand the sense and the relevance of *John* 7: 15–24 far better if we assume that it originally came after *John* 5: 47; and with that in mind we turn to the passage itself.

The criticism was that Jesus was quite uneducated. It is exactly the same accusation that was made against Peter and John when they stood before the Sanhedrin (*Acts* 4: 13). Jesus had been to no rabbinic school. It was the practice that only the disciple of an accredited teacher was entitled to expound scripture, and to talk about the law. No Rabbi ever made a statement on his own authority. He always began: " There is a teaching that ... " He then went on to cite quotations and authorities for every statement he made. And here was this Galilaean carpenter, a man with no training whatever, daring to quote and to expound Moses to them.

Jesus could very well have walked straight into a trap here. He might have said: " I need no teacher; I am self-taught; I got my teaching and my wisdom from no one but myself." But, instead, he said in effect: " You ask who was my teacher? You ask what authority I produce for my exposition of scripture? *My authority is God.*" Jesus claimed to be God-taught. It is in fact a claim he makes again and again. " I have not spoken on my own authority. The Father who sent me has himself given me commandment what to say and what to speak " (*John* 12: 49). " The words that I say to you I do not speak on my own authority " (*John* 14: 10).

Frank Salisbury tells of a letter he received after he had painted his great picture of the burial of the unknown warrior in Westminster Abbey. A fellow artist wrote: " I want to con-

gratulate you on the great picture that you have painted—or
rather the picture that God has helped you to paint." All great
productions of the human mind and spirit are given by God. If
we glory in being self-taught, if we claim that any discovery we
have made is our own unaided work, we are, in the last
analysis, glorifying only our own reputation and our own
selves. The greatest of men think not of the power of their own
mind or hand; they think always of the God who told them
what they know and taught them what they can do.

Further, Jesus goes on to lay down a truth. Only the man
who does God's will can truly understand His teaching. That is
not a theological but a universal truth. *We learn by doing*. A
doctor might learn the technique of surgery from textbooks. He
might know the theory of every possible operation. But that
would not make him a surgeon; he has to learn by doing. A
man might learn the way in which an automobile engine works;
in theory he might be able to carry out every possible repair
and adjustment; but that would not make him an engineer; he
has to learn by doing.

It is the same with the Christian life. If we wait until we have
understood everything, we will never start at all. But if we begin
by doing God's will as we know it, God's truth will become
clearer and clearer to us. We learn by doing. If a man says: " I
cannot be a Christian because there is so much of Christian
doctrine that I do not understand, and I must wait until I
understand it all," the answer is: " You never will understand it
all; but if you start trying to live the Christian life, you will
understand more and more of it as the days go on." In
Christianity, as in all other things, the way to learn is to do.

Let us remember that this passage really ought to come after
the story of the healing of the impotent man. Jesus has been
accused of wickedness in that he healed the man on the Sabbath
day; and he goes on to demonstrate that he was seeking only
the glory of God and that there is no wickedness whatsoever in
his action.

A WISE ARGUMENT

John 7: 19–24

" Did not Moses give you the law—and not one of you really keeps it? Why do you try to kill me? " The crowd answered: " You are mad! Who is trying to kill you? " Jesus answered them: " I have done only one deed and you are all astonished by it. Moses gave you the rite of circumcision (not that it had its origin in Moses—it came down from your fathers) and you circumcise a man on the Sabbath. If a man can be circumcised on the Sabbath, without breaking the law of Moses, are you angry at me for making the entire body of a man whole on the Sabbath? Stop judging by appearances, and make your judgment just."

BEFORE we begin to look at this passage in detail, we must note one point. We must picture this scene as a debate between Jesus and the leaders of the Jews, with the crowd standing all around. The crowd is listening as the debate goes on. Jesus is aiming to justify his action in healing the man on the Sabbath day and thereby technically breaking the Sabbath law. He begins by saying that Moses gave them the Sabbath law, and yet none of them keeps it absolutely. (What he meant by that we shall shortly see.) If he then breaks the law to heal a man, why do they, who themselves break the law, seek to kill him?

At this point the *crowd* break in with the exclamation: " You are mad! " and the question: " Who is trying to kill you? " The crowd have not yet realized the malignant hatred of their leaders; they are not yet aware of the plots to eliminate him. They think that Jesus has a persecution mania, that his imagination is disordered and his mind upset; and they think in this fashion because they do not know the facts. Jesus does not answer the question of the crowd which was not really a question so much as a kind of bystanders' interjection; but goes on with his argument.

Jesus's argument is this. It was the law that a child should be circumcised on the eighth day after his birth. " And on the eighth day the flesh of his foreskin shall be circumcised "

Leviticus 12: 3). Obviously that day would often fall on a Sabbath; and the law was quite clear that " everything necessary for circumcision may be done on the Sabbath day." So Jesus's argument runs like this. " You say that you fully observe the law which came to you through Moses which lays it down that there must be no work done on the Sabbath day, and under work you have included every kind of medical attention which is not necessary actually to save life. And yet you have allowed circumcision to be carried out on the Sabbath day.

Now circumcision is two things. It is medical attention to one part of a man's body; and the body has actually two hundred and forty-eight parts. (That was the Jewish reckoning.) Further, circumcision is a kind of mutilation; it is actually taking something from the body. How can you in reason blame me for making a man's body whole when you allow yourselves to mutilate it on the Sabbath day? " That is an extremely clever argument.

Jesus finishes by telling them to try to see below the surface of things and to judge fairly. If they do, they will not be able any longer to accuse him of breaking the law. A passage like this may sound remote to us; but when we read it we can see the keen, clear, logical mind of Jesus in operation, we can see him meeting the wisest and most subtle men of his day with their own weapons and on their own terms, and we can see him defeating them.

THE CLAIM OF CHRIST

John 7: 14, 25–30

When the festival was now half way through, Jesus went up to the Temple precincts and began to teach. So some of the people of Jerusalem said: " Is not this the man whom they are trying to kill? And look! He is speaking publicly, and they say nothing to him! Can it be that the authorities have really discovered that this is the Anointed One of God? But he cannot be because we know where he comes from. When the Anointed One of God comes no one

knows where he comes from." So Jesus, as he taught in the
Temple, cried: " So you know me? And you know where I come
from? But it is not on my own authority that I have come; but he
who sent me is real—and you do not know him. *But I know him,*
because I have come from him, and it was he who sent me." So
they would like to have found a way to arrest him; but no one laid
a hand upon him, because his hour had not yet come.

WE have already seen that the likelihood is that verses 15–24
should come after 5: 47; so, to get the connection, we begin at
verse 14 and go on to verse 24.

The crowd were surprised to find Jesus preaching in the
Temple precincts. Along the sides of the Court of the Gentiles
ran two great pillared colonnades or porticoes—the Royal
Porch and Solomon's Porch. These were places where people
walked and where Rabbis talked and it would be there that
Jesus was teaching. The people well knew the hostility of the
authorities to Jesus; they were astonished to see his courage in
thus defying the authorities; and they were still more astonished
to see that he was allowed to teach unmolested. A thought
suddenly struck them: " Can it be that after all this man is the
Messiah, the Anointed One of God, and that the authorities
know it? " But no sooner had the thought struck them than it
was dismissed.

Their objection was that they knew where Jesus had come
from. They knew that his home was in Nazareth; they knew
who his parents and who his brothers and sisters were; there
was no mystery about his antecedents. That was the very
opposite of popular belief, which held that the Messiah would
appear. The idea was that he was waiting concealed and some
day would burst suddenly upon the world and no one would
know where he had come from. They believed that they did
know that the Messiah would be born in Bethlehem, for that
was David's town, but they also believed that nothing else
would be known about him. There was a rabbinic saying:
" Three things come wholly unexpectedly, the Messiah, a
godsend, and a scorpion." The Messiah would *appear* as
suddenly as a man stumbles on a godsend or steps on a hidden

scorpion. In later years when Justin Martyr was talking and arguing with a Jew about his beliefs, the Jew says of the Messiah: " Although the Messiah be already born and exists somewhere, yet he is unknown and is himself ignorant of his Messiahship, nor has he any power until Elijah comes to anoint him and to make him known." All popular Jewish belief believed the Messiah would burst upon the world mysteriously. Jesus did not measure up to that kind of standard; to the Jews there was no mystery about where he came from.

This belief was characteristic of a certain attitude of mind which prevailed among the Jews and is by no means dead— that which seeks for God in the abnormal. They could never be persuaded to see God in ordinary things. They had to be extraordinary before God could be in them. The teaching of Christianity is just the reverse. If God is to enter the world only in the unusual, he will very seldom be in it; whereas if we can find God in the common things, it means that he is always present. Christianity does not look on this world as one which God very occasionally invades; it looks on it as a world from which he is never absent.

In answer to these objections, Jesus made two statements, both of which shocked the people and the authorities. He said that it was quite true that they knew who he was and where he came from; but it was also true that ultimately he had come direct from God. Second, he said that they did not know God but he did. It was a bitter insult to tell God's chosen people that they did not know God. It was an incredible claim to make that Jesus alone knew him, that he stood in a unique relationship to him, that he knew him as no one else did.

Here is one of the great turning-points in Jesus's life. Up to this point the authorities had looked on him as a revolutionary Sabbath breaker, which was in truth a serious enough charge; but from now on he was guilty not of Sabbath-breaking but of the ultimate sin, *of blasphemy*. As they saw it, he was talking of Israel and of God as no human being had any right to speak.

This is precisely the choice which is still before us. Either, what Jesus said about himself is false, in which case he is guilty

of such blasphemy as no man ever dared utter; or, what he said
about himself is true, in which case he is what he claimed to be
and can be described in no other terms than the Son of God.
Every man has to decide for or against Jesus Christ.

SEARCHING—IN TIME

John 7: 31–36

> Many of the crowd believed in him. " When the Anointed One of
> God comes," they said, " surely he cannot do greater signs than
> this man has done? " The Pharisees heard the crowds carrying on
> these discussions about him; and the chief priests and Pharisees
> despatched officers to arrest him. So Jesus said: " For a little
> while I am to be with you, and then I go back to him who sent me.
> You will search for me and you will not find me. You cannot come
> where I am." So the Jews said to each other: " Where is this fel-
> low going to go that we will not be able to find him? Surely he is not
> going to go to the Jews who are dispersed among the Greeks
> and teach the Greeks? What can this word of his mean—' You
> will search for me and you will not find me ' and ' You cannot
> come where I am '? "

CERTAIN of the crowd could not help believing that Jesus was
the Anointed One of God. They believed that no one could
possibly do greater things than he was doing. That was in fact
the argument which Jesus himself used when John the Baptist
was in doubt about whether he was the one who was to come or
if they had to look for another. When John sent his messengers,
Jesus's answer was: " Go and tell John what you hear and see "
(*Matthew* 11: 1–6). The very fact that there were those who
were trembling on the brink of acceptance moved the authorities to action. They sent their officers—most likely, the Temple
police—to arrest him. Jesus said that he was only with them for
a little time; and the day would come when they would search
for him, not to arrest him, but to obtain what only he could
give, and it would be too late. He would be gone where they
could never follow.

Jesus meant that he would return to his Father, from whom by their disobedience they had shut themselves out. But his hearers did not understand. Throughout the centuries the Jews had been scattered across the world. Sometimes they had been forcibly removed as exiles; sometimes in the time of their country's misfortune they had emigrated to other lands. There was one comprehensive term for the Jews who lived outside Palestine. They were called *the Diaspora*, the dispersion, and scholars still use this term to describe the Jews who live outside Palestine. That is the phrase the people used here. " Is Jesus going away to the *Diaspora*? Will he even go the length of going away and preaching to the Greeks and so become lost in the masses of the Gentile world? Is he going to run away so far that he will be completely out of reach? " It is amazing how a taunt became a prophecy. The Jews meant it for a jest, but as the years went on it became blessedly true that it was to the Gentiles that the Risen Christ went out.

This passage brings us face to face with *the promise and the threat of Jesus*. Jesus had said: " Seek and you will find " (*Matthew* 7: 7). Now he says: " You will seek me and you will not find me " (verse 34). Long ago the ancient prophet had put the two things together in a wonderful way: " Seek the Lord *while he may be found* " (*Isaiah* 55: 6). It is characteristic of this life that time is limited. Physical strength decays and there are things a man can do at thirty that he cannot do at sixty. Mental vigour weakens and there are mental tasks to which a man can address himself in his youth and in his prime which are beyond him in his age. Moral fibre grows less muscular; and if a man allows some habit to dominate him there may come the day when he cannot break himself of it, even if at the beginning he could easily have ejected it from his life.

It is like that with us and Jesus Christ. What Jesus was saying to these people was: " You can awaken to a sense of need too late." A man may so long refuse Christ, that in the end he does not even see his beauty; evil becomes his good and repentance becomes impossible. So long as sin still hurts us, and the unattainable good still beckons us, the chance to seek and find is still there. But a man must have a care lest he grow so used to sin that he does not know that he is sinning and neglect God so long that he forgets that he exists. For then the sense of need dies, and if there is no sense of need, we cannot seek, and if we cannot seek, we will never find. The one thing a man must never lose is his sense of sin.

THE FOUNTAIN OF LIVING WATER

John 7: 37–44

On the last, the great day of the festival, Jesus stood and cried: " If anyone thirsts, let him come to me and drink. As the scripture says: ' He who believes in me—rivers of living water shall flow from his belly.' " It was about the Spirit, whom those who believed in him were to receive, that he said this. For as yet there was no Spirit because Jesus was not yet glorified. When they heard these words some of the crowd said: " This is really the promised Prophet." Others said: " This is the Anointed One of God." But some said: " Surely the Anointed One of God does not come from Galilee? Does the scripture not say that the Anointed One of God is a descendant of David, and that he is to come from Bethlehem, the village where David used to live? " So there was a division of opinion in the crowd because of him. Some of them would have liked to arrest him, but none laid hands on him.

ALL the events of this chapter took place during the Festival of Tabernacles; and properly to understand them we must know the significance, and at least some of the ritual of that Festival.

The Festival of Tabernacles or Booths was the third of the trio of great Jewish Festivals, attendance at which was compulsory for all adult male Jews who lived within fifteen miles of Jerusalem—the Passover, the Festival of Pentecost, and the Festival of Tabernacles. It fell on the fifteenth day of the seventh month, that is, about 15th October. Like all the great Jewish festivals it had a double significance.

First, it had an *historical* significance. It received its name from the fact that all through it people left their houses and lived in little booths. During the Festival the booths sprang up everywhere, on the flat roofs of the houses, in the streets, in the city squares, in the gardens, and even in the very courts of the Temple. The law laid it down that the booths must not be permanent structures but built specially for the occasion. Their walls were made of branches and fronds, and had to be such that they would give protection from the weather but not shut out the sun. The roof had to be thatched, but the thatching had to be wide enough for the stars to be seen at night. The historical significance of all this was to remind the people in unforgettable fashion that once they had been homeless wanderers in the desert without a roof over their heads (*Leviticus* 23: 40–43). Its purpose was " that your generations may know that I made the people of Israel dwell in booths, when I brought them out of the land of Egypt." Originally it lasted seven days, but by the time of Jesus an eighth day had been added.

Second, it had an *agricultural* significance. It was supremely a harvest-thanksgiving festival. It is sometimes called *the Festival of the Ingathering* (*Exodus* 23: 16; 34: 22); and it was the most popular festival of all. For that reason it was sometimes called simply *The Feast* (1 *Kings* 8: 2), and sometimes *The Festival of the Lord* (*Leviticus* 23: 39). It stood out above all others. The people called it " the season of our gladness," for it marked the ingathering of all the harvests, since by this time the barley, the wheat, and the grapes were all safely gathered in. As the law had it, it was to be celebrated " at the end of the year when you gather in from the field the fruit of your labour " (*Exodus* 23: 16); it was to be kept " when you make your ingathering from your threshing floor and your wine press " (*Deuteronomy* 16: 13, 16). It was not only thanksgiving for one harvest; it was glad thanksgiving for all the bounty of nature which made life possible and living happy. In Zechariah's dream of the new world it was this festival which was to be celebrated everywhere (*Zechariah* 14: 16–18). Josephus called it " the holiest and the greatest festival among the Jews " (*Antiquities of the Jews*, 3: 10: 4). It was not only a time for the rich; it was laid down that the servant, the stranger, the widow and the poor were all to share in the universal joy.

One particular ceremony was connected with it. The worshippers were told to take " the fruit of goodly trees, branches of palm trees, and boughs of leafy trees, and willows of the brook " (*Leviticus* 23: 40). The Sadducees said that was a description of the material out of which the booths had to be built; the Pharisees said it was a description of the things the worshippers had to bring with them when they came to the Temple. Naturally the people accepted the interpretation of the Pharisees, for it gave them a vivid ceremony in which to participate.

This special ceremony is very closely connected with this passage and with the words of Jesus. Quite certainly he spoke with it in his mind, and possibly even with it as an immediate background. Each day of the festival the people came with their palms and their willows to the Temple; with them they formed a kind of screen or roof and marched round the great altar. At the same time a priest took a golden pitcher which held three *logs*—that is, about two pints—and went down to the Pool of Siloam and filled it with water. It was carried back through the Water Gate while the people recited Isaiah 12: 3: " With joy you will draw water from the wells of salvation." The water was carried up to the Temple altar and poured out as an offering to God. While this was being done *The Hallel*—that is, Psalms 113–118—was sung to the accompaniment of flutes by the Levite choir. When they came to the words, " O give thanks to the Lord " (*Psalm* 118: 1), and again to the words, " O work now then salvation " (*Psalm* 118: 25), and finally to the closing words, " O give thanks to the Lord " (*Psalm* 118: 29), the worshippers shouted and waved their palms towards the altar. The whole dramatic ceremony was a vivid thanksgiving for God's good gift of water and an acted prayer for rain, and a memory of the water which sprang from the rock when they travelled through the wilderness. On the last day the ceremony was doubly impressive for they marched seven times round the altar in memory of the sevenfold circuit round the walls of

Jericho, whereby the walls fell down and the city was taken.

Against this background and perhaps at that very moment, Jesus's voice rang out: " If any one thirst, let him come to *me* and drink." It is as if Jesus said: " You are thanking and glorifying God for the water which quenches the thirst of your bodies. Come to me if you want water which will quench the thirst of your soul." He was using that dramatic moment to turn men's thoughts to the thirst for God and the eternal things.

THE FOUNTAIN OF LIVING WATER

John 7: 37–44 (*continued*)

Now that we have seen the vivid background of this passage we must look at it in more detail.

The promise of Jesus presents us with something of a problem. He said: " He who believes in me—rivers of water shall flow from his belly." And he introduces that statement by saying, " as scripture says." No one has ever been able to identify that quotation satisfactorily, and the question is, just what does it mean? There are two distinct possibilities.

(i) It may refer to the man who comes to Jesus and accepts him. He will have within him a river of refreshing water. It would be another way of saying what Jesus said to the woman of Samaria: " The water that I shall give him will become in him a spring of water welling up to eternal life " (*John* 4: 14). It would be another way of putting Isaiah's beautiful saying: " And the Lord will guide you continually, and satisfy your desire with good things, and make your bones strong; and you shall be like a watered garden, like a spring of water, whose waters fail not " (*Isaiah* 58: 11). The meaning would be that Jesus can give a man the refreshment of the Holy Spirit.

The Jews placed all the thoughts and the emotions in certain parts of the body. The *heart* was the seat of the intellect; the *kidneys* and the *belly* were the seat of the inmost feelings. As the writer of the *Proverbs* had it: " The spirit of man is the lamp of the Lord, searching all his innermost parts " (*Proverbs* 20: 27). This would mean that Jesus was promising a cleansing, refreshing, life-giving stream of the Holy Spirit so that our thoughts and feelings would be purified and revitalised. It is as if Jesus said: " Come to me and accept me; and I will put into you through my Spirit a new life which will give you purity and satisfaction, and give you the kind of life you have always longed for and never had." Whichever interpretation we take, it is quite certain that what this one stands for is true.

(ii) The other interpretation is that " rivers of living water shall flow from his belly " may refer to Jesus himself. It may be a description of the Messiah which Jesus is taking from somewhere which we cannot place. The Christians always identified Jesus with the rock which gave the Israelites water in the wilderness (*Exodus* 17: 6). Paul took that image and applied it to Christ (1 *Corinthians* 10: 4). John tells how there came forth at the thrust of the soldier's spear *water* and *blood* from Jesus's side (*John* 19: 34). The water stands for the purification which comes in baptism and the blood for the atoning death of the Cross. This symbol of the life-giving water which comes from God is often in the Old Testament (*Psalm* 105: 41; *Ezekiel* 47: 1, 12). Joel has the great picture: " And a fountain shall come forth from the house of the Lord " (*Joel* 3: 18). It may well be that John is thinking of Jesus as the fountain from which the cleansing stream flows. Water is that without which man cannot live; and Christ is the one without whom man cannot live and dare not die. Again, whichever interpretation we choose, that, too, is deeply true.

Whether we take this picture as referring to Christ or to the man who accepts him, it means that from Christ there flows the strength and power and cleansing which alone give us life in the real sense of the term.

In this passage there is a startling thing. The Authorized Version and the Revised Standard tone it down, but in the best Greek manuscript there is the strange statement in verse 39: " For as yet there was no Spirit." What is the meaning of that? Think of it this way. A great power can exist for years and even centuries without men being able to tap it. To take a very relevant example—there has always been atomic power in this world; men did not invent it. But only in our own time have men tapped and used it. The Holy Spirit has always existed; but men never really enjoyed his full power until after Pentecost. As it has been finely said, " There could be no Pentecost without Calvary." It was only when men had known Jesus that they really knew the Spirit. Before that the Spirit had been a power, but now he is a person, for he has become to us nothing other than the presence of the Risen Christ always with us. In this apparently startling sentence John is not saying that the Spirit did not *exist*; but that it took the life and death of Jesus Christ to open the floodgates for the Spirit to become real and powerful to all men.

We must notice how this passage finishes. Some people thought that Jesus was the prophet whom Moses had promised (*Deuteronomy* 18: 15). Some thought that he was the Anointed One of God; and there followed a wrangle about whether or not the Anointed One of God must come from Bethlehem. Here is tragedy. A great religious experience had ended in the aridity of a theological wrangle.

That is what above all we must avoid. Jesus is not someone about whom to argue; he is someone to know and love and enjoy. If we have one view of him and someone else has another, it does not matter so long as both of us find him Saviour and accept him as Lord. Even if we explain our religious experience in different ways, that should never divide us, for it is the experience that is important, and not our explanation of it.

UNWILLING ADMIRATION AND TIMID DEFENCE

John 7: 45–52

So the officers came to the chief priests and the Pharisees. They said to them: " Why did you not bring him here? " The attendants

answered: " Never did a man speak as he speaks." So the
Pharisees answered: " Surely you too have not been led astray?
Has anyone from the authorities believed in him? Or anyone from
the Pharisees? *They* have not; but the mob which is ignorant of
the law and which is accursed believes in him! " Nicodemus (the
man who came to him before) said to them, for he was one of
them; " Surely our law does not condemn a man unless it first
hears a statement of the case from him, and has first-hand
information about what he is doing? " They answered him:
" Surely you too are not from Galilee? Search and see that no
prophet arises from Galilee."

WE have certain vivid reactions to Jesus.

(i) The reaction of the officers was bewildered amazement.
They had gone out to arrest Jesus and had come back without
him, because never in their lives had they heard anyone speak
as he did. Really to listen to Jesus is an unparalleled experience
for any man.

(ii) The reaction of the chief priests and Pharisees was
contempt. The Pharisees had a phrase by which they described
the ordinary, simple people who did not observe the thousands
of regulations of the ceremonial law. They called them *the
People of the Land*; to them they were beneath contempt. To
marry a daughter to one of them was like exposing her bound
and helpless to a beast. " The masses who do not know the law
are accursed." The rabbinic law said: " Six things are laid down
about the People of the Land: entrust no testimony to them,
take no testimony from them, trust them with no secret, do not
appoint them guardians of an orphan, do not make them
custodians of charitable funds, do not accompany them on a
journey." It was forbidden to be a guest of one of the People of
the Land, or to entertain such a person as a guest. It was even
laid down that, wherever it was possible, nothing should be
bought or sold from one of them. In their proud aristocracy and
intellectual snobbery and spiritual pride, the Pharisees looked
down in contempt on the ordinary man. Their plea was:
" Nobody who is spiritually and academically of any account
has believed on Jesus. Only ignorant fools accept him." It is

indeed a terrible thing when a man thinks himself either too clever or too good to need Jesus Christ—and it happens still.

(iii) There was the reaction of Nicodemus. It was a timid reaction, for he did not defend Jesus directly. He dared only to quote certain legal maxims which were relevant. The law laid it down that every man must receive justice (*Exodus* 23: 1; *Deuteronomy* 1: 16); and part of justice was and is that he must have a right to state his case and cannot be condemned on secondhand information. The Pharisees proposed to break that law, but it is clear that Nicodemus did not carry his protest any further. His heart told him to defend Jesus but his head told him not to take the risk. The Pharisees flung catchwords at him; they told him that obviously no prophet could come out of Galilee and taunted him with having a connection with the Galilaean rabble, and he said no more.

Often a man finds himself in a situation in which he would like to defend Jesus and in which he knows he ought to show his colours. Often he makes a kind of half-hearted defence, and is then reduced to an uncomfortable and ashamed silence. In our defence of Jesus Christ it is better to be reckless with our hearts than prudent with our heads. To stand up for him may bring us mockery and unpopularity; it may even mean hardship and sacrifice. But the fact remains that Jesus said he would confess before his Father the man who confessed him on earth, and deny before his Father the man who denied him on earth. Loyalty to Christ may produce a cross on earth, but it brings a crown in eternity.

FURTHER READING

C. Kingsley Barrett, *The Gospel According to Saint John* (*G*)

J. H. Bernard, *St John* (ICC; *G*)

E. C. Hoskyns (ed. F. M. Davey), *The Fourth Gospel* (*E*)

R. H. Lightfoot, *St John's Gospel: A Commentary* (*E*)

G. H. C. Macgregor, *The Gospel of John* (MC; *E*)

J. N. Saunders (ed. B. A. Mastin), *The Gospel According to Saint John* (ACB; *E*)

R. V. G. Tasker, *The Gospel According to Saint John* (TC; *E*)

B. F. Westcott, *The Gospel According to Saint John* (*E*)
The Speaker's Commentary (MmC; *G*)

Abbreviations

ACB : A. and C. Black New Testament Commentary
ICC : International Critical Commentary
MC : Moffatt Commentary
MmC: Macmillan Commentary
TC : Tyndale Commentary

E : English Text
G : Greek Text